THEIR RULING PASSIONS

Baron Stockmar

THEIR RULING PASSIONS

A STUDY IN WIRE-PULLING	*Baron Stockmar*
A STUDY IN FANATICISM	*Lord George Gordon*
A STUDY IN EGOISM	*Dr. Samuel Parr*
A STUDY IN AVARICE	*Joseph Nollekens*
A STUDY IN AMBITION	*The Young Disraeli*

by

PERCY COLSON

Foreword

by

JAMES LAVER

With 32 Illustrations

Biography Index Reprint Series

BOOKS FOR LIBRARIES PRESS
FREEPORT, NEW YORK

First Published 1949

Reprinted 1970 by arrangement with the
Hutchinson Publishing Group Ltd.

INTERNATIONAL STANDARD BOOK NUMBER:
0-8369-8040-9

LIBRARY OF CONGRESS CATALOG CARD NUMBER:
70-136645

PRINTED IN THE UNITED STATES OF AMERICA

CONTENTS

LIST OF ILLUSTRATIONS

I have read Mr. Percy Colson's studies of five eccentric characters with the greatest interest. And, having made that statement, I am compelled to question its validity. Why should I be interested in these five characters, in these five oddities? Why should the author himself be interested? What's Hecuba to him or he to Hecuba? Why should either of us concern ourselves, or expect the reader to be concerned, with the details of the life of Dr. Parr?

The ancients understood these things differently. Plutarch, when he was writing his lives, selected only those persons who were capable of a certain generalization; who were capable, that is, of being elevated into ideal types. He was not even very careful whether he told the truth about them or not. It was enough for him that they pointed a moral and adorned a tale.

It is, however, a mark of modernity (that is, perhaps, of decadence) that we are interested in personality as such. We are fascinated by the spectacle of character in action and, so far from desiring that our heroes should be consistently heroic, we almost prefer them to be human, all too human. Perfect symmetry in human life repels us and perhaps not only because we suspect such symmetry of being artificially imposed. We have no temptation, when we paint our Cromwells, to leave out the warts. Rather it is the warts that fascinate us. So far from generalizing we particularize. We seek the universal, if we seek it at all, through the individual, and, I suppose, it is this tendency more than any other which separates us, in spirit, from the ancient world, and from the world inhabited by the Hindus or the Chinese.

Hence our interest in the secondary characters of history. The real demi-gods escape, as it were, our scalpels. We know enough, God knows, of the warts on the moral face of Napoleon, but somehow it does not matter. He remains the image of an emperor, cast in imperishable bronze. Let us therefore leave Napoleon and concentrate on Fouché, or even on Talleyrand. These men at least were sufficiently human to yield up their secret, sufficiently like us to reveal us to ourselves. In a word, they were characters, and the word carries us deeper into the philosophy of the world stage than might, at first sight, be imagined. For it is a commonplace of the theatre that the hero is never a "character." "Characters" are played by "character actors," by "feature players" as the jargon of the films has it; that is, by someone less than the *"jeune premier."* All the parts in the present volume are played by "character actors," and our interest in them is precisely that they always act "in character."

At first there were only four of them; and that is how I came to know Mr. Percy Colson. He called upon me one day, out of the blue; or, to be more precise, he walked out of the Cromwell Road into my office in the Victoria and Albert Museum. I thought that, perhaps, he had a Rembrandt etching he desired to dispose of, or that he wanted a miniature dated. Nothing of the kind. His mission had no connection with the visual arts.

He announced, *à propos de rien*, that he had written a quartet and wanted to turn it into a quintet. I objected, truthfully, that my knowledge of music was of the slightest. I felt rather like that character of Noel Coward's, who was extremely susceptible to music, because he knew so little about it.

Colson waved my objections aside. He had written a book, he explained, about four characters—four oddities, he called them. They were Lord George Gordon, Nollekens, Baron Stockmar, and the Young Disraeli. I asked what was the connection between them.

"I don't know," said Colson. "They are just—characters." He wanted me to propose a fifth and, drawing a bow at a venture, I suggested Dr. Parr. And Colson, gathering up his traps, departed without another word. A few weeks later he sent me the finished manuscript.

Had I known him then as well as I do now, I think I would have suggested—Colson himself. For in the meantime I had learned a little about him. Years ago, some eighteen years ago to be exact, a book appeared with the falsely apologetic title of *I Hope They Won't Mind*. It was a book of reminiscences rather less sugary than such publications usually are. Indeed, to say so is to underestimate its sharp tang. The anonymous author had obviously known a great many people, particularly in the musical world, and some of them he had regarded, as the French say, without indulgence. There were stories of Caruso, and Ysaye, and Kreisler and Melba—particularly about Melba. The author even felt called upon to defend her: "I do not for a moment believe that she ever told Clara Butt to sing 'muck' to the Australians, as was stated in that singer's memoirs last year. Such advice to Clara Butt would be so entirely unnecessary." The poisoned dagger in the velvet glove!

It emerged that the author had been fortunate in his epoch, had come to London in the 'eighties, when Regent Street was one of the most beautiful streets in Europe, when Devonshire House, Stafford House,

Dorchester House, and Lansdowne House, were kept up in state by their owners and when St. James's still preserved it's eighteenth-century dignity and charm. It emerged also that the author had found himself free of a pretty extensive world, his passport thereto being undoubted breeding, a ready wit and a consuming passion for music. Obviously he had had a very good time, in spite of chronic impecuniousness. There was something about him of the eighteenth century abbé watching the world with a cheerful cynicism, which, in the end, became rather endearing.

When I learned that the author of *I Hope They Won't Mind* was Percy Colson, many things became clear. For here was my eighteenth-century abbé in person, unfrocked not for anything he himself had done, but by the mere progress of history. A man with a gimlet eye and a story about everybody; a man in whom scepticism had almost reached the point of an act of faith; a talker, a lover of the good things of life and, what is perhaps more important, a lover (in spite of everything) of humanity; a man for whom the human beings about him did not need to be good, or noble, or even successful, but just to be—human beings. If they were a little odd in their habits or opinions it went down on the credit side of the ledger. Such a man, I thought, would be very capable of exercising his talents on people of the past as well as on people of the present; and, having read his book, I think so still.

BARON STOCKMAR
(*A Study in Wire-pulling*)

"The satisfaction of his essential being lay in obscurity, in invisibility—in passing unobserved, through a hidden entrance, into the very central chamber of power, and in sitting there, quietly, pulling the subtle strings that set the wheels of the whole world in motion."

Queen Victoria by Lytton Strachey.

"Well said, old mole! Canst work i' the earth so fast?"

(Shakespeare)   *Hamlet.*

THERE are in history many instances of clever, ambitious men who have cared nothing for publicity; powers behind the throne. Men who preferred pulling the strings that make the puppets dance, to dancing with them. Such a man was Monseigneur Talbot, Pio Nono's wily secretary, whose influence at the Vatican was invoked by all those in the know who sought the favour of His Holiness and who did so much to further the schemes of his friend, the equally wily Cardinal Manning. High among these sometimes rather sinister intriguers was Baron Stockmar, the Prince Consort's friend and mentor. Not that there was anything sinister about the baron; he was an idealist—for England rather a dangerous one, for his ideal was a united Germany under Prussia, working hand in glove with England to keep Europe in order. Now this last most desirable consummation has been the aim of many statesmen, but they have always been defeated by German conceit, touchiness, racial jealousy, and inability to allow for any point of view but their own. That Stockmar should have failed to understand this was not surprising. He was a German of the Germans, supremely self-satisfied and full of that Teutonic assumption of omniscience which is so irritating to other nations. From the moment that he wormed his way into the good graces of the young Prince Albert, he set himself with infinite tact and patience to stimulate his patriotism and arouse in him his own passionate desire for a united Germany. It was not long before he established complete ascendancy over the youth—the influence of George Villiers over James I was not more complete.

The name Stockmar is a Swedish name. The family traced its descent from a Stockmar who accompanied Gustavus Adolphus from Sweden to Saxony and settled there. This Stockmar was already thoroughly German in his love of royalty and soon became high in favour with that petty ruler who was wont to say "If I can lay my head in the lap of a Stockmar, I shall be safe." The family prospered and became successful merchants and professional men.

Christian Friedrich—afterwards Baron—Stockmar, was born in 1787, his father being a worthy Coburg lawyer. The youth was educated at the Coburg gymnasium and afterwards studied medicine at Wurzburg and Jena. In later years, when he had become *persona grata* in high political circles, he wrote: "It was a clever stroke to have begun by studying medicine. Without the psychological and physiological experience which

I then obtained, my *savoir-faire* would often have gone a-begging."
Young Christian, even as a boy, had perfect faith in his lucky star.
One day while the family were dining, he said, pointing to the homely
dinner service:

"Some day I must have all these of silver."

He could have had them of gold had he chosen to profit financially
from the position to which he subsequently rose. In 1812, during the
war then raging in distracted Europe, he became town and country
physician in Coburg, and organized there a military hospital. He was,
by the way, one of the first to recognize the importance of cleanliness
and fresh air in hospitals. It was during this period that he formed a
friendship with Prince Leopold, with whose destinies he was to be
closely linked. It was his war experience, too, that gave him his deep
sense of the humiliation of his country and of the wretched state of
German affairs, and made him resolve to devote himself with all the
resources of his thorough, painstaking, critical and sceptical nature, to
the service of the Fatherland.

Prince Leopold, born in 1790, was the youngest son of Francis,
Duke of Saxe-Coburg and brother of the Duchess of Kent, Queen
Victoria's mother. He first visited England in 1814, in the suite of the
Emperor of Russia, when the allied sovereigns arrived in London to
celebrate their victory. During his visit he met and was attracted by the
charms of Princess Charlotte, daughter of the regent. That she was heiress
to the throne in no way lessened her attractions in his eye. Her engagement to the rather disreputable Prince of Orange had just been broken
off, and the omens were favourable. But the regent looked on this Coburg
princeling as rather small beer and gave him no encouragement. So he
made friends with the Duke of Kent and on his return to Paris corresponded with the princess, through the duke. The next year he managed
to get invited to England, became engaged to her, and married her in
1816. Perhaps the regent was, after all, not sorry after her unhappy
entanglement with the Prince of Orange—"Young Frog," according to
Creevey—to marry her to this respectable and good-looking scion of
the Coburgs. She was lively, generous and fond of pleasure. Her tempera-
ment was ardent and she had had more than one love affair. Her childhood had been miserable; how could it have been otherwise at that
Court?

"My mother was bad," she wrote, "but she would not have been
so bad if my father had not been infinitely worse."

The alliance was an excellent one for Leopold and his family. With
it, and that of Prince Ferdinand to the Queen of Portugal, began the
amazing luck of the Coburgs. After their marriage the young couple

settled at Claremont, near Esher, which, with £50,000 a year, the Government had settled on them.

Leopold was an appalling prig, cold, formal and selfish, and he soon tamed the poor girl. They had continual rows which all ended with her complete submission. Everything, he said to her, was for *her* good, not his—the "this hurts me more than it hurts you" attitude. Certainly he was not the ideal husband for the affectionate, tomboyish, warm-hearted girl. He had the Coburg certainty of never being in the wrong, and his eyes were steadily fixed on the main chance. There were those who were not impressed with his assumption of sincerity and altruism.

"His pomposity fatigues and his avarice disgusts," wrote that acute observer, Greville, and George IV hated him.

But Stockmar, whom he sent for and appointed physician to his household, could see no fault in him. Naturally, he saw in Leopold a ladder leading to dazzling heights.

"His (Leopold's) calmness and right-mindedness astonish even the English, who," he said, "were not given to admiring foreigners." And he continued astonishingly: "They call him a complete English gentleman, our hope in these dangerous times."

At first Stockmar's position at Claremont was humble enough. A German doctor, a nobody, he was looked down on by the other members of the household; even Leopold kept him in his place. His duties as physician to the household were not very onerous, for he wrote: "I am solitary, often alone for days together." Unfortunately this physician could not heal himself. His eyesight was bad and all his life he had suffered from dyspepsia, which, at a comparatively early age, warped his naturally cheerful, optimistic disposition and turned him into a hypochondriac. His personality did not attract. Like the average middle-class German, he was rough and unpolished and his table manners were atrocious. And so he did not greatly impress the distinguished people who visited Claremont. But he had plenty of time to exercise his extraordinary power of observation. The Queen-Mother—Charlotte, wife of George III—he described as "small and crooked, with a true Mulatto face." The regent was "very short, though of a fine figure and with distinguished manners; does not talk half as much as his brothers, speaks tolerably good French. He ate and drank a good deal at dinner." The Duke of York, he said, "held himself so badly that he (Stockmar) was always afraid he would tumble over backward. Very bald, and a not very intelligent face." The Duke of Clarence was "the smallest and least good-looking of the brothers." The Duke of Cumberland was "a tall, powerful man with a hideous face and one eye completely out of place," and the Duke of Gloucester had "prominent and meaningless eyes—a very unpleasant face with an animal expression; large and stout, but with weak, helpless legs. He wears a neckcloth thicker than his head." Altogether a charming family. Of the Duke of Wellington he wholly approved.

Happy or unhappy, the married life of Leopold did not last long. In the spring of 1817 Princess Charlotte gave birth to a dead boy and died herself from exhaustion. This tragedy Stockmar rightly put down to the incompetence of the English doctors. He had very wisely refused to attend her, knowing that if her accouchement turned out badly he, as a German, would be blamed. In those days the great resource of the medical profession was to bleed the patient; this they did even in cases of anæmia—they had bled poor Charlotte white.

Her death caused the question of the succession to the throne to become of urgent importance. Four of the sons of George III lived in sin with their mistresses and showed no anxiety to turn respectable, marry, and contribute a possible heir. The Duke of Clarence—the next in succession—seemed in no hurry to do so. There remained the Duke of Kent, a quarrelsome, stupid parasite. With great self-sacrifice and altruism, he consented to discard his mistress, Madame St. Laurent, and save the situation! He took to wife the widowed Princess Victoria of Leiningen, a sister of Prince Leopold—another step upward for the Coburgs. The result of their union was, it is needless to say, the future Queen Victoria.

For a long time after the death of Charlotte, Leopold remained in England. He wanted to go to Coburg, but Stockmar advised him not to do so, feeling that the protracted period of mourning should be passed at Claremont, where he would be consoled by the consciousness that the entire grief-stricken nation shared his grief; "were he to leave the country, it would be looked upon as ingratitude." After all, he still had the £50,000 a year—about double the total revenue of Coburg.

In the early years of the nineteenth century, the affairs of Greece were—as is not unusual—in a very disturbed state. Even Byron was powerless to relieve them. They wanted a king to put things in order, and the ambassadors of the three powers—England, France and Russia— asked the president, Capo d'Istria, if he could recommend an honest and hard-working out-of-work royalty. Capo d'Istria—inspired, it was said by Stockmar, who had already acquired an intimate knowledge of the tricky ways of European statesmen—suggested Leopold, who was enchanted. Who more suitable than he to reign over the land of Plato? So in 1829 two Greeks were sent to Naples, which he was then visiting, to treat with him. They communicated with Canning, who disliked the idea no less than he disliked Leopold, and advised him to have nothing to do with Greece. But Leopold had made up his mind to be a king if he could. After all, there were worse jobs. A king—even of Greece—was still a somebody in 1829.

The negotiations were long and tortuous, and throughout their course Stockmar played a leading part behind the scenes, interviewing one minister, writing to another and making endless journeys to see the royal and *hautes puissances* concerned in the matter.

Leopold—naturally enough—wanted to be invited by the Greek people themselves, to be their monarch, but they exhibited a regrettable lack of enthusiasm. The president seemed to expect substantial political and territorial advantages to be guaranteed by the Powers and by the king-elect and, of course, everyone wanted to be bribed. Leopold too, wanted a lot, and told Lord Aberdeen that he was not inclined to risk the dangers of the position unless he got it. Lord Aberdeen told him curtly that the Powers had no intention of *negotiating* with him; it was a case of take it or leave it. Leopold was furious. He had badly over-estimated his own importance and had expected the support of the Opposition. But Lords Palmerston, Durham, Brougham and Lansdowne all failed him. Eventually, in spite of Stockmar's frantic endeavours to persuade everyone that Leopold was the one hope of Greece, the affair fizzled out. Leopold did not shine in the negotiations. Greville wrote in his diary:

"Leopold is a poor creature. His intrigues about Greece were despicable, plotting in all sorts of underhand ways to get the miserable crown without knowing what it was, and after he *did* know and when it turned out better than he expected at the time he wanted it, he backed out again." In *The Creevey Papers* we read: "I left FitzClarence at Gosforth and continue to like him as well as ever. He said the king was getting very old and cross and that 'Prince Leopold was a damned humbug'. Sefton, he said 'had gone down to the House to hear the royal message . . . and to show Leopold up for having jibbed at last to taking Greece upon himself'."

The fact of the matter was that Stockmar did most of the plotting. Leopold was frightened; courage was not the strong point of this "Happy Prince." So he and Stockmar returned to Claremont.

Strange as it may appear, within a year after the Greek fiasco Leopold got another chance—Belgium this time. The Belgian revolution, which took place at the end of September 1830, caused considerable alarm in Europe, then seething with trouble. A letter to Leopold from Princess

B

Lieven (wife of the Russian Ambassador, a clever and dangerous *intriguante*) describes the effect it produced in London:

Ah Monseigneur, que de mauvaises nouvelles depuis la dernière lettre que j'eus l'honneur d'écrire à V.A.R.! Je dinais hier au Pavilion.[1] *Le Duc de Wellington y vint, très calme, très assuré que les affaires Belges devaient être terminées que Bruxelles devait s'être soumis. Après le diner arriva un courrier de Londres, portant les nouvelles que l'armés du Roi s'était retirées. Les mêmes nouvelles portaient qu'un grand nombre de militaires français avait dirigé la défense de Bruxelles. Sans voir trop noir dans l'avenir, on peut se dire qu'une guerre général sera la conséquence inévitable de cet état de choses.*

The fears of Princess Lieven were not realized, the reasons being that the Liberal movement caused the Duke of Wellington's Government to fall; the Polish insurrection which kept Russia busy; and the—for once—peaceful policy of the King of Prussia. The great Powers called a Conference, which accepted in principle the independence of Belgium and the separation of Holland and Belgium. Nobody, however, seemed particularly anxious to reign over Belgium. The Belgians wanted the Duc de Nemours, son of Louis Philippe, but that monarch respectfully declined the honour on account of his son. Nor did the Prince of Orange want it. However, there was always Leopold—his name, so Stockmar tells us—had already been mentioned, but the suggestion was very coldly received in England. Gradually the Grey Ministry, which had succeeded that of Wellington, became resigned to the idea, though the court looked on Leopold with unfriendly eyes. He wanted the crown badly; says Greville, "Lord Lansdowne told me that short of going in direct opposition to the wishes and advice of all the Royal Family and of the Government, he would do anything to be king'd, and, what is equally absurd, that the others cannot bear that he should be thus elevated."

In April the envoys arrived in London, and after a preliminary coaching by Stockmar were received by the prince at Marlborough House. This time Leopold, under the guidance of Stockmar, behaved more intelligently. After carefully studying the Belgian Constitution, and apparently seeing rocks ahead, he had qualms.

"Read the Constitution and give me your opinion," he said. Stockmar, who was never known to refuse his opinion, read it. "True, sir, most true," he said. "This Constitution greatly limits the power of the king," and he advised the clear-sighted prince to have confidence in the people and play a canny game.

It was not without great opposition that he was elected, but elected he was, and accompanied by Stockmar he left London for his new sphere

[1] The Brighton Pavilion—with George IV.

of action. Stockmar was rewarded for his share in the negotiations by being created a baron.

Before leaving Claremont, Leopold made a noble resolution; he resigned his £50,000 a year ! The reason for this, we read in the Stockmar memoirs, was political. A king—even a King of Belgium—he felt, would hardly meet with the consideration which was his due if he continued to be a pensioner of England—he who pays the piper is at least entitled to call the tune. But Stockmar was hard put to it to persuade him to give it up, and, left to himself, his avarice would probably have prevented him letting go of £50,000 a year. There were other grounds, too, which made the step advisable, the baron told him. The death of Charlotte and Leopold's accession to a throne had removed the only pretext on which the pension could have been continued. As Stockmar wrote: "they were merely waiting for the king's departure for Brussels to move a resolution in both Houses respecting the inexpediency of continuing the allowance; the motion of the House of Commons was already on the paper. And certainly the resolution would have been carried." So, on the whole, altruism was the best policy.

Leopold and the baron made their entrance into Brussels on the 21st July. The baron was to be confidential adviser and was also to organize the household. He did not spare his advice. But the troubles of Leopold were not over. Hardly had he been in Belgium a month when the Dutch invaded the country and, but for the aid of Louis Philippe, the Belgian army would have been completely routed. The London Conference succeeded in bringing about an armistice, and finally a treaty for the separation of Holland and Belgium was concluded.

Throughout the Belgian affair, Stockmar had played an active and clever rôle. There is no doubt that he was an extraordinarily able man and a born statesman. Had he not been he could never have wielded the influence he did most certainly wield. Although of relatively humble birth, at the age of forty-three he was already *persona grata* in European political circles. During the troubled, unsettled times after a great war, there are always opportunities for men such as Stockmar. This is as true to-day as ever it was, but it is now less easy for them to play an active part outside their own country. When things began to settle down in Belgium, the baron returned to London to arrange the pension question, and he managed to get the Government to pay Leopold's debts. On the very day of his arrival he saw Palmerston, and attacked him for the lukewarm attitude of England *vis-à-vis* the Dutch invasion. "Our confidence in England is shaken," he said. But Palmerston did not seem to mind much. The baron, by the way, had had considerable difficulty in persuading Leopold not to throw up the sponge when things became dangerous. Even in 1837, he was not too happy in his new situation. Greville says:

"My brother writes me from Paris that Leopold is deadly sick of his Belgian crown and impatient to abdicate, thinking it better to be an English prince with £50,000 a year than to be monarch of a troublesome, vulgar little kingdom which all its neighbours regard with an evil or covetous eye."

II

IN 1834 Stockmar went to Coburg to pay a long-deferred visit to his wife and family—he had married in 1821. Years sometimes passed without his seeing his wife and child which, as his son tells us, "must have been a great sacrifice for so warm-hearted a man." But if Frau Stockmar was not favoured with much of his company—and who shall say that her state was the less gracious?—she had the consolation of knowing that his conduct was pleasing to the Almighty. "He never lost his German characteristic of shaping his actions according to the highest motives."

While all these exciting events were happening, two children were growing up, both of whom were fated to play important parts on the English stage—Victoria, daughter of the Duchess of Kent, born 24th May, 1819, and her cousin Albert, son of the Duke of Coburg, brother of the duchess, born some three months later. His brother Ernest, heir to the duchy, was fourteen months older.

The luck of Leopold and his sister in the marriage market—if luck it can be called to have married the foolish and unscrupulous Duke of Kent—had convinced the Coburgs that small beer as they were in the comity of nations—not that they would have acknowledged it—they had a decidedly marketable product in their princelings. Their great ambition was to marry one of them to Princess Victoria. Belgium was all very well; so was Portugal, whose young queen Prince Ferdinand had married. But the throne of England—ah, that was, indeed, quite another kettle of fish! England was a Protestant country, a fact which, though of no great consequence, simplified matters. They were ready to adopt any country, any creed, provided they could better themselves. But they had to mind their step during the lifetime of the old king (William IV) who had no use for them, especially for the Duchess of Kent whom he detested and he lost no opportunity of letting her know it. Leopold, aided by the indispensable baron, made the first move in the game. He arranged for Albert and his brother to visit their Aunt Kent at Kensington Palace. The king, though sure that those pushing Coburgs were up to something, felt obliged to invite them to spend a day at Windsor. He treated them very casually, falling asleep in the middle of dinner.

Victoria liked them, especially Albert. She admired "his large blue eyes, his beautiful nose and his white teeth." But after all, he was only a boy—not quite seventeen—and she had not yet thought of marriage. The brothers remained in England for a month and Albert hated it.

He found English society, which considered the Coburgs far too unim-
portant to fuss over, cold and oppressive, and being shy, self-conscious
and inordinately proud of being a Coburg, he could make no headway
in it. Early to bed was the Coburg motto, and he could not keep awake
after ten o'clock. Then, too, the elaborate English meals upset his weak
stomach. He met the Duke of Wellington and Disraeli, whom he
described as "a vain Jew." The visit concluded, the brothers left for
Paris, as glad to go as the Court was glad to lose them.

Leopold and Stockmar were fairly well satisfied with the results of
the visit, and Leopold encouraged Albert to keep up a correspondence
with his important cousin.

Victoria came of age on 24th May, 1837, and the happy event was
marked by congratulations and presents from the Coburg family,
including Albert. Uncle Leopold's present arrived on the following
day. It was Stockmar! The baron was charged by Leopold to ingratiate
himself with the young princess, and with the subtlety of which he
was a past master, to sing discreet praises of Albert, tell how he had
been completely conquered by her charms, and keep his image ever
before her eyes. Leopold would rather have done it himself had it been
possible, but he could *write*, and write he did, deluging her with letters
of advice on every detail of her life. And so they wove their web, strong
in the conviction that they were acting solely in the interests of Victoria.
Personal ambition, of course, played no part in their schemes. But how
satisfactory it would be if pure altruism paid a dividend! Surely the
labourer is worthy of his hire?

Stockmar had not arrived on the scene any too soon. The old king
died within less than a month, and lo, Victoria was Queen of England!
Albert wrote her a letter of congratulation, full of pious platitudes, and
cousinly affection. So well had Stockmar done his work that he was
invited to take up his residence in the palace. He remained there for
fifteen months, to the great annoyance of Lord Melbourne and Her
Majesty's ministers, who cordially disliked the German influence at
Court. In 1838, things began to move. Victoria, by this time, had come
to imagine that the idea so cleverly and persistently hinted to her by
Leopold and the baron was her own. She suggested to Stockmar that
he should take Albert for a tour in Italy and report to her. He asked
nothing better. It would now be strange indeed if the Coburg chickens
did not come home to roost.

And so in 1838 Albert and Stockmar set out for Italy, Stockmar
hoping to discover during the tour how far Albert was fitted for the
position proposed for him; above all, if he were capable of being
moulded to further his (Stockmar's) ambition—the regeneration of

Germany. Albert at that period was a shy, amiable youth, full of good intentions. But he was slack and hated exertion of any kind, mental or physical. The fact is his mind was tired—he had been over-educated—but it was crammed with facts, which he had an extraordinary capacity for acquiring and remembering. He would have won endless prizes in modern newspaper competitions. To be asked the exact dimensions of St. Peter's, Rome, the drainage system of Jerusalem, or how many people could sleep abreast in the Great Bed of Ware would have enchanted him. He was rather delicate; his stomach, especially, being weak, and he was apt to be sick after any unusual excitement—an additional claim on the sympathy of the sallow, dyspeptic little baron. Another bond of union lay in the fact that in both of them the sense of humour was entirely lacking. Curiously enough, he showed a strong dislike for the society of women. Never had he formed even a boyish attachment—still less a liaison—with one. His virtue was, indeed, appalling; not a single vice redeemed it.

It is interesting to note that this quite intelligent youth seems to have gained nothing from his visit to Italy, except, perhaps, a love for Italian primitives—at that time very little appreciated. In after years he was to become one of the first amateurs of his period to realize their beauty and collect them. Greville, making the tour some eight years before, had enjoyed himself immensely. To begin with, he had what he described as "a childish liking for Catholic pomp." The Catholic Church both fascinated and repelled him. But then, everything interested Greville; pictures, people, politics, theatres, scenery—he has something worth while to say about all of them.

Not so our Albert. His bigoted Lutheran mind was horrified by Catholicism, he was aghast at its superstition, nor could he even vaguely understand the admirable philosophy of life it offers. Had he lived in the days of Freud he would, perhaps, have seen how little difference there is between psycho-analysis and the Confessional—the balance being in favour of the Confessional. Florence, apparently, gave him the most satisfaction. The galleries, he said, "intoxicated him with delight." He played on the organ in the *Badia*—it was "a noble instrument; it brought all heaven before his eyes." In Rome he had an audience of the Pope (Pio Nono) and they discussed the origin of Greek art. His Holiness considered that it was derived from the Etruscans, but Albert put him right, informing him that the Greeks were inspired by early Egyptian art. This, of course, decided the question once and for all. But on the whole Albert was disappointed in Italy, "alike in climate, scenery, feeling and skill." It was not Coburg!

Perhaps both he and Stockmar were saddened by the political

conditions prevailing there and by the Italian hatred of Austria, which included everything Teutonic. The tide of Italy's fortunes was then at the lowest ebb ever experienced during her long and eventful history. Apart from her imperishable heritage of art, nothing remained to remind her corrupt and apathetic people of the great days of old, the might of Venice, and the glory of the Renaissance. Without power, prestige or wealth, she was at the mercy of any of her neighbours strong enough to come and take what they wanted. By the beginning of 1806 Napoleon had conquered all Northern and Southern Italy; in 1808 he formally annexed the Papal States, and the Pope was arrested and kept a prisoner for two years. Napoleon's disasters, however, resulted in the Pontiff's restoration to power and he returned to Rome in 1814. Incessant war and the exactions of the various rulers had resulted in a terrible state of poverty and misery, and the restored governments—especially Austria— had acted with but little tact towards the soldiers and officials of Napoleon's régime, pursuing a policy of revenge and oppression, instead of conciliation. Perhaps the only exception to this unhappy state of affairs was Tuscany, where the just and lenient rule of the Grand Duke brought peace and happiness to the people, for—patriotism and politics notwithstanding—most people live just as contentedly under alien rule as under that of a fellow countryman, provided that it enables them to live and work in peace.

Stockmar, unlike his pupil, was not disappointed with the tour. He had gone to study Albert, not art, and the result of his studies had been eminently satisfactory. He could hardly have found a better way of advancing the interests of the Fatherland than that of stimulating the patriotism of this serious and intensely German youth, who seemed to be destined for so important a position, of course, always provided that his union with Victoria became a *fait accompli* and that he succeeded in gaining Victoria's love and trust and, through her, a real influence in English politics. Albert's mind, he had found, was an empty vessel, waiting eagerly to be filled from the well of knowledge—and Stockmar's well was deep.

What was there in this unpolished middle-class doctor of fifty-one that so attracted the nineteen-year-old Albert? It is one of the most puzzling facts in history. The baron certainly did not flatter him. On the contrary, he never hesitated to find fault and criticize him in his heavy, sententious German manner. And, far from resenting criticism, young Telemachus was humbly grateful to his mentor and promised to be a good boy in future. Stockmar must have possessed to an abnormal extent that strange magnetic power some people have over others. His personality was undoubtedly a very strong one; Leopold—a far more virile individual than Albert—had yielded to it. Circumstances had favoured the baron. They had been alone together in this—to Albert—unsympathetic land, and Coburg called unto Coburg. But this does not account for the doglike devotion Stockmar inspired in him; it is wholly inexplicable.

Leopold had already broached the subject of the marriage to Albert before he left for Italy, and he, worthy youth, "looked at the question from the most elevated and honourable point of view." He had already made the discovery that "troubles must be inseparable from all human positions," and very sensibly thought that, that being the case, he might just as well endure them as Victoria's husband, as in some less exalted sphere. But the difficulty now was Victoria herself. The "blue eyes, the beautiful nose and the white teeth" had faded from her memory. Why should she marry? She had tasted power and liked it, and she had no notion of sharing the privileges of her delightful position with a partner. There is a story of a small boy who ran to his father, screaming: "Mummy's fallen down the well, what *shall* we do?" "Leave well alone, my son," said father. That was Victoria's attitude. But it was time she married. After all, it was not for nothing that she was the daughter of the Duchess of Kent, whose supposed relations with her secretary, Sir John Conroy, caused a good deal of scandal at Court, and her father had been notorious for his gallantries—better a Consort than a Conroy. She was not an Elizabeth, and might not have carried off virginity with the same *aplomb* as her illustrious predecessor!

Albert, too, was not the only suitor in the field. There was the Duc de Nemours. True, he was a Catholic, but that difficulty could easily have been got over and an alliance between France and England would have settled many difficulties. Perhaps French influence in England would have made it a far pleasanter country to live in? It is an interesting speculation. So Leopold and Stockmar thought it was high time to act; they despatched Albert and Ernest to England with a letter recommending them to Victoria's *bienveillance*. "They are good and honest creatures *and not at all* pedantic!"

They arrived at Windsor Castle in the evening, and this time Victoria received a *coup de foudre*. Eyes, nose and teeth carried all before them. The courtship was of the shortest. Victoria promptly proposed to her "dear cousin," and, without even murmuring the conventional phrase "this is so sudden," he accepted her. The wedding took place on 10th February, 1840.

The news of the engagement was received in the country with the utmost coldness; no one wanted another German at Court, least of all, a Coburg. Difficulties began at once, the first unpleasantness arising over

Albert's settlement. Victoria suggested £50,000 a year, which was vigorously opposed by the Tories, who got it reduced to £30,000, much to Albert's annoyance. Even that was considered £10,000 too much. "It was not only the Tories; the whole nation supported them," Lord Melbourne told Albert. Then there was the quarrel over his precedence; this was finally settled by Victoria, who exercised the royal prerogative. To crown all, Melbourne appointed George Anson to be his private secretary, and Anson hated Germans. So no wonder poor Albert clung to Stockmar, who, apart from the fascination he exercised over him, had lived in England and—he thought—understood the English. The sycophantic Sir Theodore Martin wrote that Stockmar's being a foreigner was a positive advantage, as he would be able to understand England with detachment and teach Albert "how to become an English gentleman!" As a matter of fact, neither of them ever became gentlemen, or understood or sympathized with the English.

So from the first Albert was unhappy. He was far too intelligent not to realize that he was not welcome. He was competent and orderly, and he had come to the land of compromise and makeshift. Exact and punctilious, he found himself among the most easy-going and casual people in Europe. Caring little for sport, he was expected to take a leading position in a society that lived for it. And he was, as we have noted, entirely destitute of humour, that blessed gift which so often saves a difficult situation in England. He was, too, a moral prig of the first order, and the drunkenness, the loose living and spendthrift habits of the aristocracy, shocked him. He demanded such moral qualities in his equerries that one gentleman, approached, said: "Thank heaven that his character was much too bad for the job!" "This damned morality will ruin everything," said Melbourne.

Although when Victoria became queen the terms "Whig" and "Tory" were beginning to be replaced by "Liberal" and "Conservative," the great Whig aristocracy was as powerful as ever. "The Whigs are all cousins," said Lord Melbourne, and a change of ministry generally meant the transfer of power from one set of cousins to another. Their houses were kept up in great state and with lavish expenditure, though some of them must have been uncomfortable enough. Greville writes to Reeve: "I have been at Chatsworth for two or three days and the magnificence of the whole thing is striking beyond everything. It is to the last degree uncomfortable; the house is not lived in, or furnished, or supplied according to our notion of comfort. There are no bells, no chairs to sit in, but great cumbrous machines that are not locomotive, no books or reviews or any of the common social food—neither morning nor evening is there anything like ease, comfort or society."

It was the same at Windsor; the Royal Household was run on almost medieval lines. Albert decided that it must be reorganized and Stockmar drew up a memorandum of a length and portentousness which was almost comic in its gravity. The Court was furious. What right had Albert to meddle? Who was this wretched German doctor who dared to poke his nose into what didn't concern him? But they had their way.

In spite of Victoria's ever-growing love for him, Albert was very lonely, and Stockmar took full advantage of his loneliness to strengthen his hold over him. He instructed him in statecraft, stood between him and the respectfully hostile Court officials, and harped continually on the unhappy condition of the Fatherland under its various petty rulers, hating one another and torn by dissensions. What could a united Germany under the rule of Prussia, its strongest state, not accomplish in civilizing and educating benighted Europe? As the baron, speaking in the dear German tongue, pictured his Utopia, Albert saw visions of a new Holy Land, illuminating the dark places of the earth, while righteousness and peace—and *Kultur!*—kissed each other. And *he* could play a part in making the dream come true—ah! that was worth working for. Both of them were sincerely convinced of the utter superiority of the German race over all other races. Surely a close collaboration between wealthy England and pious Germany could keep Europe at peace and put those odious French in their place—not to speak of the impossible Palmerston?

It is hardly to be wondered at that Her Majesty's ministers viewed with some apprehension the growth of the German influence.

"King Leopold and Baron Stockmar are good, intelligent people," said Lord Melbourne, "but I dislike very much to hear it said by my friends that I am influenced by them." But Melbourne was always civil to Stockmar, who, with characteristic German boorishness, repaid his courtesy by calling him "the Procurante." All the same, the influence was there, and Melbourne knew it. In every one of the memoranda Albert drew up for the reform of everything, the hand was the hand of Albert, but the voice was the voice of Stockmar, who, unlike Albert, was quite indifferent whether he was liked or not. He had that invaluable gift, for the pushing *parvenu*, the hide of a rhinoceros. His health, however, was wretched; he suffered agonies from heartburn which made meals a misery to him. And as Albert's digestion was also bad, it was a case of two stomachs that ached as one. But ill or well, Stockmar never relaxed, nor did he allow Albert to do so.

Though generally clever and tactful, he sometimes went too far. When the Prince of Wales was born, he persuaded Victoria and Albert

not to have a single English godparent. The choice of the King of
Prussia especially was intensely unpopular in the country. Stockmar's
only friend at Court was Dr. Prätorius, Albert's German secretary,
and afterwards he transferred his favour to the doctor's successor, the
Jew, Carl Meyer. Dr. Prätorius was an extraordinarily ugly man. One
day, when Victoria was reading the Bible to the little Princess Royal,
they came to the passage: "And God created man in his own image."
"But surely not Dr. Prätorius, dear Mamma?" said the child.

A great source of annoyance and embarrassment to Her Majesty's
ministers was Stockmar's—and through him Albert's—insistence on the
personal authority of the monarch. In a memorandum written in 1850,
he urged Albert to persuade the Queen to exercise more effectively
the royal prerogative. "The sovereign," said he, "should be in the
position of a permanent premier . . . it would be unreasonable that a
king, as able as any of his ministers, should be prevented from making
use of such qualities as he possessed at ministerial councils. He must lose
no opportunity of *asserting the power of the throne.*" George III thought
the same; so did Albert, who, in a speech at the hundred-and-fiftieth
anniversary of the Society for the Propagation of the Gospel (and
British interests) in Foreign Parts, made the amazing statement that
William III—who had presided over his own council—"was the greatest
monarch the country had to boast of!" Stockmar told Melbourne that
he was too ready to yield to his supporters and so to overlook the damage
which such a course might inflict on the Queen and the Crown. The
Queen, he said, "must not identify herself with any party." Fortunately
Victoria was wise enough to realize that in a constitutional monarchy
the Crown is bound to identify itself with the Government in power.

Stockmar's friend, that arch-meddler Leopold, had at long last had
his claws cut. Victoria had grown tired of "Dear Uncle's" endless letters
of advice, insidiously advocating policies advantageous to himself. She
had gently, but firmly, given him to understand that she preferred
managing her own affairs. Her action was not displeasing to Stockmar,
who did not like any infringement of his own monopoly.

The education of the Prince of Wales gave him a great opportunity
for imposing his views on the subject. Victoria could think of no system
better than that of which her "dearest master" was so admirable an
example. Memoranda of vast length were drawn up, and Stockmar
wrote: "I have for months pursued my plan with unflagging obstinacy.
I could not do this without rendering myself odious, but the difficulties
in the way could not stop me. The result is that there is now every
prospect that nine-tenths of my proposals will be adopted." The scheme
would have sent Eton on strike immediately. Lady Lyttleton had hoped

that—as was at one time suggested—the kindly, child-loving Archdeacon Samuel Wilberforce would have been asked to supervise Bertie's education, but Stockmar scouted the idea. However, in the event it did not matter—Bertie refused to be educated!

As years went by, Stockmar succeeded in making himself indispensable to Victoria, as well as to Albert. *His* were the opinions embodied in the innumerable memoranda with which Albert deluged the Cabinet; from *him* originated the dreary moral priggishness that, like a miasma, spread over Court and country; *his* was the still small voice bidding Albert "never relax." Had it not been for him it is doubtful if Albert would ever have been anything more than the husband of his wife. He came and went as he chose, refusing to wear Court dress on the grounds that knee-breeches and silk stockings would not protect his legs properly, and he might catch cold. And such was his insolent certainty of the hold he had, that he never even took the trouble to inform his royal hosts of his departures, or pay them the courtesy of taking leave of them. And far from resenting his rudeness, Victoria, for all her overweening sense of her own importance, and Albert, that walking book of etiquette, bombarded him with letters imploring him not to leave them comfortless. "Alas!" writes Victoria, "the inestimable, good, dear Stockmar has gone without a word! My poor Albert!" Yet she would crush with devastating coldness the least fancied slight to her royal dignity on the part of one of the Court circle. Albert too, after one of the baron's rude flittings, wrote to him: "Come, as you love me, as you love Victoria, as you love Uncle Leopold, as you love *your German Fatherland*," and on another occasion, "I will send after you only one word of the dismay occasioned by your sudden disappearance. There was an outcry throughout the house from great and small, young and old! 'The baron is gone!' " Then came variations upon it: "I wanted to say this and that to him." "He promised he would stay longer." "I went to his room and found it empty." "I would have travelled with him." "He promised to carry a letter to my father." "*J'ai encore commencé un travail qu'il demandait.*"

It was said in the palace that if Albert was wanted, he was always to be found in Stockmar's room.

Was the Court really so desolated by his absence or were the courtiers trimming their sails to the favourable wind? Still, like Brutus, Stockmar was an honourable man, indeed, he was so honest that there were not wanting those who did not altogether trust him.

Perhaps royalties like being "treated rough" occasionally; it is a novelty for them. They are hardly ever contradicted; the give-and-take of good talk is not for them. The incidence of royal birth and the exigencies and etiquette of Court life tend to make them less intelligent than they might be, and some of the more intellectual among them are, no doubt, conscious of this. But Victoria was not intellectual; her mind was thoroughly middle-class. She was more at home with John Brown than she would have been in, for instance, the brilliant circle that revolved round Lorenzo de' Medici. Her saving grace was her common sense, which almost amounted to genius.

III

DURING the years that Albert was consolidating his difficult position, he never for a moment lost sight of the object so dear to his and to Stockmar's heart—the regeneration of the Fatherland. Regeneration is, perhaps, hardly the right word. The conquests of Napoleon had entirely broken up the old German Empire; the various princes had become practically independent rulers, though they were still loosely held together in Confederations with a Diet, held at Frankfort, in which Stockmar had been invited to sit for Coburg. In that fateful year 1848— the year of Louis Philippe's abdication—every throne in Europe seemed to be quaking and a strong united Germany would certainly have been a stabilizing influence.

At the last sitting of the Diet, Stockmar said: "Now is the time, after the dissolution of the Diet, for the separate Governments, especially the small ones, to acknowledge themselves as impossible and superfluous and to sacrifice themselves for the greatness of Germany. This would be a patriotic task and the only worthy conclusion of the Diet." Stockmar's son says in his memoirs that "his father was directly alluding to the Vocation of Prussia." Later in the year, Stockmar said: "I still consider it possible to unite the whole of the constitutional states of Germany as a confederate state under the presidency of the King of Prussia as Emperor. Prussia, by the nature of things, is called to be the central power of Germany."

It is, perhaps, surprising that a man with so large an experience of statecraft and the pretensions of petty princes should have been optimistic enough to expect them to show such altruism, their sole bond of union being their mutual hostility. Be that as it may, difficulties began at once. Not the least of them was the King of Prussia himself— Frederick William—who was equally unpopular with his own people and with the rest of Germany. He considered that he had been badly treated by everyone. Both southern and western Germany had heaped abuse on him, and his vacillating disposition made him almost impossible to deal with.

"The poor King of Prussia has entirely broken down. He has never yielded or acted except when it was not only too late, but when it would have been better to do nothing. Metternich and the Emperor of Russia were the ruin of him and of Germany," wrote Stockmar. He goes on to say how secure and glorious—"powerful

31

enough to uphold all Germany"—he could have been had he acted otherwise. "In Germany nobody will hear of him now."

But he did not despair; he resorted to his usual panacea for all evils, a memorandum, embodying his plan for the unification of Germany. Its essential points were that Germany should constitute an empire consisting of *immediate* and *mediate* territories. The *immediate* territory would consist of the original[1] possessions of the emperor, the other states, hitherto belonging to the Bund, would constitute the *mediate* territories. To the central power of the empire was to be delegated vast authority, including the international representation of Germany, the right of treaties and of diplomatic intercourse in peace and war, the army, navy and fortresses, customs, post—indeed, practically every department of government was to be in the hands of the emperor, who was to exercise his authority over the whole empire.

The working of this plan depended, of course, on the willingness of all the non-Prussian states to acknowledge Prussia as the leading power and on the ability of their representatives in the Imperial Parliament— very much under Prussia—to sit together in peace and legislate for the common good. For Prussia, too, the plan involved considerable sacrifices, and sacrifice made no appeal to that arrogant, truculent little kingdom, whose population was the least civilized of all the Teutonic states.

Albert, taught by Stockmar, was beginning to think for himself; he also drew up a plan and—while his mentor was still at Frankfort— sent it to the Courts of Austria, Prussia and Saxony. His plan differed from that of Stockmar. He wanted the emperor to be elected either for life or for a limited number of years, and considered that the said emperor should deal only with external politics, leaving each state free to manage its own home affairs. There should be a Diet of the Empire with three Chambers, so as to express the collective will of the whole German people, yet so arranged that the representatives of each state and people should retain their own standing and traditions. Both his and Stockmar's hopes were set on Prussia. In the meantime confusion prevailed everywhere. The first Holstein war had begun; Prussia attacked Denmark on the plea that Holstein belonged to Germany. There was rioting in Berlin and Frankfort, and Paris had suffered new disorders. "The world is worse than ever," wrote Albert.

And so their dreams proved illusory. In March 1849, it was decided that the title of "Emperor of the Germans" should be offered to the King of Prussia. But so many states were opposed to the idea that Frederick William declined the empty honour. State after state had

[1] Not belonging to Prussia.

Queen Victoria, the Prince Consort and their three children;
Princess Victoria, Prince Albert Edward and Princess Alice

·Queen Victoria with Prince Albert a year before his
death

withdrawn its deputies and finally the remains of the assembly were broken up.

But the seed had been sown, though neither Albert nor Stockmar were to see the harvest. After their efforts it was impossible that things should continue as they were indefinitely. Perhaps—indeed, almost certainly—their plans and suggestions, and their incessant propaganda for their beloved Prussia, brought about the final unification of Germany many years sooner than it would otherwise have been accomplished. The part they played was not without influence in the formation of the most dangerous, arrogant, ruthless, greedy and warlike empire the world has ever seen.

The activities of Stockmar and the prince did not meet with much sympathy in England. Lord Aberdeen told Greville that "the prince's views were generally sound and wise, with one exception, which was his violent and incorrigible German Unionism and his abetting of German dangers. He will not hear of a moderate plan—a species of federalism, based on the Treaty of Vienna and the old relations of Germany, and insists on a new German Empire with Prussia at its head."

When the question arose of Prussia dominating the German Federation, the King wrote to Victoria, asking for her support. Palmerston—who loathed Germany and all its works—heard of the letter from Bunsen, the Prussian Ambassador, and told the Queen that she must not correspond with foreign royalties except on purely personal matters. With the aid of the reluctant Albert, he drafted a reply, and insisted on her sending it to the King. But Prussia continued to obsess the prince's German mind.

Albert was now fully fledged; he had his fingers in every pie. Not a single dispatch was sent from the Foreign Office, which he did not see and, if he thought necessary, alter. Not a report of any ambassador was kept from him. And every day he received bundles of papers from other State departments. Besides all this, he kept up a regular correspondence with his German relations, with British ambassadors in foreign countries, and with the governors of colonies. And a letter from Albert was no scrap of paper. The memoranda he wrote on Oriental questions alone amounted during three years to fifty folio volumes. Writing to Stockmar in 1854, he said: "I have just worked out a plan for reorganizing the army in the Crimea. I have completed a memorandum on Examinations and New Rules of Admission for the Diplomatic Body. I am now engaged in preparing an address on the influence of science and art on our manufacturers."

In addition to these activities, he lost no opportunity of speaking in public. From the Society for the Propagation of the Gospel, he skipped

c

lightly to the cattle show, sandwiching, in between, advice to artists at the Royal Academy Dinner, not to speak of addressing the "Society for Improving the Condition of Domestic Servants and Teaching them Thrift"—a little difficult, perhaps, on mid-nineteenth-century wages. Well might Stockmar be proud of his pupil!

In 1850, Sir Robert Peel died. Both Victoria and Albert were devoted to him.

Victoria wrote to Stockmar in Coburg: "You do not answer my anxious letter. Pray *do* listen to our *entreaties* to come. It will do you good to be with my *beloved prince*. He *longs* for you." One fancies that Victoria did not often undergo the experience of having her letters unanswered.

But neither Albert nor Stockmar ever became popular. During the Crimean War, the strong undercurrent of hostility towards them burst its bounds. Albert was a foreigner, a German. He did not ride, shake hands, or dress like an Englishman. Then too, he neither betted nor gambled, and took no interest in horses. Stockmar—surely an adventurer and a spy—was his bosom friend and adviser; some said his master. He was the cunning agent of Russia and in the pay of the Emperor. Once—when he had not left Coburg for six months—he was reported to be hidden at Buckingham Palace, plotting with Albert. Stockmar was partly to blame for Albert's unpopularity; he had taught him everything except the arts of geniality and conciliation, and of making friends instead of enemies of the powerful English aristocracy. His beloved Prussia, too, had behaved very badly about the war, the King being afraid to quarrel with his brother-in-law, Nicholas.

"Prussia, unhappy country," wrote Albert. "The King is the tool of Russian dictators, partly from fear of Russia, partly from an absurdly sentimental feeling for the Emperor as representative of the Holy Alliance."

The engagement of the Crown Princess to Prince Frederick William of Russia did not improve matters. It was regarded with cold hostility. *The Times* called the *Hohenzollern* "a paltry German dynasty," and assumed that the prince—though heir to the throne after his father— was to enter the service of Russia.

In 1857 Princess Alice died, and later on in the year came another blow—Stockmar left England for ever. He was seventy years old. For twenty years he had been the power behind the throne and—through Albert—had exercised a powerful influence on English affairs. It was ime to go home. For four years the bereaved and inconsolable Victoria and her "Beloved Prince" struggled on without him, and then came to

Victoria the worst tragedy of all—the death of her husband. Albert, whose health had for some time been rapidly deteriorating and who—notwithstanding Victoria's adoration—had never known happiness in England, contracted typhoid fever. His enfeebled constitution could offer no resistance to the disease and in October 1861, he died, old and worn out at the age of forty-two.

IV

Messieurs, le temps me presse,
Adieu, la compagnie,
Grâce à vos politesses!

YES. *Grâce à vos politesses!* The baron did not want them; he had never
had any use for them. The death of the Prince was a terrible blow to
him. Albert was his creation, his tool, and now he was dead; the purpose
for which they had worked so long, in season and out of season, was
unfulfilled. When they had set out on their Italian tour, Albert was an
ingenuous boy, innocent, intelligent, full of good intentions, and so
pliable that he had been as wax in his (Stockmar's) hands. With tireless
pertinacity he had, as we have seen, striven to kindle in the boy's heart
his own passionate patriotism and his ambitions for the Fatherland.
With that object he had taught him to despise the gaiety and the pleasures
of youth; not for him the "days of wine and roses"—he must never relax.
He had turned him into a dull, industrious political machine, and the
machinery had run down. The happy, unsophisticated lad had changed
into a sick, worried man, old at forty. And it was *his* work.

Had he chosen, what could he not have made of Albert? He could
have taught him how to gain the affections of the easy-going, kindly
English people, so quick to respond to the graciousness of princes. He
could have shown him how to conciliate instead of antagonizing the
aristocracy, and warned him not to indulge in his passion for reforming
abuses, and to refrain from interfering with what did not concern him.
Albert was a real lover of art, especially music, and he could have made
the Court one of the pleasantest in Europe, a centre of culture—not
Kultur—and of all that makes life worth living. From it would have
spread a civilizing influence throughout the country. And under Stockmar
he had turned it into—Coburg! Had the baron any misgivings as, with
the ceaseless reiteration of the old and sick, he recalled the events of
the past? Probably not—he was too thoroughly self-centred.

And yet he was a good man; he had no personal ambition, he sought
no financial reward. But his *idée-fixe* obsessed him and to it he was
ready to sacrifice ruthlessly everything and everybody. That he was
detested both in Belgium and England did not cause him a moment's
worry. In 1858, when he was paying a visit to the Crown Prince and
Princess of Prussia, a friend of his, with whom he had been seen crossing
the bridge that leads from the palace at Potsdam, was afterwards asked
by an Austrian diplomatist: "Who was that man walking with you this

morning?" "Stockmar," was the answer. "Then why on earth didn't you pitch him into the river?"

In every country in which he carried on his activities he was supposed to be spying on behalf of some other country. But he had his admirers. One of them wrote to him with true German obsequiousness: "Highly esteemed, thoughtful, deeply versed in all worldly wisdom, and nevertheless nobly simple friend."

"*Vous avez mené une existence souterraine,*" a friend once said to him. Of this he was well aware. In one of his letters he wrote: "The peculiarity of my position compelled me to efface the best things I attempted and sometimes succeeded in accomplishing. Even now, people often tell me of such and such things, and how this or that arose and came to pass, and in so far as they only speak of the last stage of their production, they are right enough. But those good people knew nothing of the first growth . . . the first and chief merit is undoubtedly due to him who, of his own motion and *solely for the eventual benefit of others*, laid the seed corn at the right time in the right soil. If men and circumstances generally combine to envelop in night and darkness the best of my conceptions and ideas, that will hardly annoy me." There speaks the true German! Omniscient, self-satisfied, never wrong.

Stockmar had journeyed far. The uncouth son of the respectable Coburg lawyer, the obscure medical student had become the adviser and confidant of kings; a man to whom the secret, tortuous tracks of European diplomacy were open roads. But happiness, which through him had eluded poor Albert, eluded him also. He lived quietly at Coburg in a complete state of hypochondria, seeing only his sisters and a few old friends. To pass the long, weary hours he sorted his papers and could hardly believe that he had ever been in relation with many of even his most distinguished and prolific correspondents; he had forgotten their very handwriting. The complicated questions of which the letters treated had either solved themselves or remained unsolved; the play was over and the actors were resting.

"I must confess that I was not prepared for such a miserable old age," he wrote. His stomach ached on for two years after the death of Albert until, in 1863, a stroke of apoplexy removed him to a higher sphere, where—if there are pens in paradise—he must most assuredly be engaged in writing memoranda on the politics of the celestial realm.

When he had breathed his last, his worthy *Frau*—who, poor soul, had been left so much to her own devices—carefully removed the elaborate nightgown in which he had been attired to receive the farewel visits of his friends. Whether because having brought nothing into the world he should carry nothing out, or because in those days German custom decreed that the garments in which one died were the perquisite of the undertaker, history does not relate. On his tombstone are the appropriate words:

"There is a friend that sticketh closer than a brother!"

BIBLIOGRAPHY

Memoirs of Baron Stockmar	By his son.
Queen Victoria	Lytton Strachey.
The Prince Consort and His Brother	Hector Bolitho.
Memoirs of William Lamb—Second Lord Melbourne	W. M. Torrens.
Life of the Prince Consort	Charlotte M. Yonge.
The Creevey Papers	
The Greville Memoirs	
Letters of Charles Greville and Henry Reeve	

LORD GEORGE GORDON

(A Study in Fanaticism)

"What excellent fools religion makes of men."
(Ben Jonson)

I

TO many of us the lives and characters of people whose names, for some reason or other, we still remember, are far more interesting than are those created by writers of fiction. What were they *really* like, those men who succeeded in earning a brief respite from the oblivion which is the ultimate fate of us all? History, generally speaking, concentrates on the high lights of a period; the great events, the principal actors. And even so, it, of necessity, leaves much to our imagination. The minor rôles in the drama it is apt to leave in comparative obscurity. And yet without them the play would be incomplete, often indeed, difficult to understand, for it is the *collective* action which leads to a logical *dénouement*.

Lord George Gordon was one of those minor actors from the historical point of view, though few men loomed larger in the public eye during the last quarter of the eighteenth century, if only as a public nuisance! Dickens in *Barnaby Rudge* gives us a brilliant description of the famous riots, but his Lord George does not remotely resemble the real Lord George, and the characters associated with him are mere caricatures: the mingling of real characters with the creations of fiction is seldom very satisfactory.

The interesting article on Lord George in the *Dictionary of National Biography*, in its brief enumeration of some of the chief events of his strange career, awakens our curiosity by hinting at the story behind the picture. Mr. de Castro, whose account of the riots[1] is now the standard work on the subject, has almost entirely excluded the personal element and passes over Lord George's later life with almost indecent haste.

A great deal of what we know of him as a man is to be found in a very rare work which, if only as a human document, is well worth reading—*The Life of Lord George Gordon with a Philosophical Review of His Political Conduct*, by Robert Watson, M.D., London, 1795. There are, I believe, only about three copies of it in existence; even the British Museum—though it boasts one—cannot trace it on the library shelves. Dr. Watson, who combined revolutionary ardour with a taste for letters, should be remembered—but is not—as editor and biographer of *Fletcher of Saltoun*. He had risen to the rank of colonel in Washington's army, and returning to England, attached himself to Gordon and ultimately wrote his biography. This delightfully intimate book reminds the

[1] *The Gordon Riots*—J. Paul de Castro (Oxford, 1926).

41

reader strongly of the more famous Dr. Watson created by Conan Doyle. We know that the idea of Sherlock Holmes came to Doyle through his friendship with Dr. Bell of Edinburgh. Can Bell have drawn his attention to the biography? The "My dear Watson" of Sherlock Holmes has the same dogged loyalty, the same complete lack of humour, and the same hero worship which characterize our eighteenth-century Watson, and he is bursting with the same admirable moral sentiments.

The picture Dr. Watson gives us of Lord George, though coloured, of course, by his friendship, is obviously a true one. He shows us the real man with all his enthusiasms, his obstinacy, his kindly, lovable nature and—though Watson does not realize that he is giving his friend away —his total lack of judgment and stability. He is readable even when his gullibility is most obvious, and he tells us the story of the fantastic scrapes in which Lord George managed to involve himself, as if they were all caused by the evil machinations of his enemies. Eccentric Lord George certainly was. Gibbon called him "a mischievous madman," Horace Walpole "the lunatic apostle," and Hume speaks of him as having become insane. To be eccentric, however, does not necessarily denote insanity—were this the case we should need a vastly greater number of asylums—and one notes that the eminently sane Dr. Johnson does not hint that the riots were instigated by a madman. If Lord George was mad, so—for instance—were Lady Hester Stanhope and poor John Mytton. But no one ever suggested that they were anything but eccentric.

But, sane or insane, Lord George was the first aristocratic Socialist in England, the first pacifist in the modern sense, and one of the first to make a protest against the extreme brutality of the criminal laws. Dr. Parr—who was in some ways at least as eccentric—had already drawn attention to them.

The standard works of reference list over a dozen persons of eminence who went by the name of George Gordon, and Gordon has always been a favourite name with Jewish moneylenders. Our Lord George Gordon was a younger son of Cosmo, third Duke of Gordon in the peerage of Scotland; he was born at the family town house in Upper Grosvenor Street on 26th December, 1751. His father died some six months later. His mother was a daughter of the Earl of Aberdeen, and therefore herself of the Gordon clan. The family is one of the oldest in Scotland. We find them mentioned in twelfth-century documents as having been witnesses to charters by the Earl of March—the title now held by the eldest son of the Duke of Richmond and Gordon— and as donors of patches of land and rights of pasturage to the monks of Kelso. In 1445 the head of the clan was created Earl of Huntley; in

1559 the earl became a marquess, and in 1684 the marquess blossomed into a duke and called himself Duke of Gordon. The dukedom, as also the two English peerages of Norwich and of Gordon, became extinct in 1836, on the death of the fifth duke, who left no heir.

Lord George passed his earliest years in the north of Scotland, his mother having left London soon after his birth. There he was taught to read and write laboriously, and at the age of seven he was sent to Eton—to Dame Elley's house; there were then no preparatory schools. It was a rough life; for delicate and sensitive boys it must have been hell. But he survived it; and in the mid-eighteenth century the death rate among children was so enormously high that only the toughest survived epidemics, ignorance of hygiene, bad feeding and doctors. He was popular at Eton, both with boys and masters. The *Morning Post* of 18th July, 1780, says, in a sketch of his life, that though not enterprising he was a cheerful and boon companion, tinctured with those qualities which serve to make a man rather amiable than great, rather happy than famous. . . . "Throughout his life no man has been blest with more friends or fewer enemies."

He did not stay long at Eton. His mother took to herself a second husband, this time a young army subaltern, named Morris. It was not for nothing that he had married a duchess, for in a short time he was, through the Gordon influence, gazetted general and appointed to the command of a regiment. King George II—who was Lord George's godfather—when nominating the officers, appointed him ensign under his stepfather. His military career was a short one, for his mother, thinking, no doubt, that it would be better to concentrate all the family influence at the War Office on her young husband, decided to put little George into the navy. So he was appointed midshipman by Lord Sandwich, and nominated to a ship sailing for the American station, serving six months in Jamaica. When, in 1772, aged twenty-one, he had become lieutenant, with characteristic eighteenth-century arrogance he thought himself entitled to a command! So he asked Lord Sandwich for promotion. He was informed that others—his seniors—could not be passed over, but, as ships were being built, he would be remembered when an occasion presented itself. This did not please Lord George; he consulted his friend Edmund Burke, who suggested that he should leave the navy and take up politics, promising him that he should be returned for some borough in the Rockingham interest. Thereupon Lord George went again to Lord Sandwich, asking him to say definitely whether or not he would give him a ship. Again Lord Sandwich was politely evasive, so, taking his commission out of his pocket, he handed it to his lordship and told him to do what he liked with it.

The next thing to do was to find a borough to represent. He returned to Scotland, and, a parliamentary election occurring soon after, he decided to contest the seat for Inverness-shire, which had long been held by Colonel Frazer of Beauly Castle. Lord George proved himself a master of electioneering tactics. Watson tells us that he visited every part of the county, played on the violin and bagpipes, spoke Gaelic, and wore the tartan and filibeg in places where they were the national costume. He gave a grand ball at Inverness, to which he invited the young and old from every part of the constituency; he even hired a yacht in order to bring from the Isle of Skye the fifteen beautiful girls belonging to the MacLeod Clan—"the pride and admiration of the north." He was an attractive youth and his charms were irresistible; too irresistible for the elderly Colonel Frazer, who, not wanting to lose the seat, went to the Duke of Gordon and offered to purchase another seat for his dangerous rival. Lord George consented, and in 1774 entered the House of Commons, as joint representative with the first Lord Melbourne, of the borough of Ludgershall in Wiltshire, a pocket borough which was the property of George Selwyn. So, at twenty-three, having been both soldier and sailor, behold him a budding politician. At this period he seems to have been amiable and high-spirited. William Hickey describes him two years later as "gay, volatile, and a follower of Bacchus," and Samuel Romily— though he did not like him—says he was "strong-willed and enthusiastic."

Lord George took his seat in difficult times. Lord North, who had been head of the administration since 1770, was thoroughly and deservedly unpopular. By 1778 the Opposition was so strong that he was expected to resign at any moment. There was the perennial Irish question, the American war, which, to the great delight of England's many enemies, was going as badly as possible, and to add to his troubles, war clouds were gathering on the Continent. Perhaps things would have gone better had not the King succeeded in keeping him in power, or had he (the King) fallen into complete imbecility a few years earlier; he was less dangerous as a lunatic. Edmund Burke attributed the whole of the grievances to "the fatal and overgrown influence of the Crown."

Trouble thus threatening on every side, it seemed to the Government a suitable moment for conciliating the Catholics and improving their legal status, with a view to enlisting their co-operation—the more so, seeing that the Quebec Act of 1774 had recognized Catholicism as the established religion of Canada. It was indeed high time that the iniquitous laws against them, which dated from the reign of William of Orange, were repealed.

Lord North first turned to the Scottish Catholics. He sent to them as confidential agent Sir John Dalrymple, a Baron of the Exchequer of

the Scottish Judiciary. Sir John interviewed the Vicar Apostolic of the
Lowlands, Baron Hay, who received the proposals favourably, but the
Pope's Vicar Apostolic, Bishop Challoner, whom he consulted on his
return to London, was timid and apprehensive of danger. It was William
Sheldon, a Jesuit-trained lawyer, who proved the most helpful. He disapproved of bringing the clergy into temporal matters; they were, he
said, the business of the Catholic gentlemen of England. So the Duke of
Norfolk, the Earl of Shrewsbury, Lord Petre and other leading Catholics
were approached, and it was decided to present a petition to the King,
offering him the lives and fortunes of his Catholic subjects. Edmund
Burke drew up the petition, which was graciously and gratefully received,
and a Bill drafted by Sir George Savile—known to fame as the *Mr.
Burchill* of Goldsmith's *Vicar of Wakefield*, the portrait by Hogarth, and
by Savile Row, which was named after his family—was rushed through
both Houses, and passed without a division.

The Act was moderate enough. Among the worst abuses it removed
were the penalties and disabilities by which Catholic priests could be
arrested and sentenced to perpetual imprisonment for keeping schools;
the laws which forbade Catholics to purchase or inherit land; and the
most objectionable clauses of the Attestation Act. It also allowed them
the right to worship in their own manner. But moderate as the reforms
were, they infuriated the Puritan element, strong throughout the country,
above all, the Evangelicals, Dissenters and Presbyterians. In Scotland the
Bill aroused a frenzy of fanaticism, which spread like wild-fire. Inflammatory publications poured from the Press; in every pulpit violent
measures against it were advocated and dangerous riots broke out—
particularly at Edinburgh and Glasgow. Catholic churches were burnt,
and Catholic ladies were compelled to take refuge in Edinburgh Castle.
So alarmed were the Scottish Catholics at the beginning of 1779, that
they wrote to the Government begging to be excused from the benefits
of the measure. Only when the Edinburgh magistrates were authorized
to publish a proclamation announcing that the proposal to ameliorate
the condition of the Scottish Catholics was entirely and irrevocably
abandoned, did the agitations reluctantly die down. Encouraged by the
success of the fanatical resistance to the Bill in Scotland, the English
religious bigots decided to adopt similar tactics. They, too, organized
societies, and the London Association of Protestants was formed. It was
rich in enthusiasm, funds, numbers and—it was convinced—divine
approbation. All it needed was a leader, and it found one in Lord George
Gordon, who had identified himself with the Anti-Catholic cause.

In 1778, when Lord George had been four years in Parliament, he
looked at the world, and behold, it was very evil! Man, that is to say,

political man, which also signified aristocratic man, had created God in his own image, and in return for the compliment expected God to play the game like a gentleman: to bless the squire and his relations and not to interfere with their feudal rights over the common herd. On the whole, God had come up to scratch, so man was contented enough.

Not so Lord George. Something had happened to him; what, and how, is a puzzle. He had entirely lost that easy good nature and desire to please which had made him so popular in his boyhood and youth. During his first two years in Parliament he had apparently taken very little interest in the debates, spending his time, rather, in studying parliamentary procedure and the tricky ways of politicians. To account for the change in him, one can only suppose that the political and social abuses and the corruption he saw on every side had worked on his impressionable, generous, but unbalanced and revolutionary nature. Perhaps too, conceit, ambition, and a desire to be in the limelight played their part—we have seen how petulantly he resigned his commission—though only twenty-one—when Lord Sandwich refused him a command.

But whatever the cause of his discontent, the time was out of joint for Lord George. Everything roused him to indignation, including the corrupt system to which he owed his seat in Parliament. Above all did he hate the privileged class into which he had been born. He began to speak in every debate, criticizing every measure proposed and disagreeing with members of both parties, with Lord North, Pitt, Fox, and even with his friend, Edmund Burke. He doubted the sincerity of Burke's "windy harangues," and felt that he was "no friend to the people." These tactics did not endear him to the House, though his constant flattery of the people was beginning to make him a popular figure outside. They said there were three parties in the country: "The Ministry, the Opposition, and Lord George Gordon."

Worst of all, he had become a religious crank. From the first he had rushed furiously into the fray against the Savile Bill. In 1780 a member complained that "the noble Lord is perpetually interrupting the business of the House by his anti-papistical tirades."

It is difficult to understand how he came by this anti-Catholic bias. His family had long withstood the flood of Protestantism—his great-grandfather was one of the Norfolk Howards—and after they became nominal Protestants they remained on the most friendly terms with the Catholics on their estates, on one of which was situated a Catholic college. And in any case, at no time in their history have the Ducal Gordons been noted for religion. Perhaps Lord George was just a "Gay Gordon" rampant!

The Protestant Association, in inviting him to become its president, spoke of his noble zeal in the Protestant interest, his spirited conduct in Parliament, the numerous societies he supported in Scotland, and implored his aid to "preserve civil liberties from the encroachments of Popery." Who could refuse so flattering an invitation? Certainly not Lord George Gordon. He protested, but not too much, at the compliment paid him, in a letter which fills three closely-printed pages and ends by saying with what pleasure he would help to assist in obtaining the repeal of a "Popish Act so pernicious in its tendency to the civil and religious liberties of these kingdoms."

And so the Protestant Association and Lord George were united; a petition to Parliament was drawn up, and Lord George, with the committee, waited on Lord North on 4th January, 1780, asking him to present and support it. After a long conference, North refused categorically either to support it, or to take any steps for the repeal of the Act. So it was decided that copies of the petition should lie open for signature, one at Lord George's house in Welbeck Street, one at the office of the secretary, and another at the Standard Tavern, Leicester Fielsd. A few days after, Lord George made an insolent speech in the House. Addressing the Speaker, he said that before long they would introduce a petition "which will extend, sir, from your chair to a window at Whitehall that kings should often think of." As day by day the position of the agitators strengthened, both Government and the Catholics —who throughout the affair behaved extraordinarily well—becamee alarmed. Lord Petre appealed to Lord George. He said the petitioners were a "mean lot," that they were trading on his (Lord George's) popularity, that the Catholics had a considerable regard for him, and that if he would join the ranks of the party he could, with his abilities and family influence, attain to any position he chose. Why not, he suggested with great moderation, give the Act time to come into operation, and see if it were really as dangerous as he anticipated? But no, Lord George and moderation were strangers. His followers might be mean, but he was not mean enough to throw them over, and so on. Before leaving, Lord Petre said: "*I am afraid riots will happen in presenting the petition.*"

Lord George then went to see Edmund Burke; they had long been intimate friends, notwithstanding his distrust of Burke's politics. But when Burke heard of the failure of Lord Petre's mission, he told Lord George that he could choose between his (Burke's) friendship and the Association. So a friendship of many years was sacrificed in an instant and never resumed. Lord George's next step was to seek an audience of the King—to which, being the son of a duke, he was entitled. On entering the presence, he bolted the door, and in a solemn voice reminded His Majesty that "the House of Stuart had been banished from the throne for encouraging Popery and arbitrary power," and requested King George to order his ministers to support the petition.

"I have taken no part in the late Bill. Parliament did it," he replied.

"But sir, you *have* taken a part, and a very capital part too, by giving your royal assent to it," said Lord George. He then told the King that one of His Majesty's judges had carried on a private correspondence with a "Popish bishop" for the diabolical purpose of arming the Papists against the colonies in America, and gave the name of the judge. Poor George, who would gladly have consigned Papists, colonies and Lord George to the devil, answered:

"I have not been privy to any secret transaction of that nature. I am a Protestant." To change the subject, he asked after Lord George's family. Not to be beguiled, Lord George asked him to say definitely whether or not he would direct his ministers to support the petition.

"I am in no way pledged in the business," said the King.

"Am I to understand, then, that your Majesty declines to speak to Lord North?"

King George bowed his assent and terminated the interview.

A few days afterwards, Watson tells us, Lord North called on Lord George in Welbeck Street and, when the elaborate eighteenth-century courtesies had been exchanged, said that he had a message from His Majesty to communicate. He then, on the King's behalf, offered him a handsome sum of money and an important Government post if he would resign his leadership of the Association, and Lord George replied, that while he was much obliged for His Majesty's gracious offer he would neither accept the money nor have anything to do with a government in which Lord North was minister. The interview doubtless ended less cordially than it had begun. If this report be true—and there is every reason to doubt it—he was throwing away a great opportunity. The fact that he was invited to be president of the Association—whose leaders were by no means negligible—proves that he was already of some political importance and, as Lord Petre had reminded him, he had everything in his favour. But he had gone too far to draw back, nor had he any wish to do so; he was intoxicated by his own fanaticism. "It is a proud thing to lead the people," Dickens makes him say.

Dickens, in *Barnaby Rudge*, gives us a description of his appearance in 1780, which, judging by contemporary portraits, is probably accurate.

He was about the middle height, of a slender make, and sallow complexion, with an aquiline nose, and long hair of a reddish brown, combed perfectly straight and smooth about his ears and slightly powdered, but without the vestige of a curl. He was attired, under his great-coat, in a full suit of black, quite free from any ornament, and of the most precise and sober cut. The

Queen Victoria and Prince Albert in wedding dress

Albert, Prince Consort

Princess Charlotte of Wales and Prince Leopold of Saxe Cobourg

Clandestine meeting of Prince Leopold and Princess Charlotte gravity of his dress, together with a certain lankiness of cheek and stiffness of deportment, added nearly ten years to his age, but his figure was that of one not past thirty. As he stood musing in the red glow of the fire, it was striking to observe his very large bright eyes, which betrayed a restlessness of thought and purpose, singularly at variance with the studied composure and sobriety of his mien, and with his quaint and sad apparel. It had nothing harsh or cruel in its expression; neither had his face, which was thin and mild, and wore an air of melancholy; but it was suggestive of an indefinite uneasiness.

That he was sincere in his hatred of Catholics is probably true. He attributed to them the amiable qualities with which Lord Clarendon endowed John Hampden—"a head to contrive, a tongue to persuade, and a hand to execute any mischief."

All efforts to persuade the government to repeal the Savile Act having failed, the Protestant Association decided that the petition must be presented without delay. Lord George called a meeting for 29th May, at the Coachmakers' Hall, at which he made a long and violent speech. "Popery is making great strides," he said; "the only way to stop it is for them to go in a firm and manly way to the House and to show their representatives that they were determined to preserve their religious freedom with their lives." "I tell you candidly," he said, "that I am not a lukewarm man, and if you wish to spend your time in debate and idle opposition you can get another leader."

He then proposed the resolution:

"That the Protestant Association do attend in St. George's Fields on Friday next, 2nd June, at ten o'clock in the morning, to accompany his lordship to the House of Commons on the delivery of the Protestant petition."

In order that they might know their friends from their enemies, he asked every true Protestant to wear a blue cockade in his hat.

The resolution, duly reported to the Government, had the effect of, for once, uniting all parties. Burke wrote to Lord Loughborough, begging him to urge the Government to announce without delay the way in which it would act in the matter, and himself suggested the answer he thought suitable. Lord North replied personally: "to inform you of the conduct we mean to observe when the petition to be presented by Lord George Gordon shall be taken into consideration." He sent Burke a copy of the resolution.

That the Association had strong supporters in the city is shown by a minute, which on the 31st May the Court of Common Council entered on their records:

It is the opinion of this Court that the passing of any Acts of Parliament, in favour of Papists, or repealing any Acts against Popery, is totally repugnant

D

to the true interests of this country; and this Court doth request this city's representation in Parliament to support any Bill that may be brought into Parliament for repealing the late Act in favour of Roman Catholics so far as relates to the establishment of seminaries for the education of youth, and the purchasing of lands within this realm of England.

II

THE great day arrived. On Friday, 2nd June, about sixty thousand of Lord George's followers assembled at St. George's-in-the-Fields, now— even such is time!—the site of the Catholic Cathedral of St. George's, Southwark. Each of them wore the blue cockade in his hat. "It is hot and disagreeable in London, with violent lightning every evening," wrote Lord Jersey to Countess Spencer, the same day.

The organization was excellent, the plan of campaign being carried out exactly as arranged. At about eleven o'clock Lord George appeared, mounted on a tall, bony horse; he was an awkward rider, stiff and angular. He carried a long gold-headed ebony stick with one of its ends projecting on either side, and his long, straight powdered hair was hanging about his pale face. He dismounted and harangued the mob, which pressed so closely round him that he was half-suffocated. He ordered one division to proceed over London Bridge, another by way of Blackfriars, and he himself took charge of those who were to approach the House of Commons by crossing Westminster Bridge. Before him marched two men carrying the petition—an enormous roll containing the signatures of at least one hundred and twenty thousand people. The procession took its way in perfect order and by half past two the whole body assembled in front of the Houses of Parliament. So far there had been no horse-play, but the genuine petitioners had been joined *en route* by another and more dangerous element of the population: young roughs out for a lark, pick-pockets out for loot, and the unemployed.

Shouts of "No Popery" were raised, and the roughs began to attack members on their way to the two Houses, insulting them in the most violent and indecent manner. Some they obliged to take oaths to vote for the repeal of the Act. Lord Mansfield, the Lord Chief Justice—who was suspected of Papist sympathies on account of his friendship with the Duchess of Norfolk and because he had recently acquitted a Catholic priest, whom he tried for saying Mass—had the windows and panels of his carriage smashed, and he himself narrowly escaped with his life. The Archbishop of York was greeted with groans and hisses; Lord Bathurst, Lord President of the Council, was, notwithstanding his great age, "pushed about rudely and kicked violently on the legs"; the Bishop of Lichfield had his gown torn off, and his brother of Lincoln, who was unpopular, fared worse.

51

The *Morning Post* of 3rd June thus describes the incident:

The conduct of the Christian associates on Friday to the Bishop of Lincoln was such as would have disgraced infidels. They took the hind-wheels off his lordship's coach, which they attempted to overturn, and when he had gotten out, tore his canonicals, struck at him repeatedly and would in all probability have destroyed him in the fury of their rage, had not a young gentleman, Mr. McNalty of the Temple, interposed and at the risque of his life, fought through the mob till he got the bishop to the house of Mr. Atkinson, an attorney. There the bishop dressed himself in a gown of Mrs. McNalty's and managed to escape by climbing over a back wall.

Others attacked and robbed were the Duke of Northumberland, Lord Townshend and Lord Hillingborough. Lord Stormont, Gold Stick in Waiting—Lord Mansfield's nephew and heir—had his carriage smashed, and the same thing happened to Lord Sandwich. How he must have regretted not having given Lord George a ship, when he had applied for promotion eight years earlier! By this time he might have been comfortably drowned, killed in the American war, or even—with luck—scalped by Indians! Lecky describes the scene at Westminster that afternoon:

No serious discussion was possible [he says]. Pale, bruised and agitated, with their wigs torn and bespattered with mud, the peers of England sat listening to the frantic yells of the multitude, who already thronged the lobbies.

Meanwhile the petition had been received by the officers of the House of Commons and laid on the table for presentation; with it went Lord George. For some time nothing happened; the members were too much engaged with the mob to pay it any attention, indeed, only the doorkeepers and a few ordinary officials were there to protect the Holy Temple of British Liberties. The doors were locked and the Strangers' Gallery empty. From time to time Lord George went to the head of the stairs to report progress. He told them of the poor success the petition seemed to be likely to meet with, mentioning the names of those who opposed it, particularly naming Burke. He told them that it was proposed to take it into consideration the following Tuesday, but, he said, "I do not like delays." Shortly after, he again addressed them:

"Gentlemen, the alarm has gone forth for many miles round the city. You have got a very good Prince, who, as soon as he shall hear the alarm has seized such a number of men, will, no doubt, send down private orders to his ministers to enforce the passage of your petition."

This was too much. General Conway, who was standing near, warned him of the danger of such language, and General Gordon, a near relation, went up to him and said: "My Lord George, do you intend to bring your rascally adherents into the House of Commons? If you do, the first man of them that enters, I will plunge my sword, not into his, but into *your* body." An old friend, General Grant, cried: "For God's sake, Lord George, do not lead these poor people into danger!" But it was no use; the fanatical strain in his character was now in complete possession.

The mob had made two attempts to force the doors, but by this time a detachment of horse and foot guards had arrived; they were roundly cursed and pelted with every available missile. Mr. Justice Addington—under whose instruction they were acting—then told the petitioners that if they would disperse peaceably, he would dismiss the soldiers. They cheered him, and large numbers of them departed. At last Lord George secured a hearing. He had, he said, a petition signed by near a hundred and twenty thousand of His Majesty's Protestant subjects, praying for a repeal of the obnoxious Act, and moved to have it taken into immediate consideration. He was seconded by Mr. Alderman Bull. Only six were for the petition and a hundred and ninety-two against it. The House then adjourned, and peace was re-established in the parliamentary precincts.

Elsewhere, trouble was brewing. A large party of roughs made for Duke Street, Lincoln's Inn Fields, and demolished the beautiful chapel attached to the Sardinian Ministry, in which—it being under diplomatic immunity—London Catholics were accustomed to worship. Others rushed to Warwick Street, Golden Square, and wrecked the Bavarian Minister's private chapel. A number of rioters were arrested and taken to the public office in Bow Street, where Sir John Fielding—half-brother of the novelist—committed them to prison.

On Saturday morning things seemed to be quietening down; but it was only a lull in the storm. On Sunday the rioting broke out again with renewed violence. Large numbers of rioters attacked the houses and chapels of Catholics round Moorfields, smashing and stealing furniture and valuables. By midday business in the city was at a standstill. A detachment of the mob started the day by marching in procession to Lord George's house, carrying relics of the chapels they had destroyed; others went to Wapping and Smithfield, wrecking and looting the houses of Catholics and of anyone suspected of Popish leanings. Two tradesmen who had given evidence against some of the rioters charged at Bow Street, had their houses and shops burnt, and Sir George Savile's house in Leicester Fields met with the same fate; the iron railings round it were torn out and used as weapons, and had he himself not managed to escape, he would probably have paid for the Act of Repeal with his life. During the day a reward of five hundred pounds was offered for the apprehension of those concerned in wrecking and plundering the chapels of the Sardinian and Bavarian ministers.

One of the most remarkable features of the riots was the absolute incapacity—or even reluctance—of the city authorities to attempt to cope with the situation. Mr. Malo, a well-known silk merchant, went to the Mansion House to warn the Lord Mayor, Brackley Kennett[1], that the mob intended to destroy the Catholic chapels in Moorfields, and afterwards to demolish the Mansion House. Kennett, who was extremely agitated, declared that he did not know what to do. "You do not know anything of the business," he said. "I have orders to employ the military if necessary, but I must be cautious lest I bring the mob to my house. I can assure you that there are very great people at the bottom of the riot." Again, on Sunday, 4th June, when an officer of the Sun Fire office, who was with his engines at Moorfields, asked Kennett for orders, he was told to be quiet and leave him alone. Lord Beauchamp, who was in command at the Tower, told Kennett that it was his duty to take action, and that he should report his conduct to the House of Commons. My Lord Mayor did not condescend to reply. Later, he said to Lord Beauchamp that "the mob had got hold of some people and furniture they did not like, and what was the harm in that?"

On Tuesday, 6th June, both Houses of Parliament, St. James's Palace, and the Bank were guarded by troops, as also the New River Head, the rioters having threatened to cut the main pipes in order that there should be no water to extinguish the fire. Every cut-purse and bully in the town had now joined in the game, and a brutish, drunken and criminal rabble was working its will in the city. The Protestant Association, alarmed at the demon it had unloosed, issued a handbill signed by Lord George, begging its followers "to refrain from unconstitutional proceedings." But it was too late. The cry now was—Destroy! Burn! Loot! A howling mob descended on Lord Mansfield's beautiful house in Bloomsbury Square. They began by piling his furniture in the street; to this they added the contents of his valuable library, containing many law books annotated by their owner, his rare manuscripts, his fine collection of pictures, and all the wearing apparel they could find. They then set fire to the pile. The cellars were then looted, the wines and spirits were brought up, and an orgy of bestiality followed. Finally they set the house itself on fire. A body of guards arrived when it was nearly all over; the Riot Act was read; the order was given to fire, and many of the mob were killed or wounded. Lord and Lady Mansfield had escaped

---

[1]Kennett started life as a waiter in a low public house; he afterwards kept a brothel, then a tavern, and finally went into business as a wine merchant, becoming an alderman and in due course Lord Mayor of London.

by a back door a few minutes before the rioters arrived. Another party had, at the same time, looted and burnt the house of Sir John Fielding, which was full of works of art. Another famous building which narrowly escaped destruction was Lambeth Palace. The mob had arrived in great force, but the Guards, a hundred strong, got there in time to save it.

Late on Tuesday afternoon the crowd marched to Newgate to rescue their comrades who had been arrested. The prison had recently been built at a cost of over £45,000, and was reputed to be the strongest in England. But it was not strong enough to resist the violence of the mob. Crabbe, then unknown to fame and having arrived in London— if not with the proverbial half-crown in his pocket, at any rate possessed of less than three pounds—gives a vivid description of what he saw. He lodged near the Royal Exchange and was returning to his rooms, when he came upon the rioters in the act of firing the house of Mr. Akerman, the governor of the prison—Boswell's great friend. He also saw Lord George in a coach, accompanied by a mob of at least five hundred, bowing right and left as he passed. He describes him as "a lively-looking young man in appearance and nothing more, though just now the reigning hero." Crabbe was shocked by the brutality of the crowd. "By eight o'clock," he says, "Mr. Akerman's house was in flames; the prison was, as I said, a remarkably strong building, but determined to force it, the mob broke the gates with crows and other instruments and climbed up the outside of the cell part, which joins the two great wings of the building where the felons are confined, and I stood where I plainly saw their operations. They broke the roof, tore away the rafters, and having got ladders, they descended. Flames all round them and a body of soldiers expected, they defied and laughed at all opposition. The prisoners escaped. I stood and saw about twelve women and eight men ascend from their confinement to the open air. You have no conception of the frenzy of the multitude. This being done and Akerman's house a mere shell of brickwork, they kept a stove of flame there for other purposes. It became red-hot, and the doors and windows appeared like so many volcanoes. With some difficulty they then fired the debtors' prison, broke the doors, and they too made their escape. Tired of the scene, I went home." In the evening he returned, and saw ten or twelve men getting on to the top of the debtors' prison while it was still burning. In the black smoke, mixed with sudden bursts of fire, they looked "like Milton's infernals, who were as familiar with flame as with each other."

Wednesday, 7th June—long remembered in London as "Black Wednesday"—dawned on a veritable reign of terror. "'Black Wednesday' was the most horrible night I ever beheld, which for six hours together,

I expected to end in half the town being reduced to ashes," wrote Horace Walpole. All shops were shut and the streets were given up to the rioters. Protestant citizens were as terrified of the mob as were the Catholics. Hundreds of householders chalked "No Popery" on their doors and shutters, while others hung out bits of blue silk, to indicate their support of the Association. In Hounsditch and Duke's Place, the centres of the London ghettoes, the Jews tactfully followed suit, chalking on their front doors "This house is a true Protestant." Grimaldi, the famous Italian clown—who had just arrived in England—went one better. With all the irony of his fellow-countryman, Goldoni, he fixed a placard on his door on which was written: "No Religion !" So utterly contemptuous of the authorities were the rioters that they sent notices to the King's Bench and Fleet Prisons to say when they would come to burn them down.

The same infernal politeness they extended to Thomas Langford, a Holborn distiller. There were ghastly doings when they brought up the contents of his vaults, which were full of brandy and raw alcohol. Dickens thus describes the scene:

The gutters of the street, and every crack and fissure in the stones, ran with scorching spirit, which being dammed up by busy hands, overflowed the road and pavement and formed a great pool into which people dropped down dead by dozens. They lay in heaps all round this fearful pond, husbands and wives, fathers and sons, mothers and daughters, women with children in their arms and babies at their breasts, and drank out of hats, pails, buckets, tubs and shoes; some men were drawn out alive, but all alight from head to foot; who, in their unendurable anguish and suffering, making for anything that had the look of water, rolled, hissing, in this hideous lake and splashed up liquid fire, which lapped in all it met with as it ran along the surface, and spared neither the living nor the dead.

That night the inhabitants of the city looked on such a spectacle of horror as has rarely been seen. Clouds of flame and smoke ascended from every direction; from the King's Bench and Fleet Prisons, from the Bridewell, the toll gates on Blackfriars Bridge and from innumerable private houses. Dr. Johnson going to see the ruins of Newgate, passed a gang of the dregs of the population, plundering the Sessions House at Old Bailey; he saw boys in their teens gaily helping to destroy a house, and three little boys armed with iron bars were marching down Holborn, shouting: "No Popery," and extorting money from shopkeepers, who were afraid to refuse lest they should be branded as Papists. The rioting was not confined to London. Fanny Burney wrote from Bath:

Since I writ this morning, to our utter amazement the new Roman Catholic Chapel in this town was set on fire at about nine o'clock. It is now burning with a fury that is dreadful. . . . Mrs. Thrale and I have been walking down with the footmen several times.

Mrs. Thrale wrote the same night:

The flames of the Romish Chapel are not yet extinguished, and the rioters are going to Bristol to burn that. I do not believe that a dog or a cat sleeps in the town this night.

At long last, firm measures were taken. The city authorities were galvanized into activity by the King, and John Wilkes—his old enemy, and erstwhile revolutionary—was to be seen taking a leading part in defending the Bank of England against the mob. Troops were poured in, the rioters were driven into concentrated areas, and by midday, Thursday, the Lord of Misrule was deposed. During the five days' rioting, some hundreds of people were killed or injured, and at least two hundred thousand pounds' worth of damage done.

It would be a mistake to believe that Lord George either instigated or sympathized with the rioting; it would be a greater mistake not to acknowledge that he must have realized that it would be highly probable. The riots were not, however, an isolated phenomenon, caused wholly by anti-Catholic bigotry. Lord Stormont said that they "had deep and foul roots." All the evidence goes to show that they were, in the main, political, provoked by the intense hostility towards Lord North's hated government, and there is little doubt but that the city tacitly connived with the rioters. The country was seething with poverty and discontent; it needed only a spark to set it ablaze, and the Savile Act served the purpose. After order was restored, there was an acrimonious correspondence between the city authorities and the Government, each blaming the other, but both were agreed as to the responsibility of Lord George. After a Cabinet meeting, a warrant was issued "for the apprehending and taking into safe custody, the Right Honourable Lord George Gordon."

On Friday they went to Welbeck Street and found him waiting for them. "If you are sure it is I you want, I am ready to attend you," he said. A hackney coach was called and he was taken to the Horse Guards. After a long examination, which took place at the War Office, before Lord North, the Secretaries of State and several Lords of the Privy Council, he was committed to the Tower, and escorted there by the largest guard ever commanded to escort a State prisoner.

Interesting sidelights are thrown on the riots by the writers of the period. Mrs. Thrale, writing to Dr. Johnson from Bath, says:

And when all the Papists are burned and the Protestants all hanged for burning them, the Jews may jump for joy. I think no one else can be pleased.

Mr. Thrale's brewery, by the way, had a lucky escape, owing to his wily manager, Mr. Perkins. When the mob arrived, he showed them about fifty pounds' worth of food and drink and persuaded them to go away while he prepared the banquet; in the meantime he managed to obtain a detachment of soldiers. When the rioters returned they did not like the look of the waiters, so made off.

Horace Walpole wrote: "Mercy on us! We seem to be plunging into the horrors of France in the reigns of Charles VI and VII, but there is no panic. Lady Aylesbury has been to the play in the Haymarket, and the duke and my four nieces to Ranelagh this evening." Walpole was singularly unsympathetic about Lord Mansfield; he mocked him for his timidity which—considering that he was over seventy and had only just escaped with his life—was not surprising. Baretti, too, was amazed at the cowardice shown by many Londoners. "Not two in all London," he said, "could resolve of joining to each other in their own defence." Johnson had a lot to say about it all. In speaking of the King, who was wholly responsible for the choice of ministers, he said:

"Such a bunch of imbecility never disgraced a country." The riots, he thought, were caused by "Protestant bigotry." He speaks of Lady Albemarle being robbed at Mrs. Keppel's own door in Pall Mall at twelve o'clock at night.

Of those arrested for taking part in the riots—a hundred and fifty-three in all—fifty-nine were sentenced to death, of whom twenty-one were executed. Oddly enough, one of them was the public executioner, Edward Dennis, alias Jack Ketch. He admitted that he helped in burning the house of a Catholic, but pleaded compulsion. He was on his way home, he said, when he was recognized and there were shouts of "There goes bloody Jack Ketch!" Someone called out: "He doesn't like losing his job"—meaning the execution of the escaped prisoners in Newgate, who were to have been hanged on 8th June. The Recorder who tried him agreed that his defence was probably true, considering "the odious light in which he stood as executioner." But the jury, swayed by their hatred of his profession, brought in a verdict of guilty. He begged for mercy, appealing to the sheriffs, aldermen, and the Lord Mayor himself, to bear witness to his exemplary character. Perhaps his conviction of his moral worth smoothed his progress on the path down which he had precipitated so many of his fellow-citizens.

The riots served one useful purpose. They called attention to the urgent necessity for the reform and reorganization of the police.

III

FOR eight months—to the great relief of the Government—Lord George languished in the Tower.

> Stone walls do not a prison make
> Nor iron bars a cage.

But he found that the massive walls of the old fortress resembled one far too closely to be agreeable. At first he was not allowed to take exercise, even on the ramparts, and no one was permitted to see him without a signed order from a member of the Cabinet. All his letters were opened and some of his correspondents were arrested. Great was the grief and indignation of Watson, whose attitude towards the rioters was more sympathetic than that of his noble friend. He seems to have regarded 7th June as a disappointingly abortive Day of Judgment. London, he says, "was wrapped in a Good Friday gloom when the news of Lord George's arrest became known. Suspicion and anxiety were visible on every countenance."

At his trial, which took place on 5th February, 1781, at the King's Bench Court, there was not a vacant seat; people had been waiting in the cold since before dawn for the doors to open. Lord George's two brothers, the Duke of Gordon and Lord William Gordon, were present; so also were the Duke of Richmond, Lord Derby, Charles James Fox, and Sheridan. The presiding judge was Lord Mansfield, who showed a laudably short memory for all he had personally suffered at the hands of the rioters. With him were associated Justices Willes, Ashurst, Buller, and a Grand Jury. All London was agog with excitement. Lord George —with singular stupidity on the part of the authorities—was allowed to drive from the King's Bench in a coach, and the streets through which he passed were lined with cheering crowds and congested with private carriages. Carefully groomed and elegantly dressed in black velvet, he bowed right and left to the spectators and entered the Court with the air of a popular actor making a long and eagerly anticipated reappearance on the stage. With a perfect sense of publicity values, he managed to arrive three-quarters of an hour late, to the great annoyance of Lord Mansfield, who had taken his seat punctually at eight o'clock. For his defence, he had retained his cousin, Thomas Erskine—subsequently Baron Erskine, and Lord Chancellor. Erskine's Junior was Mr. Kenyon. For the Crown were the Attorney-General and the Solicitor-General.

Lord George was all smiles; it was delightful to be once more the centre of attraction. When the jury were called, he objected to no less than nineteen of the names, including one man who was a rope maker. "He is too interested by profession!" said Lord George.

The indictment, drawn up in the inflated and obscure phraseology of the best legal documents, accused George Gordon, "commonly called Lord George Gordon," of not having the fear of God before his eyes and of having conspired—being seduced by the devil—against the peace and tranquillity of the kingdom." The Attorney-General made out a good case against him. He justified the Savile Act, saying that its only fault was that it did not go far enough. Passing to the Protestant Association, he reminded the jury that though it was "the inherent right of the subject to petition Parliament," yet Parliament must not be dictated to. He brought many witnesses to testify to the encouragement Lord George had given to the rioters. One said that he (Lord George) had accused the King of breaking his Coronation Oath; another, that he declared his readiness to go to the gallows for the cause, "and that when some of the leaders asked him: 'Do you wish us to go away?' he answered: 'You are the best judges of what you ought to do,' and that 'it might be a question of now or never.'" The Reverend Thomas Bowen, acting Chaplain to the House of Commons on 2nd June, testified that he had heard one of the leaders say to Lord George that, if he would tell them that it was necessary for them to go, they would do so, and many other witnesses gave evidence that he made no effort to disperse his followers before the situation became dangerous. But the most telling point against him was the evidence of one Richard Pope, who swore that he had applied to the prisoner for protection for his house. He produced a paper which he had written beforehand, which Lord George signed in a coach, on witness assuring him that it would be of service to him.

All true friends of Protestants will be particular and do no injury to the house of any true Protestant. As I am well assured, the proprietor of this house is a staunch and worthy friend to the cause.

(*Signed*) G. Gordon.

All the witnesses agreed that even before the rioting became general, it was dangerous for anyone not wearing the blue cockade to venture abroad.

It was late afternoon when Mr. Kenyon began his speech for the defence. It was not natural, he said, that a person of Lord George's character and position, a member of the legislature too, could be actuated by the motives which the prosecution attributed to him. He censured the Attorney-General for "addressing himself to the passions of the jury by improper and exaggerated description." With great skill, he discredited the evidence of the Crown witnesses. "If juries are to believe witnesses because they will swear to facts, juries are become of very little use indeed. Those who are acquainted with the legal profession, see and lament that *there is no fact whatever that witnesses may not be brought to prove.*" With regard to Bowen's assertion that he had heard Lord George say that the Scotch had no redress until they had pulled down the Mass-houses, Kenyon, while not impeaching his (Bowen's) integrity, "suggested" that he imagined things that had never taken place. No one else had heard Lord George say it. "The Attorney-General had said that, 'if a man turned out a wild beast, he was guilty of murder if a man were killed by it.' " "That," he said, "is not the law of the land, or of humanity."

Mr. Kenyon told how Lord George had tried to see the King to express his horror of the rioting, but was refused audience. As to the "protection" he had signed, surely he was justified in doing so if he thought it would help to avert violence. So greatly was he shocked at what he saw that on 2nd June he nearly collapsed and was taken into the carriage of a Mrs. Whittingham, in a fainting condition. Sir Phillip Jennings Clarke heard him beg the mob to go home, saying: "While you assemble in this tumultuous way, the House will never consent to your petition."

When Kenyon had finished, Mr. Erskine rose, and according to writers of the day made one of the most brilliant and sensational speeches recorded in legal history. He spoke for over two hours and, when he sat down, his reputation was made and Lord George's acquittal practically assured. Lord Mansfield, though tired and peevish from want of sleep, summed up with strict impartiality.

"I tell you," he said, "as the joint opinion of us all (the four judges) that if this multitude assembled with intent, by acts of force and violence, to intimidate, to awe, to force, to induce, or to compel the King, lords and commoners to repeal an Act, that is certainly high treason. If there was no intent of intimidation, either in the mob or prisoner, then he is to be acquitted. If you find he had any hand in inciting the people to commit those acts of violence, and that he intended it, you will find him guilty. If you are of opinion, upon the evidence, that the scale hangs doubtful between them, then it should hang on the favourable side."

After an absence of three-quarters of an hour, the jury filed back into Court.

"Do you find the prisoner guilty or not guilty?" the foreman was asked.

"Not guilty," he replied.

"So say we all," echoed the rest.

The verdict was greeted with frenzied cheers of delight, and when the excitement had quietened down Lord George addressed the jury. He congratulated them on their verdict, with which, he said, he entirely agreed. Once again he was the hero of the hour. The Protestant Association—by no means dead—sent him a long address, and Watson tells us that "wherever he went, the ringing of bells announced his arrival and deputations came to greet him with the freedom of their cities." Perhaps in the chorus of congratulation no voice gave him greater pleasure than that of Dr. Johnson, who said that even if he were indirectly responsible for the riots, he was "far better pleased that Lord George Gordon should escape punishment than that a precedent should be established for hanging a man for constructive treason."

With a sigh of relief, Lord George returned to Welbeck Street. Life held out to him infinite possibilities of interfering with his fellow-men; he was only thirty, he belonged to the ruling classes and, though not rich, he was certainly not poor, as his expenditure had never exceeded his income. He had inherited five thousand pounds and an annuity of five hundred a year. With this, as he said in the House of Commons, "though one of the poorest members, I am one of the most independent." His misfortunes had not taught him tact. Within six months after the trial he wrote to Lord North, saying that he wished personally to present to the King a very valuable book entitled *Scotland's Opposition to the Popish Bill*. Would Lord North kindly inform him if he should do so at His Majesty's public *levée*, at his residence, or when he was sitting upon his throne. Lord North, he continued, should advise His Majesty to congratulate the Scottish artillery division in London, on their opposition to the Popery Bill. This was too much for Lord North. He replied curtly in the third person, saying that if the book was to be presented it must be done at a *levée*.

Notwithstanding Lord George's acquittal, the Government, to a man, held him responsible for the riots. Not so the people. In the following September a majority of the Livery of London nominated him as a candidate for the city. The Government was furious. Every ministerial influence was set to work: bribes, threats, and promises were lavished and at a meeting of Lord George's friends at the Paul's Head Tavern, a number of king and constitution men, including Alderman Wooldridge, intruded themselves. There was a scene of wild confusion and the alderman made a violent speech, vowing to frustrate Lord George's business—he (Lord George) was not present. The follownig day the Lord Mayor wrote him a humble apology, but at the same time said that great caution was necessary to *restrain the indiscretion of some jealous friends*. Lord George took the warning to heart. The electorate, he knew, was by no means unanimous; then, too, elections in London were expensive. There were other ways of taking part in public affairs; on every side he saw abuses calling for the intervention of God, assisted by Lord George Gordon. So, all things considered, he declined the proposed honour.

The check to his parliamentary career, and the failure of all his efforts for the repeal of the Savile Act, left Lord George at a loose end. For the moment, no cause seemed to demand his immediate championship. That, for the privileged classes, London was a very pleasant dwelling-place, did not seem to occur to this earnest young man. In Fleet Street a more discerning biographer than his friend Watson was collecting the wit and wisdom of Dr. Johnson; at Strawberry Hill, Horace Walpole was writing his famous letters to Madame Du Deffand, and entertaining the wits of, perhaps, the most brilliant and cynical society London has ever known; at Westminster, Charles James Fox, William Pitt and Edmund Burke were crossing swords, supping gaily afterwards at Brooks' or Crockford's, while at Drury Lane, David Garrick was amusing this delightful world with the comedies of Sheridan. And Joshua Reynolds and Romney were immortalizing the features of these interesting people. Why did Lord George remain so unaware of all this? So uninterested in it? His not very intelligent brother, the duke, and his charming wife, were in the centre of things, and he himself had both personal charm and magnetism. But unfortunately for him, he did not "fit" in the irreligious, tolerant London society of the late eighteenth century.

The exciting events in which he had taken part had told on him; he needed a holiday. Why not go to Paris? The Scots, he knew, were far more popular there than they were in England. So to Paris he went, perhaps not wholly unmindful of the much advertised attractions of the French female. He had always enjoyed feminine society, indeed, there were those who said he liked it too well. Though he never married, there is abundant evidence that his religious complex was not due to sex-repression; eroticism and religious fanaticism often make very good bed fellows, so psycho-analysts tell us. Hannah More, with her customary charity, said that he was extremely debauched, and Horace Walpole spoke superciliously of his "loose morals." Another tribute, though not of the same nature, was paid him by Mrs. Elizabeth Montagu. When—on the occasion of his excommunication[1]—he referred to the Archbishop of Canterbury as the Whore of Babylon, she remarked:

"If Lord George Gordon has called the Archbishop of Canterbury

[1]*See* page 68.

the W—— of Babylon, it is very uncivil, *as it is the only W—— his lordship dislikes!"*

But after all, there is very little to prove that Lord George was more licentious than the majority of the men of his class. Contemporary journalism has, however, recorded the initial, if not the name, of one of his girl friends. The *Town and Country Magazine* was publishing a series of plates portraying certain well-known people concerned in various fashionable intrigues, under the title of "The Meretricious Fair." Number XVII of the series, issued in July, 1780, showed "Lord Crop"—very clearly intended for Lord George, as the accompanying letterpress shows—and "Miss E——." The lady was a well-known *courtesane* of the day. Her face, we are told, was fascinating, though delicate, her person desirable, though not robust. Lord George had visited her and fallen a victim to her charms. But she "preferring the species to the individual, refused to give up to one person what, in her view, was meant for mankind." So Lord George had to resign himself. He paid frequent visits to her house in the Tottenham Court Road.

Paris, to return to his visit to that city, did not please him. He was presented to Marie Antoinette, and, while paying homage to her beauty, "the trappings of despotism" did not dazzle him. The Court was "a whited sepulchre." Above all was he shocked by the French clergy. "What ill use they make of their ill-gotten power! What outrages the Church of Rome offers to Nature!" So he returned to England, "more than ever resolved to prosecute his plans for general reform."

During the year 1763 he wrote pamphlets on every conceivable political subject, addressed to the "Friends of Freedom" in the various European capitals; he also studied the Jewish question. For some time past, Jews, oddly enough, had attracted him. He admired the way they had preserved their religion intact throughout the ages. The implacable God of the Calvinists and the fierce old Hebrew Deity had much in common. *He* would have had no truck with the lethargic, tolerant Protestant bishops, still less with the Scarlet Woman! He "smote his enemies in the hinder parts and put them to perpetual shame." That is exactly the spot on which Lord George longed to smite Catholics! You knew where you were with a god like that, thought his lordship. In the following year he renewed his disastrous activities. The twenty-five-year-old William Pitt was now Prime Minister—as the office had come to be called—and possibly no two men have ever been born more calculated to dislike each other. The brilliantly clever, but cold and ambitious, son of Lord Chatham despised this tiresome fanatic, with his violent enthusiasms, undesirable connections, and want of balance,

Queen Victoria at the age of eighteen

The Princess receiving the news of her accession to the throne
on 30th June, 1837, from the Archbishop of Canterbury and
the Lord Chamberlain

but realized that he could be dangerous. Lord George saw in Pitt an example of aristocratic government at its worst.

He attacked Pitt with regard to the iniquitous taxation. The price of food was increasing, the streets were crowded with beggars, and starvation was rife. He presented his compliments to Mr. Pitt. He had just received further instruction from Glasgow against the tax on linens and cottons. The following extracts will advise Mr. Pitt on the situation:

We are sorry to inform your lordship that if the new tax passes into law, it will not be in the power of the Civil Magistracy in different places of Scotland to keep the peace. . . .

Your lordship will take the trouble to request your brother, the Duke of Gordon, to go to Mr. Pitt and inform him of the dreadful prospect we have of mobs and tumults from the working people in this country. . . .

Lord George hopes to hear from Mr. Pitt before he goes out this night.

In reply, Mr. Pitt presented his compliments to Lord George and informed him that "the Lord Advocate had sent to Glasgow all the information necessary and that he, therefore, had nothing to trouble his lordship with on the subject."

The taxes were abandoned, and that his efforts had been partly responsible for this is proved by the letter of thanks he received from representatives of the trades in question.

His next proceeding was to protest against the restoration to their owners of estates belonging to Scottish nobles who had taken part in the rising of '45. This infuriated his family. Many of these highland chieftains were his near relations, and they rightly considered that his action showed a deplorable lack of family feeling! Shortly afterwards he found another way of exasperating the Government and aristocracy; he supported Fox when he challenged the right of the great Whig families to regard votes as property to be bought and sold at will. This ancient privilege would, if abolished, deprive the Government of an enormous advantage at by-elections. A howl of indignation arose and Fox, for the time being, was almost as unpopular in social and political circles as was Lord George himself.

Time had not lessened Lord George's hatred of Catholicism; indeed, the failure of his attacks on the Church in England had increased it. In 1784 he turned his attention to Holland, where the Emperor Joseph of Austria was behaving in the high-handed manner in which Austrian monarchs in the days of their greatness were wont to behave, and making new and entirely unjustifiable claims on Dutch territory in order to pay for his recent war with Great Britain. Now the Emperor was a Papist, and therefore capable of anything; he could have but one object—the subjugation of a small Protestant people. Lord George "sounded the

E

Tocsin," Watson tells us. He called on the Dutch Minister and suggested that he and the Dutch Consul should go to St. James's and approach the King on the subject. The prospect of such a step naturally alarmed the minister, who received the suggestion rather coldly. So he took matters into his own hands. He arrayed himself in the uniform of a Dutch naval officer, and—like Scott's *Minstrel Boy*—flung over his shoulder a large belt, in which he placed the highland broadsword that had belonged to his father and which "had opposed with success the usurpation of the See of Rome." Thus oddly accoutred, and accompanied by the minister—who had yielded to his insistence—he went to the Guard Room at St. James's Palace, and persuaded the third regiment of the Guards to present arms to His Excellency and to cut their ribbons into Dutch cockades. Drawing his rusty sword, he saluted the minister and swore to protect Dutch interests. This strange scene over, he returned to Welbeck Street and wrote memorials to the countries concerned.

He had many sympathizers, so found no difficulty in obtaining support. His cause, they thought, might result in the employment of the hundreds of sailors who were wandering over the country, ready to turn their hands to anything.

Once again he wrote to Pitt:

Sir. Several hundred seamen have addressed me to-day, many of them lately arrived from India—come in coaches. Acting lieutenants, mates and midshipmen are among them. The following is a copy of the generality of their addresses;

"*We, the seamen whose names are underwritten, are able, willing and ready to serve the United Protestant States of Holland against the King of the Romans. And your petitioners will ever pray for—Lord George Gordon!*"

Mr. Pitt replied, with a singular lack of cordiality, that he did not consider it his duty to correspond with Lord George on the subject, and reminded him that:

Any steps he had taken to induce seamen to serve against the Emperor had been taken without the smallest degree of authority or countenance from His Majesty's ministers.

He concluded:

It is for your lordship to consider what consequences may be expected for them.

The Government took every precaution; closed the ports and cleverly spread rumours among the sailors that Lord George had taken advantage of them for his own ends. A large crowd of them arrived at Welbeck Street to take vengeance, howling and banging at his door. Lord George was quite equal to the occasion. Going out to them, he asked for silence, and told them that the rumours lied; he was, as ever, the "Friend of the People." Pitt and his satellites were perfidious liars! Tyrants! Bloodsuckers! The old charm worked once more; the sailors went away, cheering him, and his lordship sat down calmly and finished his breakfast.

In the meantime the question was settled without the aid of Lord George's navy, as the Emperor entered into negotiations with the Dutch and all immediate danger was averted. Nothing daunted, he wrote an extraordinary letter to that monarch. He had, he said, information that His Majesty was being poisoned by Italian priests in his own house. "If this is true," he wrote, "fly to the hotel of Count Wassenaar and Baron Van Leider, Dutch Deputies, and lodge with them, and you will be as safe and happy as Rahab was with Joshua's spies in Jericho. *If you will turn to me, I will turn to you.*" He concluded by hoping the God of the Jews would lead him into the way of peace, and was "his sincere friend and humble servant, G. Gordon!" Whether or not the erring Emperor turned to his "humble servant, G. Gordon," history does not relate.

The Dutch affair was the last occasion on which he actively attacked Catholicism. Perhaps he was beginning to realize that the Catholic Church had survived—and would survive—far more formidable foes than Lord George Gordon.

But naturally he was not popular at the Vatican—so much was he disliked, Watson tells us, that "the Pope sent two faithful Jesuits provided with a pardon for all crimes, past, present and to come, if they could succeed in ridding him of this troublesome president of the Protestant Association!" Perhaps Watson had overestimated the importance of Lord George in the eyes of the Holy Father? But be that as it may, he was on his guard and became very careful what he ate and drank. According to Watson, the two papal emissaries took up their abode in Welbeck Street and, with all the patience of Mother Church, awaited their opportunity. Let Watson tell the story:

> They sent a vial filled with a certain liquid to which were affixed instructions written by his [Lord George's] apothecary, with the strictest injunction to take it immediately. As it was brought by a stranger, who hastily departed, it created suspicion and at the very moment when he was about to swallow the draught he hesitated, and sent for the apothecary; the imposition was detected, the medicine analysed and found to contain the most deadly poison!

Providence having once again intervened so politely on his behalf, he resumed his tireless labours for the good of humanity. This time he certainly did excellent work by opposing the innumerable taxes which the Government—at its wits' end to find money—imposed on the wretched and already over taxed people. A tax on the Scotch distilleries, which amounted practically to prohibition, was, through his exertions, considerably modified. He opposed other taxes too, among them those on windows, candles, stamps and postage, and although he did not meet with success in every case, he undoubtedly aroused the public to resist the exactions of its ministers. His greatest triumph was against Pitt's hated shop tax. Beginning at Bond Street, Lord George went on to the city and persuaded shopkeepers to shut their shops and put up long poles decorated with black crepe, bearing notices with the inscription: "This shop to let." The infuriated and embarrassed Cabinet were obliged to yield to public opinion and drop the measure.

Soon after this, Lord George managed to get into trouble with the leading lights of the Church of England, who disliked him at least as much as he disliked them. He had been attending the lectures of a popular dissenting minister, a Mr. Wilson, with whom he had become intimate. Wilson contracted a fatal illness, and when dying sent for him to consult him about the disposal of his property. As he had made no will, a dispute arose, and it was necessary for Lord George to appear before the then extremely powerful Ecclesiastical Court at Canterbury. He refused to do so, offering, however, to give evidence before a civil magistrate. Highly incensed, the Archbishop of Canterbury caused him to be solemnly excommunicated with bell, book and candle, at the Church of St. Mary-le-Bow on 4th May, 1788.

"To expel me from a society to which I never belonged," said the victim, laughing, "is an absurdity worthy of an archbishop."

IV

HE who singlehanded takes arms against a sea of trouble, must choose his weapons with discrimination. The last two causes to which Lord George devoted his tireless energies were to bring him again into conflict with the law, and this time more seriously, for in the "Prisoners' Petition" he attacked the majesty of the law itself.

In the eighteenth century the penal code was brutal in the extreme. Death or transportation was the penalty for the most trivial offence; they could be inflicted for the theft of goods worth five pounds or over, and young boys and old offenders were treated exactly alike. That the judicial system was not all it should be, had already been recognized by a few people. John Howard was quietly making a tour of England, visiting the prisons and making notes. His tour was to lead eventually to a complete reform of the system. Lord George also saw the necessity for reform, but *he* could do nothing quietly. It was characteristic of him that he was uninterested in the worst abuses of justice—the inhuman cruelty to young offenders; the debtors, thrown into jail and left there indefinitely; the ghastly, insanitary prisons. But the sad fate of those condemned to transportation moved him to tears of grief and indignation. He visited Newgate and talked to some of them, finding that one and all shared his opinion as to the injustice of their sentences. So he had no difficulty in persuading them that a petition —blessed word!—addressed to someone or other would be just the thing. Why not addressed to Lord George himself? Who knew more about petitions than he? He graciously accepted his own suggestion and drew up a document, "The Prisoners' Petition to the Right Honourable Lord George Gordon, to preserve their Lives and Liberties and prevent their Banishment to Botany Bay."

It was written in his usual high-flown, bombastic style, calling on high heaven for redress, and but for one sentence would have met with the ridicule it deserved; that sentence referred to the Statutes of the Almighty being "*falsified and erased by lawyers and judges.*" There they had him. It had been impossible to convict him of direct complicity in the riots, but this was different. He had grossly libelled the judicature and the administratives of the law, and thus, indirectly, the King. A writ was therefore issued against him.

His other offence—also a libel—was even more serious. It was against royalty, in the person of Queen Marie Antoinette. The trial to which it gave occasion shook all France, and according to Goethe, "laid the foundation of the State in ruins." How Lord George became involved in it requires some explanation.

The leading actors in this complicated drama—the Diamond Necklace affair—were the Queen, the Cardinal Prince de Rohan, the Comtesse Jeanne de la Motte de Valois, as she called herself, though her husband's claim to the name and title were more than doubtful, and the Court jewellers, Böhmer and Bassange. The plot was born in the fertile brain of—let us call her—Jeanne.

The Court jewellers, knowing Marie Antoinette's passion for precious stones, had been for some years collecting the most perfect diamonds they could discover, in order to make the finest necklace in existence and to induce the King to buy it for her. When it was completed they submitted it to His Majesty, who was frightened at the price—one million six thousand livres—and definitely refused to buy it. Repeated efforts and a reduction in price were of no avail and the necklace remained on their hands. In the meantime the astute Jeanne had heard of their trouble and set herself to invent a scheme for turning it to her own advantage. Now it so happened that she enjoyed the patronage of the Prince Cardinal de Rohan, a man of delightful personality, handsome, witty and enormously rich. He had been sent as Ambassador to the Court of Vienna, where his French gaiety and social popularity offended the Empress, the bigoted, haughty, and intensely disagreeable Marie Thérèse, mother of Marie Antoinette, who made her daughter's life—already difficult enough—a burden to her until she succeeded in getting him recalled to Paris. On his return the young Queen, at her mother's request, refused to receive him.

This naturally made things in Paris difficult for the Cardinal. He poured out his soul to the sympathetic Jeanne, who assured him she could help him to overcome the difficulty. She was, she told him, in the Queen's confidence; he must wait a few days and she would think out a plan. Her first step was to visit the jewellers. A great nobleman, she told them, who had lost the favour of Marie Antoinette, was anxious to regain it by helping Her Majesty to obtain the necklace which she was dying to possess. The jewellers were, of course, delighted, and agreed to entrust her with it, so that she might show it to the Cardinal. The transaction, she said, must be absolutely secret and her name must on no account be mentioned. She then went to the Cardinal and showed him the necklace. The Queen, she said, had told her she could not live without it and was willing to pay in instalments, but unfortunately the jewellers insisted on the money being guaranteed by a personage of undoubted position and financial standing. If *he* would care to be that personage, it would mean his complete restoration to the royal favour. The Cardinal was overjoyed and promised to go himself to the jewellers and fix the price and conditions of payment. Jeanne in the meantime gave them back the necklace. The contract was duly drawn up and Jeanne undertook to submit it to the Queen. A few days later she brought it back; on it was written "Approved" and the signature "Marie Antoinette De France." The jewellers were to bring the necklace to Jeanne's house the following evening, and a messenger from the Queen would call for it. The messenger—who was a friend and accomplice—arrived, was handed the packet and departed. Having obtained possession of it, the precious couple proceeded to remove the diamonds from their setting and sell them. Paris, London and Amsterdam were flooded with diamonds.

But greatly to his dismay, the Cardinal's position at Court did not improve; neither did the jewellers receive a penny of their money, and at last, not daring to approach the Cardinal, they went to Versailles and begged an audience of Her Majesty. She declined to receive them personally, but sent a lady-in-waiting to whom they told their story. After seeing Marie Antoinette, the lady informed them that they had been swindled. The Queen had neither ordered nor received the jewels. On this, they went to the Cardinal. Horror-stricken and worried to death, he sent for his friend, the famous Comte Cagliostro, and asked his advice. "Your only course is to go to the King and tell him what has taken place," he said.

Within a few days Paris was wildly excited by the news that the great Cardinal-Prince had been arrested; Madame "de la Motte de Valois" and her husband committed to the Bastille on a *lettre de cachet*; and that Cagliostro had also been sent to prison for complicity in the affair.

The trial resulted in the triumphant acquittal of the Cardinal and of Cagliostro; Jeanne was sentenced to be stripped naked and whipped by the public executioner; to be branded on the shoulder with the letter V (*voleuse*)—though it also stood for Valois; to be deprived of all her property and confined for life in the prison of the *Salpêtrière*. De la Motte was sent to the galleys.

It was a terrible ordeal for Marie Antoinette. Not only had the corruption of the Court been exposed and some of the greatest names in France smirched; she was only too well aware that she was almost universally believed to have been concerned in the conspiracy. Mirabeau called the affair "the prelude of the Revolution." After the trial, Cagliostro—ordered to leave Paris—went to England where he had many friends, not the least among them being Lord George Gordon. This Cagliostro, whose real name was Joseph Balsamo, was a remarkable personality. He was intended for the priesthood, but honest toil not appealing to him, he left his native place, Palermo, and for some years led a gay and adventurous life. Little was heard of him until, aged about forty, he blossomed into the "Comte" de Cagliostro, magician, healer, and *Grand Seigneur*. Soon all Europe was ringing with reports of his uncanny powers; of the cures he had effected and of his kindness to the poor. He claimed to possess the science of ancient Egypt, of universal medicine, and the secret of the Philosopher's Stone. When asked who he was, he replied: "I am he who is." He had visited London before—in 1781—and had had an enormous vogue in the most exclusive circles.

The eighteenth century, the age of rationalism, was also the Golden Age of Charlatanism. In 1780 a rival of Cagliostro's, one James Graham, was so successful that he was able to take Schomberg House, Pall Mall, which he fitted up as a "Temple of Health and Hymen." His magic paraphernalia included "the Celestial State Bed." If you slept in it—presumably not alone—you would beget children of heavenly beauty. But the fee being five hundred guineas, clients were few. Children were expensive enough. Attractive little creatures, though, even when they could not compete with Adonis or Helen of Troy. One must take one's chance and hope for the best!

Cagliostro had met Lord George on his first visit to London; on this second visit his trial and imprisonment—even though he was acquitted—had somewhat diminished his popularity with the fashionable world. This, and the fact that he had suffered at the hands of the "tyrants, blood-suckers and enemies of freedom," was enough for Lord George. He visited him constantly, placed his coach at his disposal, and accompanied him everywhere.

One day in September, during this second visit, Sophie von la Roche, a charming German blue-stocking, called on Cagliostro at his house in Knightsbridge, then one of London's outer suburbs, with large tracts of meadowland. When shown into the drawing-room, she noticed a young man with closely-cropped hair and blue eyes. He was dressed entirely in black. Instead of introducing them, Cagliostro asked her to what religion she belonged.

"I am a Protestant," she said.

"Lucky for you," answered her host, laughing, "for this is Lord George Gordon, who cannot abide Catholics. You would not have been able to stay here for a moment."

A few days later she again lunched with Cagliostro, and again met Lord George. An interesting conversation took place. After asking him how he liked various members of the Government—including the King—

and finding him singularly unenthusiastic about all of them, she said:

"I am surprised that you, with your gentle appearance, could be responsible for the death of so many of London's inhabitants, and for bringing misfortune to hundreds of others."

"Ah, madame," he answered, "that was not my fault nor was it my intention; but when the English mob is roused to ire it can no longer be restrained."

"Then, my lord, a noble Englishman, with knowledge of the mob-mind and a love of religion, should not release so unruly a spirit in rebellion."

Lord George took the reproof meekly, saying he liked her for her frankness.

At lunch the subject of Jews and their religion came up. The menu consisted of macaroni, stewed lamb, fresh young codling, pork, roast veal, and vegetables. Lord George, however, ate nothing but cress sprinkled with salt, which was symptomatic of a change that had taken place in the mind of the Protestant champion. Judaism—alone among the religions practised in the western world—pays particular attention to the subject of diet. Various animal foods must not be eaten; meat and butter may not be served together, and animals must be slaughtered in the *Kosher* manner. But there are no rules as to vegetables. Lord George had, for a long time, been greatly interested in the Jewish religion; he had made a high-flown appeal to Jewish financiers—interlarded with phrases from the Old Testament—to induce them to refuse financial support to the Government, in order to promote peace. He was Israel's friend, he said. "*Shemah Israel,*" whatever that may mean. Unfortunately these hard-headed business men were unmoved by his eloquence.

This Jewish predilection seems to have arisen when he was passing through Ipswich, where was established a small Jewish community which was a centre for the activities of the Jewish pedlars who travelled the Suffolk countryside, dazzling the eyes of farmers' wives and village maidens with their cheap finery. The most remarkable person in this community was Mrs. Sarah Lyon, a vigorous old lady who was destined to live to the age of a hundred and five and to be painted both by Constable and by Gainsborough. Her son, Isaac Tittermann, provided *Kosher* meals for strangers. In order to advertise his wares, he inscribed over his doorway a passage in Aramaic from the traditional Passover Eve liturgy:

"Let all who are hungry enter and eat."

Lord George, though not hungry, was curious; he entered, made inquiries, and was fascinated by what he saw and heard. From that time on, his mind constantly dwelt on the Children of Israel. He began to study

Hebrew, and seems to have been in close touch with Nathan Solomon, of the New Synagogue in Leadenhall Street. It was some time between this Ipswich visit and 1786, that he made his odd decision to adopt Abraham as a father.

For a Protestant fanatic like Lord George to have taken such a step seems almost unbelievable. Yet, perhaps, the transition is not so surprising after all. Religious fanaticism is rather a disease than a depth of conviction. Hence, it is among the bigoted, intolerant and emotionally unstable, not the *innately* religious, that conversion from one creed to another tends to occur. Lord George was fanatically obsessed with the problems of his own salvation, and fanatics are apt to be swept away by waves of religious enthusiasm. Revivalism provides us with many such—practically pathological—cases.

Having made his decision, he went to see David Tevele Schiff, Rabbi of the great synagogue in Duke's Place, St. James's, asking to be admitted to the Jewish fold—this must have been in the summer of 1786—and was surprised that his application was received without enthusiasm. That such was the case is easy to understand. The position of the Jews was already precarious enough. Were they to be accused of proselytizing it might become still more precarious. Perhaps, too, the Rabbi was a little afraid of Lord George; this eccentric scion of nobility might well be a dangerous acquisition to Jewry. He was a sensible man and begged his lordship to reconsider the question.

The Rabbi Schiff's rebuff offended Lord George. Later on, in a letter to Angel Lyon on the wearing of beards, he virtually accused him of accepting bribes from the wealthy members of his synagogue. But not to be deterred from his purpose, he went to the Hambro Synagogue—a less orthodox community. The Reader of the congregation, Aaron Barnett, father of John Barnett, the composer, gave him the usual tuition in the faith; he was circumcised, took the ritual bath, and pronounced the prescribed benediction. In place of his former dignified name, he was given that of Israel, son of Father Abraham! On the following Sabbath he attended the synagogue in Magpie Alley, Fenchurch Street, it was crowded with old-clothes men, pedlars and pawnbrokers, all agog to catch a glimpse of the noble convert. The Hazan chanted the ancient formula, calling down a blessing upon him, and Lord George made an offering of *one hundred pounds*! Such a sum was not often mentioned in this poor synagogue; the congregation heard the announcement with bated breath.

His conversion caused a great sensation. Once again he was the centre of interest, but no longer a popular hero; indeed he became a figure of fun. Numerous broadsheets—those crude ballads which in the eighteenth century were to a large extent the literature of the lower classes—were published, covering him with ridicule, and caricaturists vied with one another in depicting the noble lord with a long beard, dressed as an old-clothes man and surrounded by a mob of Polish Jews. "Moses chusing his Cook" shows Lord George in the company of ten of his new co-religionists whose piety is scandalized at seeing the attendant bring in a sucking pig for their dinner. Here are some verses from a very rare broadsheet that had an enormous success throughout the country:

> Ye Jews, Turks and Christians, I pray you draw near,
> When a comical ditty you quickly will hear,
> Concerning Lord George, who for Protestant laws
> His life said he'd lose in so glorious a cause.
> Derry down, etc.

> In seventeen hundred and eighty's fam'd year,
> At the head of the Protestants he did appear,
> When prison came down and houses did burn.
> Who'd have thought that his lordship a *smouchy*[1] wou'd turn.

> Next the poor Queen of France, who to us ne'er did ill,
> Was attacked by Lord George with his venomous quill,
> But O! had he done it this side of the water
> He'd have closed his career in a Frenchify'd halter.

> So we wish them much joy of this new convert Jew,
> Tho' my tale it is odd, yet I'm sure it is true.
> So farewell, my lord, since to Newgate you're taken,
> You may find it a hard case to save your own bacon.

Apropos of "the poor Queen of France," let us return to the libel against her, for which Lord George got into trouble with the French Government.

Cagliostro was not finding his second visit to London so pleasant as the first. On his previous visit he had made a bitter enemy of the proprietor and editor of the *Courier de l'Europe*, a man named Morand, as pretty a blackguard as you would find in a day's march. Brilliantly clever and utterly unscrupulous, he had been a criminal since his early boyhood. Expelled from France, he went to London, where he lived by blackmail. Morand attacked Cagliostro without mercy. "The exposure of a swindler as dangerous as Cagliostro is a useful service to society" he wrote. Lord George, of course, burned with indignation—he had not then declared himself a Jew—and longed for a chance to vindicate injured innocence. The chance soon came.

[1] Slang for Jew.

Shortly after Cagliostro's arrival, the French *Chargé d'Affaires*, M. Barthelémy, sent him an intimation that he was at liberty to return to France, and requested him to call at the Embassy. Accompanied by Lord George he drove to the *Hôtel de France* in Piccadilly, but declined to discuss the business except in the presence of his friend. M. Barthelémy consented, and a letter from M. Breteuil, the leader of Marie Antoinette's faction, giving the permission, was read to him. Cagliostro demanded a copy of the letter, which was refused. Thereupon Lord George rushed into print. He wrote a violent letter to the *Public Advertiser* (22nd August, 1786) in which he accused Breteuil and his minions of having stolen a great part of Cagliostro's fortune. The Queen, he said, was still violently against him. The honour of the King, the Parliament and the French people was at stake. A few days later he returned to the attack. This time he went too far: "The friendship and benevolence of Comte de Cagliostro in advising the poor Prince Louis de Rohan to be on his guard against the Comtesse de Valois and *the intrigues of the Queen's faction—who still seek the destruction of that noble prince—has brought upon the Comte and his amiable Comtesse the hateful revenge and perfidious cruelties of a tyrannical government.*" Lord George was quite aware of the danger he ran. He wrote to the editor of the paper, promising to be responsible for the expenses of "any prosecution" taken against him.

The French Government was prompt. A writ was issued, citing both articles, at the suit of the French Ambassador and M. Barthelémy, Cagliostro, the victim of the wicked French Court, discreetly disappeared!

It was some time before Lord George was put on trial on either of the two charges; justice in the eighteenth century was very leisurely. Not until January, 1787, did things begin to move, and even then it was Lord George himself who set them in motion. He presented himself at the Court of King's Bench and stated that he had received a summons to appear personally in that Court, to answer to an information exhibited against him on the King's behalf for certain crimes and misdemeanours. He had, he said, come himself as he did not intend to be at the expense of a counsel. His reason was that one of the learned gentlemen who had defended him at his last trial—Sir Lloyd Kenyon—had since been raised to a high situation, and the other, his cousin, Mr. Erskine, had some time ago been retained for the prosecution. As Erskine owed his present position to his brilliant success in the previous trial, Lord George might well have sighed, "Blow, blow, thou winter wind."

Naturally this born litigant made all sorts of difficulties. He appeared with Blackstone's *Commentaries* tied up in a handkerchief and said the Court had mixed the charges; the Attorney-General was "incompetent."

The Court told him that his first step was to *appear*. "I appeared yesterday," he replied. Then he said he had been described as "George Gordon," and he had as much right to the prefix to his name as the Lord Chief Justice, styled William, Earl of Mansfield. "Can the process be intended for the *Right Honourable Lord George Gordon?*" he asked, and walked away. A second summons was issued and he again made the same objection. "You must *appear* before you can be heard," Mr. Justice Buller told him. "Use your eyes," answered Lord George. Legal etiquette, however, must be observed, and since he had not *filed* his appearance it was obviously absurd for him to pretend that he was present in Court. When he had complied with the regulations, the information was read. It charged him with inserting libels in the *Public Advertiser* of 22nd April, 1786, on the Queen of France. Did he plead guilty or not guilty? After a lot of quibbling, he entered a plea of Not Guilty to both charges.

V

THE case had a preliminary hearing in May. Lord George, in his examination, spoke of those "noble strangers," Cagliostro and his wife; he said that permission for Cagliostro to return to France was given only so that he might be again thrown into the Bastille; he asserted blandly that the character of the Queen of France was notorious. The judge interrupted him, telling him curtly to keep to the subject. The problem before the jury was a simple one. They found him guilty and he was committed for trial.

The "Prisoners' Petition" case was tried on 6th June. Prosecuting for the Crown, the Attorney-General said that although the petition was supposed to be addressed to Lord George, he had written it himself "with a view either to raise a tumult among the prisoners within, in an endeavour to procure their deliverance or, by exciting the compassion of those without, to cause a disturbance and produce the same effect." He suggested that the public had already seen the effects which an appeal to the passions of the mob was capable of producing. British justice, far from being severe, was more merciful than that of any other country. "The reason why executions are more frequent in England is *because the laws are milder. We do not torture prisoners*," he asserted naivey! He went on to say that Lord George had paid several visits to Nelwgate. "Why should a noble lord trouble about such people?" he asked. When he had finished speaking, Pitt was called. He told the Court that Lord George said to him: "Don't you think it is cruel that so much blood should be spilled?" And that he had replied: "I cannot help it, my lord, nor you neither."

Lord George defended himself adroitly. He said that his attention had first been drawn to the extreme barbarity of the penal code when a servant of his had cheated him of eighteenpence. He had been sent to the chemist to buy some article and said it had cost four and sixpence, though he had paid only three shillings for it. "I forgave him when on making inquiries I found to my horror that the lad could have been hanged for the offence." He had tried to see Lord Mansfield on the subject, but—not unnaturally—the Lord Chief Justice refused to receive him. Other judges had told him that the laws were against the laws of God, but agreeable to the law of the land. He had not talked to the prisoners, having been refused permission to do so. His object had been reformation, not rebellion.

Mr. Justice Buller summed up very briefly. There was no question as to the defendant's having written and published the libel. Did it, or did it not, refer to His Majesty's judges? The jury found him guilty without leaving the Court. A week later he again appeared to answer the charge of having libelled Marie Antoinette. The Attorney-General opened with a long hymn of praise of the "most high, mighty and puissant Marie Antoinette—a great and illustrious princess, eminently distinguished and renowned for her wisdom, prudence, justice, clemency, chastity and every regal virtue."

If Her Majesty followed the trial, as no doubt she did, how she must have wished that the French people could be brought to endorse the Attorney-General's opinion of her! He went on to say that the French Ambassador and the *Chargé d'Affaires* were of equal virtue, so far as it was possible for subjects to approach the sovereign, in intellectual and moral worth. But alas! Lord George Gordon, incapable of appreciating this exalted pattern of all the virtues, had dared to asperse her character and alienate the affections of her subjects by "unjustly, maliciously, scandalously," etc., etc.

Lord George's defence was, as he must have known, hopeless. All he could do was to repeat his accusations: "Everyone knew that the Queen of France was a very *convenient* lady; the ambassador's reputation in Paris was of the worst; Cagliostro was their victim."

He spoke to deaf ears. This time everyone was against him; the current of sympathy which during the riots trial had flowed between him and the public, had been cut off. Who was this Cagliostro? "A damned Italian impostor!" The French Queen and the frog-eating ambassador were also foreigners, but then Marie Antoinette was a woman. Lord George had not played fair. After a short charge from the judge, a verdict of guilty was instantly returned. He was told that he must come up for judgment on the following day, when the judge would have had time to consider his sentence.

It has never been explained why, after he had been found guilty, he was allowed to leave the Court without bail, but when to-morrow came Lord George had flown. Most likely, the authorities connived at his escape. If he were in hiding, either at home or abroad, he could do no harm; all they asked was that he should cease from troubling. Then, too, the Gordons were a powerful and popular family, and though Lord George had done them no credit they had no desire to see him in jail. Certainly no great efforts were made to find him. A few days later a messenger from Holland brought word that he had landed there. But Amsterdam did not want him; he was too dangerous a guest, so they ordered him to quit the city. The burgomaster, however, called on him and suggested that he should try Antwerp. This he declined on being told by a Dutch friend that if he set foot there the Emperor's police would immediately arrest him. The magistrates of Amsterdam then sent him to Harwich with a file of guards. He arrived there on 22nd July. Strange to say, even then he was not arrested. That the authorities knew of his movements seems pretty evident from a paragraph which appeared in the *Morning Herald* of 27th July, 1787:

> Lord George Gordon is arrived in town from Holland and is said to be going down to his brother's seat in Scotland where he will remain till November next. Lord George Gordon says he is returned to England in obedience to the States-General, rather than involve his own country in the horrors of a general war!

In December, 1787, some four months after Lord George's return to England, there was a delightful, but not very unusual, commotion in and around that part of Birmingham known as "the Froggery." It was a far from fashionable neighbourhood, remarkable chiefly for the bare, unlovely synagogue situated there and maintained by a handful of Jews, most of whom lived in a poor thoroughfare known as Dudley Street. In one of its dingy houses lived an old Jewess who hawked capers and anchovies in the city. With her lived her son, who had a great reputation among his co-religionists for his profound knowledge of the Mosaic law. This house was the centre of the excitement. From it there issued Mr. McManus, a well-known Bow Street runner, and in his charge was a sallow man of average height, with long, reddish-brown hair and a straggling incipient beard; he was dressed in the Jewish fashion. McManus pushed through the curious crowd with his charge and, entering a waiting hackney coach, they drove off.

The old lady, with Oriental gestures and lamentations, told her neighbours in voluble Yiddish how pious and kind her guest had been; how he had been continuously occupied in studying the Hebrew language and Jewish literature under her son, how generous he had been, maintaining the whole family in affluence, how he had observed even the most minute precepts of the law of Moses, except that, being in hiding, he had not attended the synagogue. But to atone for this sin of omission, he had promised to build them a brand new one to replace the present wretched edifice.

It was thus that Lord George Gordon reappeared on the scene after his long retirement. He had returned from Holland, ostensibly at least, as a pillar of the Protestant Cause. He left Birmingham as Israel Ben Abraham Gordon. In spite of the fact that it was Saturday, and that Jews do not travel on the Sabbath, McManus insisted on their starting

Lord George Gordon

(*a*) At the Maypole Inn. Illustration by "Phiz" in *Barnaby Rudge*

(*b*) Priestly garments, images of saints and household goods were cast into the flames

immediately, so Lord George provided himself with *Kosher* food to eat *en route*. On their arrival, he was conveyed to Mr. Justice Buller's private house, where he passed the night. Very early the following morning he was taken to the King's Bench Prison, where he was quite at home. On the third morning some of his family came to see him; also some members of the Protestant Association, amazed and mortified at the shocking transformation of their erstwhile leader. Jews, too, flocked to King's Bench, but were not allowed to enter. However, they sent him *Kosher* food. It was not until 28th January, nearly a month later, that he was brought up for sentence. It was a cold, grey morning and his short transit from the prison to the Courthouse passed almost unnoticed. Where was the excited, thrusting mob struggling to gain admission to the show, or at least, a glimpse of the principal actor? Where were the highly decorated coaches and carriages filled with fashionably dressed lords and ladies? And could this grotesque, prematurely aged person wrapped in a long heavy overcoat, his beard extending under his chin from ear to ear and differing from the colour of his hair, be the elegant young man who seven short years ago had smilingly bowed his acknowledgments to the cheering crowds, assembled to do him honour? The *Morning Herald* said the following day:

His lordship made both in dress and aspect an appearance truly *Mosaic*. His beard extended a considerable way from his chin and his countenance seemed solemn and sanctimonious.

In Court the atmosphere was even colder than it was outside. Mr. Justice Amherst commented on the scandalous nature of the libels, and told him that had he read his Bible to good effect he might have behaved better, the one *great aim of religion being to teach obedience of the law*. He regretted the disgrace Lord George had brought on his illustrious family. The sentence ran:

Being convicted of composing and publishing a scandalous paper called the *Prisoners' Petition*, this Court does order and adjudge that for your offence aforesaid you be imprisoned in His Majesty's jail of Newgate for three years. And being convicted of trespasses, contempts and misdemeanours against the royal comfort of her Most Christian Majesty and M. Barthelémy, this Court does here order and adjudge you to be fined in Five Hundred Pounds and further imprisoned in Newgate for the space of two years, from and after the termination of the aforesaid judgment, and that you give security for fourteen years' good behaviour, yourself in Ten Thousand Pounds and each of your securities in Two Thousand, Five Hundred Pounds.

It was a stiff sentence but, all things considered, a well-merited one. Perhaps, had Lord George not committed the crowning folly of adopting

F

the Jewish faith, it might have been less severe. That he had done so certainly seemed to justify people in considering him insane.

And so the grim gates of Newgate Prison closed on Lord George Gordon. On the night of 7th June, 1780, his followers had stormed and fired it; on 28th January, 1788, he entered it himself—never, except for the briefest intervals, to leave it alive.

Curiously enough, Lord George being at last safely under lock and key, every effort was made to get him released. The French Government, which had lent its countenance to the proceedings partly to appease the wounded vanity of M. Barthelémy, and partly out of *amour propre*, would gladly have seen the sentence remitted. They had one and all been delighted at this attack on the hated Marie Antoinette and they intimated to the Foreign Office their willingness that since the national honour had been satisfied, justice should be tempered with mercy. Lord Grenville, however, to whom the very name of Lord George was anathema, would not hear of it. The Italian saying *sta bene dove sta*[1] seemed to fit the case exactly. But they gave him another chance. Soon after his imprisonment, Watson tells us, Pitt, wishing to appear generous and knowing that popular opinion was shocked at the severity of the sentence, intimated to the Duke of Gordon that the royal clemency would be extended to his brother if he would make a public recantation of his opinions and promise to make no further trouble. It was an extraordinarily handsome offer, but, with all the obstinacy of the fanatic, Lord George scouted "the infamous proposition." "To sue for freedom was an admission of guilt—never should his conduct disgrace the principles he had espoused—the tender mercies of the wicked were cruelties," and so on.

At first he was lodged among the common felons and confined in a gloomy, sunless room, so damp that the stone walls were covered with a moist green crust. "But though confined to a dungeon," says Watson, "his mind was not inactive. If kings and priests were determined to persecute him, he, on his part, was resolved never to cease from exposing their follies and their crimes." Fortunately for him, he was soon able to expose them from more comfortable quarters. Money and influence did their work and he was given lodgings more suited to his rank; indeed, when John Wesley visited him, he found his room "more like the study of a recluse than a prison." They talked of "Protestantism and Papacy, light and darkness," as they put it. Wesley, like so many of his contemporaries, seemed to have a curious sympathy for this impossible creature, and politely ignored his slumming excursion among the tents of Israel. All the same, they were sad, squalid dwellings, those

[1] He is well out of the way.

eighteenth-century prisons, and yet, in spite of their filth, perhaps more bearable than a modern prison. Although, as in the case of Lord George, those who could afford it could buy practically all the material comforts they wanted, while poor prisoners were herded together in a state of indescribable dirt and wretchedness, they enjoyed the privilege of human companionship and of contact with the outside world. Prison officials of to-day tell us that only by segregating prisoners can you prevent the lesser criminals from being corrupted by the greater. The gentlemen who have enjoyed the hospitality of Maidstone or of Wormwood Scrubs do not endorse that opinion.

Lord George received many visitors, both from his English and Scotch admirers and from foreigners. "I am become one of the shows of London for strangers and foreigners to stare at," he wrote. The poorer Jews, said Watson, "looked upon him as a second Moses, destined by Providence to guide them to the promised land." On the whole, life in that strange prison seems to have passed pleasantly enough for him. It was, apparently, not unlike that led by the American millionaire crook of to-day when, having failed to bribe adequately some powerful authority, he finds himself in jail. Much of the sympathy lavished on him was wasted. He was amply provided with money, lived in good style, and kept an excellent table. Watson, who visited him every day, tells us that he rose at eight, read the newspapers at breakfast, attended to his correspondence and constantly wrote articles on political subjects. At twelve visitors began to arrive and continued to throng his rooms until late in the evening. More than once the royal dukes, York and Clarence—and assuredly the eccentric, kindly and tolerant Duke of Sussex—honoured him with their company. On the rare occasions when he happened to be alone, he played the violin, or took part in some ball game with other prisoners. At two he dined, always inviting at least half a dozen visitors to join him.

His visitors, a contemporary journal tells us, were composed of all ranks, and included peers, Jews, Gentiles, legislators, labourers, officers and soldiers, and all fared alike. The dinner, plain and simple, consisting of two courses; the liquor, porter or table beer, with sometimes a glass of wine. Lord George himself drank nothing but porter and he dined on meat and fish alternately. About six o'clock he went to bed. Once a fortnight he gave a formal dinner party at which etiquette was strictly observed. The guests invited were any distinguished persons who, like himself, had had unsuccessful encounters with the law, notabilities from the outside world, and members of his own family, who, now that he was no longer in a position to disturb their tranquillity, found it very amusing to dine with him at Newgate. One can imagine with what excited shrieks of pretended fear, what gathering up of silken skirts; what fluttering of fans and play of gold and jewelled pomander-boxes, filled with scents and essences to guard against the dread jail fever, these fine ladies and gentlemen passed the gloomy portals of the prison. On these gala occasions dinner was followed by music or dancing. Lord George was fond of music and "was allowed to be an excellent judge of both vocal and instrumental music." "A bagpiper attended him every fortnight and regaled his guests with plaintive selections on his pipes!" Other music was provided by the Duke of York's band. Lord George often entertained visitors from the Court circle, "whom it is not safe to name. They expressed their opinion on the administration with great freedom."

It is difficult to understand why, even in that easy-going period, the Government permitted Newgate Prison to become a sort of club, in which disgruntled politicians, dangerous revolutionaries, debtors and criminals were free to discuss their (the Government's) delinquencies. All the most notable *sans-culottes* in England forgathered in Lord George's rooms—some being near neighbours! There were to be seen Horne Tooke, the shrewdest of the Wilkes agitators, an old-fashioned Radical, who appealed to Magna Carta yet ridiculed Paine's *Rights of Man*, Charles Piggot, an ardent champion of the French Revolution and one of Edmund Burke's most formidable opponents; Joseph Gerald, Dr. Parr's protegé, who was afterwards sent to Botany Bay; Daniel Isaac Eaton, who was indicted for publishing Paine's book; John Frost, who attended the trial of Louis XVI, as representative of the Corresponding Society, and was denounced by Burke as "ambassador to the murderers," and "Peter Pindar" (John Wolcot) whose mordant satires on George III had delighted London.

Together with these odd idealists were several of Lord George's fellow-eccentrics. Noteworthy among them was Martin van Butchell, who for many years kept the mummified body of his first wife as the principal ornament in his parlour, and, of course, there was the faithful Watson, like Boswell, eagerly gathering material for his biography. Among this queer fry walked Lord George, puffing his long churchwarden pipe, still the perfect Scottish gentleman, except for his beard and gaberdine. There is a picture of him extant, in which he is shown with many of his entourage, benevolently watching a game of rackets in the Court, which was one of the amenities of that strange prison.

The illustrious, be they chaste as ice, cannot escape calumny, even when they are doing time. The report went round that Lord George kept two Jewish maidservants, who stayed with him day and night— Watson says that they left every evening at nine o'clock. There is a portrait by the famous miniaturist, Ozias Humphrey, of a very pretty Jewess carrying a tray and decanter, described as "Polly Levy, Jewess in attendance on Lord George Gordon during his confinement in Newgate." Whatever his personal relations with his servants, Lord George treated them with great kindness. One day, Watson tells us, "when the Duke of York was there with some of his courtiers he (Lord George) walked up to his maids and began to talk on indifferent subjects; there was a turkey roasting at the fire, and as the duke saw the cook employed in conversation, he very obligingly turned it, and showed that he understood the business of the kitchen as well as the achievements of war." Posterity, perhaps a little better informed concerning the duke's military abilities, may well hope his culinary skill was not quite as bad.

Watson gives us an attractive picture of his hero. His temper, he says, "was extraordinarily even, his conversation modest and he was always ready to learn of others. An excellent linguist, he could converse with Frenchmen, Italians and Germans in their own tongues. He was easy of access, punctual in his dealings and attentive to what the world calls trifles; equally exact about a farthing, or about a hundred guineas. He had his papers so placed that he could find them in the dark." His fellow-prisoners loved him—no wonder, for he seems to have been infinitely kind and generous to them, and at Newgate his patience and generosity were taxed to the fullest extent. They laughed at him and his eccentricities, but their laughter was kindly. Perhaps he learnt to laugh with them? Well for him if he did, for his lack of humour was certainly one of the contributing causes to his misfortunes. The world is all too serious—especially in the dark days in which we live. It needs a new Boccaccio, a Chaucer, a Rabelais, to teach us with pleasant smiling irony to laugh at ourselves.

Life in Newgate had its lighter moments; Lord George seems to have had a magnetic attraction for cranks. Watson made notes about some of the queer people who visited him. "One evening," he writes, "a young lady from the Oxford Road waited upon his lordship and requested the favour of a private audience. As she was an entire stranger he thought proper to decline, and signified that as there were none but friends present she might safely communicate what she had to say. After much hesitation, she assumed a solemn air and with a hollow tone of voice, said that six months ago she had conceived by the Holy Ghost, without any communication with man."

This had naturally worried the poor girl, and she had been very unhappy and miserable until the previous night, when the Archangel Gabriel had appeared to her and exhorted her to be of good cheer. He told her that the end of the world was at hand and revealed many things "hidden in the womb of time," especially concerning Great Britain, France, and that sink of iniquity, Rome—"the home of the 'Holy Fisherman,' who holds the keys of paradise in one hand and the gates of hell in the other; who consistently pretends to be the 'Servant of Servants,' whilst he arrogates to himself a dispensing power over the lives and properties of man—this spiritual tyrant, whose professional practice is ever to devise new crimes!"

One gathers that, on the whole, Gabriel and the Vicar of Christ were not on the best of terms! He went on to tell the lady that the child to whom she was about to give birth was destined to announce the glad tidings of universal redemption, and oddly enough, ordered her to go at once to Lord George Gordon—apparently being unaware that his lordship had embraced Judaism—and ask his lordship's advice on the matter. Thereupon Gabriel spread his wings and flew away. Lord George was somewhat embarrassed by his visitor's story, and asked Dr. Watson—as confirmed a moralist as ever was his namesake, Sherlock Holmes's Boswell—to reason with her on the impropriety of her conduct. Watson, not so gullible as usual, remarked that the baby was evidently well on the way, even if it were the gift of a less celestial lover. On his trying to demonstrate the improbability of the episode, she indignantly reminded him that the history of revealed religion was just as incredible. But alas! Both Watson and Lord George hardened their hearts, and the immaculate virgin retired disconsolate.

Another gentleman named King, who was suffering from the pangs of an incurable disease, accompanied by the pangs of conscience, came to unburden his rather murky soul. He had been employed by the Government to spy on Lord George, and to try and entrap him. He assured him that London was swarming with Jesuit spies, for whom no employment was too mean. Lord George refused to believe it, telling his visitor that Jesuit priests were generally men of family and education and most unlikely to engage in such despicable work. So he too, departed.

To the rites of his new religion Lord George was pathetically faithful; it is a curious phenomenon that converts are more meticulous in such matters than those to the manner born. He fasted with the prophets, rejoiced with all the savage joy of the Psalmist when the enemies of the Almighty were put to shame, and wailed with the best on the day of atonement. Every morning he was seen with the phylacteries between his eyes; his Saturday's bread, his meat, his wine, were all Jewish, and on his wall were the ten commandments in Hebrew, the bag containing the phylacteries, and the *tallith*—the praying garment. Indeed he was a Jew of Jews! Most of all did he rejoice in his magnificent beard, which now reached to his waist. No beardless Jew was allowed to approach him. Did not the Mosaic code enjoin that: "Ye shall not round the corners of your heads, neither shalt thou mar the corners of thy beard"?[1]

[1]Leviticus, XIX, 27.

VI

Lord George's interest in politics and his passion for playing a part in public affairs never deserted him. From Newgate he issued handbills, larded with quotations from the Old Testament, so applied as to reflect on the King and the Government. This the prison authorities stopped, so he turned his attention to French affairs; to the rape of Poland about to be completed, to the iniquities of the Empress Catherine of Russia in crushing the Poles, indeed to every national and European event in that exciting period. Great was his joy in 1789, at the taking of the Bastille —"a day which gave new life to man and which shook the pillars of superstition"— and, as may be imagined, the misfortunes of the Royal House of France did not trouble him unduly.

His five years' sentence came to an end on 28th January, 1793, and he appeared before the judges to give security for his future good behaviour. The Court was crowded, and the arrival of this Scottish aristocrat with his gaberdine and his astonishing beard caused a sensation. He was ordered to remove his hat. This he refused to do, basing his refusal on the Oriental usage of twenty centuries ago which regarded an uncovered head as discourteous to the Most High. The officers of the Court then removed it, whereupon Lord George produced a white night-cap which he bound round his head with a red and white handkerchief. Having, more or less, won the first round, he was asked if he had the necessary securities in Court to the amount of two thousand five hundred pounds each. He said he had, and indicated two greasy Polish Jews of the poorest class. On the judge refusing to accept them, he asked leave to address the Court. His two sureties, he said, were men whose characters were beyond reproach and—unless the Court judged them from the low standard of pounds, shillings and pence—would be found completely satisfactory. "As it was a mere fiction," he continued, "which the Court themselves chose to adopt, by supposing me worth ten thousand pounds, the same fiction ought, in justice, to be held good in proportion to the sureties—*unless the Court really intended imprisonment for life when they demanded such excessive and unprecedented bail.*"

And this, no doubt, was what the Court had intended. Other people came forward and offered to replace the rejected Jews, but in every case they were declared unsuitable on one pretext or another. Lord George's family could, of course, have arranged the matter easily enough, but Pitt had taken care to buy their support. Honours had been heaped upon them, the duke and duchess were Court favourites, his brother, Lord William, had been made High Admiral and Ranger of Hyde Park, his uncle commander-in-chief in Scotland, and his sisters had been given pensions. That they should prefer this troublesome and unpredictable relation to be safely under lock and key was quite understandable. He had violated every canon of his caste and, to crown all, had turned Jew! His other offences they might have forgiven, but that was the limit, "the most unkindest cut of all!"

Back at Newgate, he was gratified to find that he had not quite lost his popularity with the masses. Letters poured in, sympathizing with his cruel lot. Watson tells us that a deputation of sailors waited on him and proposed that they should come in their thousands and rescue him, but that he declined to allow them to risk their lives and liberties. Most likely the thousands existed only in Watson's optimistic imagination.

But though Lord George did not know it, the order of release was soon to arrive. Jail fever—endemic in the filthy eighteenth-century prisons—laid its clammy hands on him and, notwithstanding the care of the devoted Dr. Lettsom,[1] Lord George, depressed and hopeless, was an easy prey. On 1st November, 1793, he died, and was buried by his family in a vault in St. James's Cemetery, Hampstead Road.

Historians have not been able to make up their minds whether or not he was mentally deranged. The late Lord Oxford and Asquith's view was that he was "eccentric to the verge of madness, ignorant and uncultured, but a sincere fanatic." De Castro does not altogether agree with him; he writes: "With every respect for so weighty an opinion it can scarcely be conceded that he was either ignorant or uncultured. His predominant characteristics were a restless energy, a perverse acuteness and an inability to distinguish fame from notoriety. He hungered and thirsted for the former, but perforce slaked his burning desire from the latter. To be always in the limelight was his passion and to ensure himself the plaudits of the multitude was his cankering ambition."

It has been argued that Lord George's conversion to Judaism was merely another manifestation of his craving for the limelight, but this can hardly be altogether true. By adopting the Jewish faith he threw

[1] Dr. Lettsom was one of the most enlightened doctors in England, and in many ways at least a hundred years ahead of his time. He was immortalized in these lines:

> Out of death lead no ways.
> When any sick to me apply,
> I physics, bleeds and sweats 'em.
> If after that they choose to die,
> Why, verily!
> I Lettsom.

away utterly and irrevocably every possibility of ever regaining either social or political consideration; henceforward nothing remained for him but contempt and ridicule.

Throughout his unhappy, turbulent life, he had been obsessed with religion. His fanatical attacks on Catholicism, his passion for tilting at windmills and for the reform of everything and everybody, his wistful glances towards the Quakers, whom he envied for the peace of mind he believed them to enjoy, and his interest in the occult, were all expressions of a religious complex which a psycho-analyst of to-day would easily diagnose. There is no doubt, however, that he honestly believed in the justice of every cause to which he devoted his fitful, ill-starred energies. Had he lived, would he have found a permanent home in Jewry? Or would that latest and queerest aberration have been but a momentary halt in the strange odyssey of our poor, sorry Don Quixote?

But it is idle to speculate on what might have happened to him.

BIBLIOGRAPHY

The Life of Lord George Gordon   Robert Watson, M.D.,
                                                 London, 1793.

The Gordon Riots   J. Paul de Castro,
                                                 Oxford University
                                                 Press, 1926.

The Morning Post, 1780

Life and Poetical Works of the Reverend George Crabbe   The Bodley Head, 1907.

Barnaby Rudge   Charles Dickens.

Diary and Letters of Fanny Burney   Edited by Austin
                                                 Dobson.

Letters of Horace Walpole   Edited by Mrs. Paget
                                                 Toynbee.

The Diamond Necklace   F. Brentano.

Cobbett's State Trials   Vol. XXI.

Sophie in London. (Being the Diary of Sophie von la
    Roche.)   London, 1933.

Lord George Gordon's Conversion to Judaism   Israel Solomons,
                                                 London, 1915.

The Dictionary of National Biography

DR. SAMUEL PARR
(*A Study in Egoism*)

"Be careful how you choose your enemies."

(Oscar Wilde)

I

THAT fortunate century, the eighteenth, is, in the minds of most of us, associated chiefly with its famous political, social and literary figures. With the Prince Regent and his mistresses, with Marlborough, the Pitts, Fox and Sheridan, with Beau Nash ruling Bath with suave authority, with elegant beaux, gossiping and taking snuff with one another at the "Old Snuff House" in the Haymarket, with Vauxhall and Ranelagh, and with Dr. Johnson.

But, as Trevelyan points out in his *English Social History*, it has another aspect. If the eighteenth century was an age of great personalities and of high civilization, it was, at the same time, exceedingly virile and in its later years very progressive. Before it drew to a close, the campaigns for parliamentary and prison reform, for the abolition of the slave trade and of cruelty to children, and for the amelioration of the wretched conditions in which the London poor lived, had all started, and the drink question was beginning to trouble the social conscience.

It was a highly individualistic age. The eighteenth-century man was expected to stand on his own feet, to be *himself*; and as he was not hemmed in by the hundred and one stupid, exasperating and unnecessary restrictions which *we*, in this feeble and knock-kneed age of all-pervading mediocrity, are forced to endure, he was apt to be a far more interesting and self-reliant being than the human robot of to-day. And not only did the century abound in men famous in every field of endeavour; it tolerated every form of eccentricity, religious, political and social. What other period has produced such oddities as Lady Cork, John Wilkes, Lord George Gordon, "Old Q," or Dr. Samuel Parr, the subject of this sketch?

Much of our knowledge of Parr is derived from an immensely long and chaotic book by his friend, Dr. John Johnstone,[1] who may perhaps be called Parr's Boswell. But a curious Boswell, for his enthusiastic admiration for the doctor's scholarship and his many good qualities is so tempered throughout the book by his desire to be truthful, that never was eulogy so damning! After reading it one feels inclined to misquote the famous lines on another doctor, and say:

"I do not like thee, Doctor—Parr"!

Samuel Parr was born in January, 1747, at Harrow-on-the-Hill,

---

[1] *The Works of Samuel Parr with Memoirs of His Life and Writings*, by John Johnstone, M.D., London, 1828.

where his father—the son of a clergyman—practised as a surgeon and apothecary. Parr senior, writes Johnstone, "was a man of violent temper; the petty tyrant of his fireside." He contrived to combine these unamiable qualities with high moral rectitude and a noble disregard for money. He was also a strong Tory, which probably accounts for Samuel's adoption of Whig principles later in life. Samuel was an appallingly precocious child. When only five years old he was admitted to the "Free School, raised and endowed by John Lyon at Harrow."

"Lyon of Harrow, Yeoman John," as the school song has it.

Children developed early in those days. We read of midshipmen of twelve and ensigns of sixteen taking part in naval and military engagements, and of university undergraduates of sixteen and seventeen. When under fourteen, Samuel became head boy.

At the time he entered the school, the headmaster was Dr. Thackeray, great-grandfather of the novelist. He retired in 1760 and was succeeded by Dr. Sumner. Among Samuel's schoolfellows were the Duke of Gordon, Lord George's brother, the Earl of Barrymore, Lord Middleton, Fletcher Norton, and William Bennet, afterwards Bishop of Cloyne. From his earliest childhood Samuel was didactic and desperately serious. He hated games; indeed the only occasion on which he was ever known to join in the amusements of the school was in a battle between Hawke's and Thackeray's houses to get some fireworks. Once a friend of the family found him sitting on the gate of Harrow churchyard, gravely watching the little victims play. "Why aren't you playing, too?" the friend asked. The infant answered solemnly: "Do you not know I am to be a clergyman?"

His best friend at Harrow seems to have been Master William Bennet, who "revelled in the gaudy and captivating diction of Hervey's *Meditations Among the Tombs*". Johnstone tells us that Samuel and his young friend "delighted in intellectual competitions and disputed logic, syllogism and metaphysical problems."

It was the same at home. Both Samuel and his brother had set their hearts on going into the Church. Their favourite game was pretending they were clergymen. They put on white shirts, Samuel tied the dinner bell to the banisters and tolled it, and they read the service between them, taking it in turns to preach. The Vicar of Harrow was so charmed when he heard of these manifestations of early piety, that he had little cassocks and surplices made for them, which, of course, enchanted them. When any of their pet animals died, they read the burial service with great solemnity.

Here are some of their favourite books at seven years old:

Catechism of Mythology.
Epitome of Modern Geography.
Epitome of Ancient Geography.
Epitome of Grecian History.
Epitome of Jewish History.
Epitome of Heraldry.
Epitome of Navigation.

It is pleasant to know that they also delighted in *Mother Goose* and *Little Red Riding Hood*.

Sam was a pretty child, much spoilt by his mother who was, it appeared, "the servant of her husband and family, waiting on them and pampering them with delicate food." Samuel's sister writes:

Sam was the darling of his mother, and her death—which happened in 1762— was severely and everlastingly felt. She was, indeed, but too indulgent to him: every wish and whim was attended to, and his appetite was so consulted as to have hot meat suppers prepared for him from early childhood. I remember when he was lying under the heavy attack of smallpox, that left its mark upon him till death, he wrote expressing pleasure in the assurance he felt that if the disease were to reach me, I should not suffer as he was suffering, as I had not been indulged in hot suppers. Before this seizure in about his twelfth year he was very fair and regular featured. I recollect well my feeling in the midst of my joy at seeing him get better, something akin to satisfaction that the prettiness which had attracted so much notice was completely spoilt.

A year after the death of his first wife, Dr. Parr married again and home life became very uncomfortable, as the children hated their step mother.

Sam left Harrow at fourteen; his father wanted him to follow his own profession, which, however, did not appeal to the boy. He had grown into a strong, muscular lad and took a singular pleasure in going to the Harrow slaughter-house and knocking down oxen; he also enjoyed seeing the said oxen slaughtered. Still, as Johnstone says, he was remarkably attached to animals. Johnstone regrets that for the honour of the profession and the benefit of mankind he did not adopt it. But he admits that he does not think Samuel would have achieved popularity as a doctor, for "though to affliction he was always kind, yet in expression he was not tender. In some of his moods his appearance would have been terrible to nervous ladies and his feelings were often too intense to authorize the supposition that he could always have restrained them before the patient. He had not courage enough for a physician and too little coolness of mind for a surgeon."

So, perhaps after all, the honour of the profession did not suffer too irreparable a loss when he declined to adorn it.

Finding that Samuel absolutely refused to be a doctor, his father was at length persuaded to let him have his own way, and in 1765 entered him as a sizar at Emanuel College, Cambridge. During his first vacation, Dr. Parr died of apoplexy, and Samuel's grief at his loss was mingled with rage when he found that he had left the whole of his money to his second wife. "Rapacious Mrs. Parr!" said his friend, William Bennet.

At Cambridge, as at Harrow, Samuel renounced all the pleasures of youth and lived laborious days, applying himself to the acquisition of that mastery of Greek and Latin for which he subsequently became famous. One of his tutors was the master of Emanuel College, Dr. Farmer, well known as a commentator and a "black-letter" collector, and afterwards as a resident Canon of St. Paul's. He was, says Archdeacon Butler, "a man of such singular indolence as to neglect the usual duties of his office as tutor of a college in sending in the young men's accounts, and is supposed to have burnt large sums of money by putting into the fire, unopened, letters which contained remittances, accompanied by remonstrances and requiring answers."

"It was with difficulty that Parr was persuaded from pouring forth the bitterness of his wrath upon a man who neglected and endeavoured to degrade him," we are told. But his scholastic abilities and hard work had not passed unnoticed. In November, 1766, the headmaster of Harrow wrote offering him the position of first assistant at Harrow school.

Mr. Holmes has this morning acquainted me with his design of leaving Harrow next Christmas [wrote Dr. Sumner]: *I immediately determined to mention the vacancy to you and offer you the employment.*

The salary I pay Mr. Holmes is £50 per annum. What profits may arise from pupils I cannot fix with any certainty. Mr. Holmes, I understand, receives £40 or £50 from them, and if you think proper to succeed him, I hope it is needless to say I shall do everything in my power to make your situation here respectable and profitable.

Fifty pounds a year does not seem a very high salary for the second master of Harrow, but it must be remembered that Harrow was not then on a par with Eton and Winchester. It was only during the reign of George III that it began to be anything more than the "Free School raised and endowed by John Lyon." When Parr entered the school, it was just beginning to come into its own.

Parr retained his post at Harrow for the next five years—he was ordained in 1769 to the curacy of Willesden and Kingsbury—and they were probably the happiest years of his life. He seems to have got on

The Gordon Rioters in action

A scene from the Gordon Riots

well with both masters and boys, though no doubt they made capital out of his lisp. With one of the masters too, the Reverend David Roderick, he formed a warm friendship. But alas, trouble was on the way. Dr. Sumner, his friend and protector, died of apoplexy in 1771. Parr, who was not quite twenty-five, could think of no one so fitted as himself to succeed the popular headmaster who, by the way, had in eleven years raised the number of boys from eighty to two hundred and fifty. So he sent off a circular letter to each of the governors, offering himself for the position, and enlisted Lord Dartmouth and the Master of Caius College, Cambridge, to support his candidature.

He was not appointed, the choice falling on an Eton master, Dr. Benjamin Heath. Furious at the slight—which he attributed to a vote he had given for John Wilkes at Brentford—he resigned his mastership, and his friend, David Roderick, left with him.

"When it was known that Heath was likely to become master," says Roderick, "the upper boys considered it as an indignity to have an Eton master put over them, when they had in their own school a person of superior learning." This notion they inculcated into the other boys, so that a petition, "ably drawn up and signed by every boy in the school, was presented to the governors on the subject." The petition, which Johnstone quotes in full, is a remarkable piece of work for school-boys, and the zeal of the younger boys for the pure scholarship of Parr was equally remarkable. There were not wanting those who were unkind enough to suggest that Parr himself had a hand, not only in inditing it, but in instigating a mild rebellion attempted by some of the petitioners. They took the carriage of one of the governors to the common and destroyed it, and some of the smaller boys tried to smash the windows of another governor's house. However, order was soon re-established. But so persistent were the rumours that Parr wrote Dr. Heath an angry letter, denying their truth and calling on him to declare publicly his disbelief in such dreadful allegations. This letter Heath did not answer, nor did he refute the rumours, and when Parr called on him he did not return his visit.

Having been, as he described it "driven away from Harrow to the great anguish of his heart," he determined to have his revenge. To this end he persuaded Dr. Sumner's brother to lend him two thousand pounds. He then applied to the Bishop of London for a licence, which, Johnstone tells us, was at first refused "with great contumely." But the bishop relented, and Parr, buying a house at Stanmore, set up what he fondly imagined would be a rival school to Harrow. He managed to induce the parents of about forty of the Harrow boys who had got into trouble on his account, to send them to Stanmore. These included Lord

Dartmouth's two boys, and the sons of the Bishop of Meath and the Dean of York. David Roderick became his assistant master.

It was a mad scheme. Stanmore—which even within quite recent years was a small country village—is only about two miles from Harrow, and the pleasant walk over fields was a favourite one with Harrovians. The boys of the two schools were bound to meet constantly, and their encounters were seldom peaceful, so it was, perhaps, the worst place he could have chosen. Then, Parr was no Dr. Sumner. Like many men who make excellent servants, he was a bad master. He could not keep authority, and his pupils did much as they liked, even going shooting and hiring horses to ride. The boys who had supported him felt, naturally enough, that he was under an obligation to them and, once the fun of the adventure had worn off, felt themselves in an inferior position to the Harrow boys. Parr did all he could to make his school a success; they did a Greek play, for which Garrick lent them the costumes, and he encouraged fights, arranging that they took place outside his study windows, but in spite of his efforts the number of boys never exceeded sixty. One gathers that he was not popular. He was a bad teacher, totally unable to adapt his teaching of the classics to the mental capacity of his pupils, whom he flogged with more than the ordinary ferocity of the eighteenth-century schoolmaster. "Temple (of Rugby) is a beast," said one of his boys, "but he is a just beast." Parr was not a just beast. He would flog without mercy, and for the most trifling faults, the boys whom he did not like, letting his favourites and the sons of important parents go scot-free. Favouritism and lax discipline are always resented by boys and they are apt to take the law into their own hands. Certainly curious things happened at Dr. Parr's school—here is a letter some of his boys sent to the father of an unpopular youth:

The late scandalous behaviour of your son hath at length occasioned this final resolution of his school-fellows. We have now decided to associate no longer with a person against whom suspicions of theft are so strong, and proof of lying and scandal are so well attested. For the first, Sir, examine his library; for the second we ourselves can bring innumerable instances. His malice, which is of the blackest and most extraordinary nature, hath been continually employed in endeavouring to violate the friendship of those whose esteem he could not obtain. But his motives of resentment are as dishonourable as the acts themselves; we despise them both. If breaking into the bed chamber and study of his master, examining his letters and papers; if mean familiarities with the servants; rifling their closets and drawers; if defamations, if deceit, if acts of the basest kind constitute the character of a villain, we know where the condemnation ought to fall.

A nice boy, you say! But there is another side to the case. This deep-dyed villain was a certain William Beloe, who some years later wrote a book called *The Sexagenarian* in which he pilloried his old schoolmaster, "that dragon of learning." The suspicion of theft was quite unjustified, but he must have been unpopular. He got into trouble at Cambridge afterwards for his sarcastic tongue. There is nothing the young hate so much as satire; they are so defenceless against it.

To add to his troubles, Parr had taken a wife before opening his school, thinking that it befitted a schoolmaster to be married. The marriage—to a Miss Marsingale—was arranged by a friend, a Dr. Askew, whose wife was an intimate friend of the lady. Alas, it was not a success. His wife was as cold and rigidly conventional as he was hot-tempered and eccentric. She was fiendishly clever in drawing attention to his foolishness and his social ineptitude. "Parr," she said, "was born in a whirlpool and bred a tyrant." Needless to say there were continual scenes. On one occasion, rising from the dinner table during a fierce discussion with her, he picked up the carving knife and going to her portrait which was hanging on the wall, cut her pictorial throat from ear to ear!

It was at Stanmore that he began to practise those eccentricities which, with his reputation as a scholar, made him so well-known a figure in later years. He smoked a vilely strong shag tobacco from morning to night. Even his friend Roderick disapproved of him, saying: "he brought upon himself the ridicule of the neighbours and passengers, by many foolish acts; such as riding in high prelatical pomp through the streets, on a black saddle, bearing in his hand a long cane or wand, such as women used to have, with an ivory head like a crozier, which was probably the reason why he liked it; at other times he was seen stalking through the town in a dirty, striped morning gown." It was at Stanmore too, that he developed his dangerous and innate genius for making enemies, which was all his life to hinder his advancement and render him unpopular with those most in a position to be useful to him. The Rector of Stanmore was a Mr. Smith. He had been very kind to Parr when he set up school, helping him to buy his house and adapt it to its intended purpose. At first they were warm friends, but it was not long before their relations became cool and at last all intercourse between them ceased. It was a pity. Smith was a clever, witty man with great personal charm. He had been brought up at Lichfield with David Garrick and Dr. Johnson, and the break in their friendship did not improve matters at Stanmore for Parr. As time went on the number of pupils dwindled; the old boys left and there were no new ones to take their place until—in 1777—the school having left him, he left Stanmore.

II

AFTER his ignominious retreat from Stanmore, Parr applied for the headmastership of Colchester Grammar School, and asked a friend—a man called Bennet Langton—to beg Dr. Johnson to speak for him. Langton did so, and Johnson kindly agreed, saying that a man of Parr's learning must be well-suited "for presiding over a seminary of education." There was only one other applicant for the position and, as he decided not to compete, Parr was elected. The Vicar of Colchester offered him two curacies. "The duty is a service at each church once a Sunday," he wrote, "but I am now under the necessity of giving up the 'business of burials' on account of my gouty feet. These must therefore be undertaken by the curate. And I am also obliged to load him with the buryings of a third parish. . . . I now give fifty pounds a year for the service of the two churches on Sundays, but I mean to make the salary fifty guineas on account of the additional duty." The "buryings" he mentioned averaged some fifty-four yearly, so the curate got about 11¼d. a corpse!

Parr took up his duties at Colchester in 1777. He repaired the schoolhouse and took another house in which to board pupils, but, we are told by Johnstone, the success of his endeavours was very inconsiderable. Still, after his turbulent life at Stanmore, he found Colchester comparatively restful. But no more than at Harrow, or at Stanmore, was he quite at his ease. He began by having a row with the trustees of the school concerning a lease. As usual, he wrote a pamphlet, which he sent to his friend and lawyer, Sir William Jones. "Too violent, too strong throughout," was Sir William's comment on the document; so the trustees won, without, as Parr wrote, "even the mockery of a skirmish." And he had longed for a battle royal!

At Colchester he made some good friends, among them Thomas Twining, Rector of Fordham, near Colchester, and one of the most delightful of eighteenth-century parsons—classical scholar, musician, literary critic, and the valued friend of Dr. Johnson and Dr. Burney. Twining wrote to his brother, who was thinking of sending his son to Parr's, "Of Mr. Parr's abilities, learning, taste, manner of teaching and finding out the disposition, talents and character of boys, I have the highest idea. How he is in point of discipline and severity, I cannot pretend to say; I have been told that he flogs too much. In conversing with him I have heard him disapprove of beating children; I have heard him say that *words* were his worst rod; that what the boys most dreaded was his *shaming them before the whole school.*" What boy would not be caned rather than shamed? But, as Johnstone says, the versatile doctor used both methods. Still, Twining confessed that if he had a son he would take the risk and send him to Parr.

He did not stay long at Colchester. In 1778 he applied for the post of headmaster of Norwich Grammar School, was appointed, and removed there the following year. Why he left Colchester Johnstone does not tell us; in all probability it was owing to his unsatisfactory relations with the trustees of the school.

Nothing daunted by his previous failures, Parr settled down to his new duties. True, he would rather have been headmaster of Harrow, but after all, he was still young—only thirty-two—and already noted for his scholarship. "His confidence in his own powers now waxed strong," says Johnstone. "Such being the natural aspiration of genius, it was not out of the order of things for him to aspire less high than his fellow schoolmaster, Milton." Then again, Norwich was an important city; he could hardly fail to make useful connections there in ecclesiastical and political circles, and politics had always attracted him; through them lay the surest path to preferment. It was unfortunate for him that he chose the wrong party. In 1783 the change of ministry and the coalition of Whigs and Tories aroused the hopes of the Whigs and—perhaps because he had always had an enthusiastic admiration for Fox—he threw in his lot with them. But Pitt was now the man of the moment, and although the Commons voted an address to the Crown to advise His Majesty not to dissolve Parliament, it was dissolved, and Fox found himself out of office.

In 1786 Dr. Parr—he had taken the degree of LL.D. at Cambridge in 1781—resigned his position at Norwich. Johnstone cannot tell us the reason. He seems to have been more successful there than either at Stanmore or Colchester, though never popular. He himself, in speaking of his successor, Dr. Forster, says: "his mild government, compared with my strictness, made him for some time popular." On leaving Norwich he took up residence in Hatton, of which Lady Jane Trafford, the mother of one of his pupils, had conferred upon him the perpetual curacy.

Parr was now thirty-eight, and, as he wrote to a friend who wanted to borrow from him. "Not a shilling richer," than when he went to Stanmore. He had, however, paid back the two thousand pounds he had borrowed to set up his school there. The income from Hatton and from his Prebend's stall did not together amount to more than a hundred a year, so he was obliged to take pupils.

In 1786 he began writing political pamphlets, the first being a preface to his edition of *Bellenden*—a Scot who flourished in the seventeenth century and who wrote a book on Cicero. In this preface he attacked Pitt and the coalition with more than his usual violence. It did not need Parr's mastery of Latin to prove that Whig and Tory could not make good bedfellows, but, one may well ask, "Why did he write all this? What provocation had he? Why did he insult Pitt, the Duke of Richmond and Lord Thurloe?" He had thrown in his lot with Fox, but it was by no means certain that he would have benefited, even had his party triumphed. Fox had not the power of *personally* disposing of preferment. He might, perhaps, have been made a canon residentiary of St. Paul's through Fox's influence; on the appointment of the regency he had had hopes of being promoted to the See of Bristol. But when his friends *were* in power, Lord Grenville declined to recommend him for a bishopric on account of his unpopularity with his clerical brethren. After all, Pitt was not only a great statesman; he was popular with the public, so besides infuriating the Pittites, Parr's violence disgusted and alarmed his own party, with whom he was by no means *persona grata*— they could not rely on him. So his preface hurt no one but himself.

The Test Act had given them a proof of his inconsistency. In 1789 he had been all out for its repeal; it was "unjust, oppressive, tyrannical." In 1790 he had changed his mind, and wrote, "I strenuously opposed the attempt to procure a repeal." He even arranged meetings to resist it, leaguing himself with the High Church Party, who loathed him— naturally enough, for at the outbreak of the French Revolution, its most fervent supporters were the Dissenters of Birmingham under Dr. Priestley, whose house was sacked, and Parr was the only clergyman in England who openly sympathized with him. With regard to the Test Act he wrote to his friend Howell:

I think Mr. Burke entirely wrong, and that he has done more harm than ever was done before. Indeed, he never was of much use to the party, and has himself domineered over Mr. Fox's better judgment. He and Sheridan are not yet reconciled I assure you. But what signifies private reconciliation? In Parliament he accused him of something like treason; and in Parliament he should be forced to support or retract the charge. The evil lies deep in jealousy of Sheridan's superior popularity and superior influence with Mr. Fox: and you see Pitt is taking great advantage: and sorry I am that Mr. Fox is to have a lead in the repeal business, for it will alarm the country and not fix the Presbyterians. Have you seen Wesley's libellous and most inflammatory pamphlet called "Theodosius"?

Yours, etc.,

S. Parr.

It says much for the kindly tolerance of Fox that he remained on good terms with his dangerous friend.

At one time Parr had been one of Burke's most enthusiastic admirers —"Burke was his chief idol," said Johnstone. But Burke's policy with regard to the Test Act, his secession from the Whig Club, and his famous book on the French Revolution, had changed him into an enemy. Burke was much criticized for leaving the party, but he was not the only member of the Whig Club who resigned membership for reasons of conscience. It was a great blow to Fox, who, later on, writing to Dr. Parr, said in his much-quoted letter:

The truth is, though I do not feel any malice against Burke, nor would I have in any degree thwarted any plan for his advantage or honour; though I feel the greatest gratitude for his continued kindness during so great a part of our lives and a strong conviction that I owe to his friendship and conversation a very great portion of whatever either of political or oratorical merit my friends suppose me to have displayed: notwithstanding all this, I must own that there are some parts of his conduct that I cannot forgive so entirely as perhaps I ought, and as I wish to do.

His public conduct may have arisen from mistaken motives of right, carried to a length to which none but persons of his ardent imagination would have pursued them. But the letter to the Duke of Portland and Lord Fitzwilliam, with the worst possible opinion of me, is what I can never think of without sensations which are as little habitual to me as to most men. To attempt to destroy me in the opinion of those whom I so much value, and in particular that of Fitzwilliam with whom I had lived in strictest friendship since our infancy; to attempt it too, at a time and in a way which made it almost certain that they would not state the accusation to me, and consequently that I should have no opportunity to defend myself—this was surely not only malice, but baseness in the extreme, and if I were to say that I have quite forgiven it, it would be boasting a magnanimity which I cannot feel.

Perhaps De Quincey is right in saying that a man so simple, plain and with a mind so homely, was constitutionally incapable of understanding the complex, subtle and slightly pompous intellect of Burke. He knew well that he owed his own success to his brilliant oratory and his *personal magnetism*. "I have always hated the idea of any of my speeches being published," he said.

Fox's letter was written after Burke's death, and Parr had been asked to write his epitaph. One or two of Burke's admirers considered the epitaph cold. "Then I have indeed been successful," said Parr, "for as I did not feel warmth, I had not attempted to express it." One of Parr's methods of expressing disapproval of Burke was, to say the least

of it, peculiar. He suspended his portrait with the head downwards!
This posthumous punishment he inflicted on two other "criminals"—
Mr. Windham, the Home Secretary, and Paley. "I never thought Paley
an honest man," he said. The three portraits hung for years in this position
at Hatton.

Even when the doctor and Burke were friends, he did not spare him
criticism. On one occasion when Sheridan, Fox, Burke and he were
discussing the speeches made in a debate at the House of Commons, he
had some disparaging things to say about most of the speakers.

"You did not mention my speech, so I suppose you have no fault
to find with it," said Burke.

"Not so, Edmund," answered Dr. Parr. "It was oppressed by epithet,
dislocated by parenthesis and debilitated by amplification."

When settling at Hatton, Parr had hoped to take an active and
leading part in the affairs of the county. But alas! In 1789 he had offended
the Earl of Warwick, the Lord Lieutenant, when, in the election for the
borough, he supported Mr. Greville contrary to the direct interests of
the Castle, using his very considerable powers of invective against Lord
Warwick. His lordship was quite equal to the occasion; he was just as
insulting, and called Parr "a Jacobin!" Parr threatened and raged, but
all to no purpose. Lord Warwick announced that he would be happy
to subscribe to any work Dr. Parr published against him. Notwithstanding this, when, in 1795, Lord Warwick nominated a number of
justices for the peace for the county, Parr, hurt and surprised that his
name was not among them, wrote an angry letter of protest. Lord
Warwick replied:

*I apprehend that the proper answer to the letter which I have just received
from you is, that I do not consider myself as responsible to any individual for the
motives of my conduct when acting in the discharge of my duties.*

Parr's desire to be a magistrate was oddly inconsistent, as he often
remarked that "no minister ought to be a magistrate."

In the meantime the political horizon grew blacker and blacker.
The country was seething with discontent and strong measures were
discussed, among them, the suspension of the Habeas Corpus Act.
Another attack on the liberties of the people, screamed Dr. Parr, and
his constant toast was "*Qui suspenderunt, suspendantur.*" This time his
friend Fox fully agreed with him. "The grounds for this," he stated in
the House of Commons were founded on "stale, ridiculous and con-
temptible facts, and a pretence on the part of the Government of an alarm
which was a gross affectation." However, as only twenty-eight members
of the House opposed it, the suspension was voted. Certainly the alarm

Newgate where Lord George Gordon was imprisoned and died

Samuel Parr

Cricket at Harrow School in 1802

Very truly yours,
Thomas de Quincey

Thomas de Quincey

felt was not unjustified. During that year—1795—a journeyman printer, one Kyd Wake, was convicted of insulting the King while he was driving in his state carriage, and sentenced to be imprisoned for five years and to stand in the pillory for one hour every day during the first three months of his sentence. Two Bills, called the "Pitt and Grenville Bills", were brought in and enacted—"an Act for the safety and preservation of His Majesty's person against treasonable and seditious practices and attempts," and "an Act for the more effectually preventing seditious meetings and assemblies." Though most of the aristocracy approved of them, they aroused a great deal of opposition. Dr. Parr arose in his wrath. "They aimed a deadly blow at the vitals of the constitution." "They nearly established a despotism and constituted a treasonable attempt against the liberties of the country," he wrote to Fox, who answered:

My dear Sir—I return you many thanks for your two letters and am very glad things were so properly settled at Warwick. If you think there is a reasonable prospect for success, I own I could wish there were some attempt to get a petition for your part of the country against the two Bills now pending. It is impossible, even for those who most wish to be blind, not to see that they are part of a decided system calculated to bring on, as speedily as possible, what Mr. Hume calls the euthanasia of the British Constitution.

I am, very sincerely, Dear Sir, yours ever,

C. J. Fox.

Notwithstanding Parr's genius for making enemies, he could be very agreeable to those whom he liked. He was a warm-hearted man and extremely generous on occasion. In 1795 his political friends, knowing, no doubt, that there was no hope of preferment for him and that he was almost entirely dependent on his pupils, raised an annuity of £300, which was paid him by the Dukes of Norfolk and Bedford.

With Parr, not to be a Whig was to be a criminal. His passion, De Quincey says, "carried him always back to Whiggism," and had he never strayed from the strait and narrow way of Whig interests he would have had his reward. The Whigs were wise in their generation and never forsook those who stuck to them through thick and thin.

But there are occasions when the safety—even the very existence—of the nation is threatened, and party strife must give way to its defence. We to-day know that only too well. Such a crisis arose when Napoleon was sweeping over Europe like an avalanche. How did Dr. Parr behave in that crisis? In the spring of 1814 he wrote:

My indignation at the English Government as the real and implacable disturbers of the peace in Europe increases daily and hourly, and from that malignant spirit which began to act in 1793, and is now reinforced by the accession of such an auxiliary as the Prince Regent, I forbode the most disastrous consequences.

And so, as De Quincey remarks: "Jena, Austerlitz, Germany, Russia, were not French—they were British Acts." Did he rejoice over Waterloo with the rest of the world, as did Wordsworth? With such a political weathercock, who can tell?

One of the most puzzling things in Dr. Parr's career is how, in that age of literary giants, he managed to get himself the reputation of being a distinguished author. Both he and his friends seemed to take it for granted; the delusion lasted throughout his life, and is, even now, not entirely dead. Never was reputation built on such a slight foundation. What did he write? Here, says De Quincey, "is a learned doctor, whose learned friend has brought him forward as a first-rate author of his time, and yet nothing is extant of his writing beyond an occasional preface, or a pamphlet on private squabbles." *Bellenden*, despite its undoubted brilliance as a Latinist's *jeu d'esprit*, is nothing but an attack on his political enemies. It was not that his duties as a schoolmaster gave him little leisure to write; he was no sufferer from literary constipation, quite the contrary, indeed! He poured out, according to Johnstone, some 5,734 octavo pages, many of them printed in small type—add what is omitted, and one may well put it at 7,000 pages. And of all this, not one page is ever read or quoted; not one wise or witty saying has come down to us.

This seems to worry his biographer, who writes:

> *It may be regretted that with such powers and such means of gathering information from every quarter, that Dr. Parr did not produce some great work; on some great subject. That, like Clarendon, he did not give the history of the awful period of which he saw the spring-tide and in part, the issue: or, like Burnet, that he did not relate in a familiar manner, the transactions of the period in which he lived: or, like Tacitus, paint in caustic and living colours the atrocities of which he was a witness, and deliver as an everlasting memorial to posterity, the characters of those who took a part in them.*

Why not, indeed? The only explanation Johnstone has to offer, is that neither did Archbishop Markham nor Dean Cyril Jackson choose to immortalize themselves! But he omits to say that they neither of them claimed high literary distinction. Parr was always *contemplating* some great work. "I intended to write Johnson's life," he said. "I laid by sixty or seventy books for the purpose of writing in such a manner as would do no discredit to myself. Often I have lamented my ill-fortune in not building this monument to the fame of Johnson and (*let me not be accused of arrogance when I add*) my own." Again:. "In regard to Johnson's life, I shall probably write it some day or other. But I will not begin till I am master of my own time. I shall write it in the spirit of a scholar. Moreover, I have not read more than one half of Sir John Hawkins, whose book I met with at Crewe Hall. It was dull, confused and impertinent and illiterate, and with all those faults it somehow or other interested me. Well, when these shallow fellows have done writing, I perhaps, shall begin to write, but not before."

He had also collected a vast amount of material for a life of Fox, on whom, one imagines, he could have written far better than he could on Johnson. But alas! and alack! The "shallow and illiterate fellows" continued to write, so Dr. Parr kept silent and left Dr. Johnson to Boswell.

Did posterity—for whom Parr was so solicitous—lose much by his literary reticence? Next to his ambition to wear a mitre was his wish to rival Dr. Johnson. The one desire was as hopeless as the other. Dr. Johnson, for all his slightly pompous style—typical of the age in which he wrote—humanized everything he touched with his wise philosophy, sincerity and love of common humanity. Even his *Lives of the Poets* continues to be read and admired; as Lytton Strachey says, "His æsthetics are almost invariably subtle, or solid, or bold. They have always some good quality to recommend them—except one—they are never right." But then, to quote Strachey again, we go to it (*The Lives of the Poets*) not for instruction or for information, "we go to it to see what Dr. Johnson thought." That is the last reason for which one would read Dr. Parr, apart from the fact that his turgid, pompous, vulgarly ornate, over-Latinized style makes him almost impossible to read. Here is an example of it—taken from the document he wrote to confound the trustees of Colchester Grammar School:

That day indeed, I expected to find a day of fierce contention, and therefore I had arrayed myself in a panoply of the trustiest armour; in the breastplate of innocence, the shield of the law, the sword of indignation, and the helmet of intrepidity. When I first entered the lists against these hardy combatants, I determined to throw away the scabbard, and firm as I considered the strength of my cause, I imagined that my antagonists would not yield in the contest.

That even in his own day Parr's pretensions to literary fame did not convince everyone, is seen in an attack on him in *The Pursuits of Literature.* "It would be ridiculous indeed to compare the Birmingham doctor with Dr. Samuel Johnson. What has Dr. Parr written? A sermon or two, rather long, a Latin Preface to *Bellenden* (rather long, too) consisting of a *cento* of Latin and Greek expressions applied to political subjects; another preface to some English tracts, and two or three English pamphlets about his own private quarrels. And this is the man to be compared with Dr. Samuel Johnson!" "I really think," says the author, "it is impossible to point to any man of learning and ability (and Dr. Parr has both) who has hitherto wasted his powers and attainments in such a desultory, unmeaning, wild, unconnected, and useless manner as Dr. Parr. I have done with him."

This aroused the wrath of his biographer. "No, the beast of prey never loses his victim till he has torn him to pieces," he writes. But it was true. Parr wrote thousands of letters in his illegible handwriting, all at breakneck speed, hitting at everyone right and left and never pausing for an instant to consider the impression his rash accusations might produce.

Though himself violently intolerant of criticism, he did not hesitate to deal it out with a liberal hand to other writers. Sir Walter Scott he hated, probably on account of his immense popularity—he was nothing, he was an "arrant charlatan and impostor." "As to Sir Walter Scott, his jingle will not outlive the next century," he wrote. Though no one nowadays considers Scott a great poet, no critic would deny his claim to be a great novelist. There were, Parr said, only five true poets living— "the race is nearly extinct." They were Moore, Byron, Crabbe, Campbell, and a Reverend Mr. Stewart, an Irish poet with whom at the moment he happened to be friends. He did not mention Gray—he had probably been reading the *Lives of the Poets*!

One asks, again, how did he acquire his reputation as a literary man? Perhaps because, like or dislike him, he was undoubtedly a strong, pushing personality and his political activities brought him into contact with many of the most notable men of his day. Being totally devoid of modesty, false or otherwise, he never ceased advertising his claims to greatness, for, like Lord George Gordon, he had a genius for publicity and was his own publicity agent. But chief among the reasons for his celebrity was his classical scholarship, which, though sterile, was admittedly first-rate. In the eighteenth century a knowledge of the classics was considered an essential part of the education of a gentleman. They were the only subjects taught seriously in the public schools and universities, and Latin quotations were used freely in the Houses of Parliament, in the pulpit and in general literature. That there was a good deal of snobbishness in this cult of the classics was recognized even in those days, especially in France. d'Alembert, the French philosopher wrote:

On s'est donné bien de la peine pour étudier une langue difficile: on ne veut pas avoir perdu son temps: on veut même paraître aux yeux des autres récompensé avec usure des peines qu'on a prises: et on leur dit avec un faux transport. "Ah, si vous sçaviez le Grec!"

One wonders what would happen if one of our legislators of to-day quoted Horace!

III

THE eighteenth century is often accused of having been an irreligious age. This, however, like all generalizations, is only partly true. Certainly the Puritan fanaticism of the mid-seventeenth century had burnt itself out. It had given place to a less emotional type of religious teaching, sleepy and easy-going, based on the ethics of the Christian faith—a religion which exactly suited the majority of churchgoers, especially the upper classes. But one must not forget that it was also the age of John Wesley, George Whitefield and other evangelical preachers, such as Roland Hill, who drew crowds to the Surrey Chapel.

"I go to hear Rowland Hill because his ideas come straight from the heart," said Sheridan to Dr. Milner, the Dean of Carlisle.

"Mr. Hill! Mr. Hill! I feel to-day 'tis the slap-dash preaching that, say what you will, does all the good," replied the dean.

Dr. Parr, like most of his brethren, was a Latitudinarian, but, unlike most Latitudinarians, he took an inordinate pleasure in ceremonial, lights and vestments—"ecclesiastical millinery", as Dr. Inge puts it. This was in accordance with his love of ostentation in private life. His two overmastering ambitions, he avowed frankly, were to wear a mitre and drive a coach and four. He preached sermons of evangelical length in which he could not help being controversial. Though a soi-disant loyal son of the Church, he hated what he called "rampant orthodoxy," that is, any of its teachings with which he disagreed. These he would slur over, reading them so indistinctly that no one could understand him. But he professed an implicit belief in the basic dogmas of the Christian faith. Again, when obliged to read Royal Proclamations that conflicted with his political opinions, he turned them into ridicule by his grimaces and the satirical manner in which he read them. His services, too, were extremely informal. "Show that lady and gentleman into my pew, Sam," he once called to his servant, while reading the lesson. But to his great credit he strictly observed the Church's injunction of charity to the poor. No needy member of his congregation appealed to him in vain. Here he was at his best, and his charity was the more whole-hearted, as the poor could not contradict or argue with him. He took part in all the social activities of his parish; smoked and jested with the old, visited and looked after the sick, gave them all a big dinner on May Day and danced round the Maypole with the girls. His oddities were a source of great amusement to the village. On one occasion he rode from Hatton to Warwick, wearing a dressing-gown over his coat, an enormous wig, a clerical hat, long woollen stockings, and jack boots with one spur.

With his clerical brethren his relations were less happy. During part of the time when he was curate of Hatton, Dr. Bridges, a Fellow of Magdalen College, Oxford, was rector of the neighbouring parish of Wadenhoe, and as he could not hold a new preferment conferred upon him *with* Wadenhoe, but could do so as curate of Hatton, the two clergymen—at that time friends!—agreed to change churches, Parr retaining the right to officiate in Hatton Church for six Sundays every year. Now Dr. Bridges was a person of Dr. Milner's type,[1] and a strict evangelical; he was also a man of family and fortune and very popular in the social world. His habit of spending his days carrying spiritual and material comfort to the poor in the slums of Bristol, and his evenings dining out, infuriated Parr. So when the church passed into his hands for the stipulated six Sundays, he did his utmost to efface the impression left by Dr. Bridges. He performed pagan rites of expiation, circling round the church nine times; he fumigated the precincts with his shag tobacco and congratulated his congregation on their release from pollution.

"Be careful how you choose your enemies," said Oscar Wilde. There is profound truth in his saying; its observance would have smoothed the paths of many ambitious but indiscreet place-seekers, Parr among them. His violent and unscrupulous attacks on public men and institutions, including the Church—an unfortunate lack of tact in one whose mind was centred on wearing a mitre—had made him enemies in high ecclesiastical and political circles.

Bishops in the eighteenth century were almost invariably either men of aristocratic birth, or men who had been chaplains either to the King or to some great noble family. "Bishops are not chosen for their learning," said Dr. Johnson. But whatever the reason for their preferment, they were expected to support the party to whom it was due. When Lord Shelborne presented Dr. Richard Watson to the See of Llandaff, he told the Duke of Grafton that he had no doubt the bishop would write pamphlets for the party. Now one of the most influential bishops—and one of the few who did not owe his bishopric to his birth —was Dr. Warburton, Bishop of Gloucester. Another, both influential and popular, was the Bishop of Worcester, Dr. Hurd. Dr. Parr had made deadly enemies of both bishops. This was particularly unfortunate in the case of Dr. Hurd, as he was his diocesan. Of Warburton Dr. Johnson wrote:

[1] Dr. Milner was head of Queen's College, Cambridge, and afterwards Dean of Carlisle. He was a saintly clergyman, too saintly for Dr. Parr who detested his evangelical principles and manner of life.

To be a bishop a man must be learned in a learned age, factious in a factious age, but always of eminence. Warburton was certainly eminent. Pope introduced him to Allen: Allen introduced him to his niece and so by Allen's influence and his own he was made a bishop.

Warburton was highly intellectual, but haughty and arrogant; a typical eighteenth-century bishop—rather supercilious, according to Boswell—and he exacted every iota of the deference he considered due to his position, and bishops in those days enjoyed a prestige little less than that of royalty, so no wonder Dr. Parr yearned for a mitre! Living in state in his palace with ample means to keep it up, he ruffed it with the best. His harassed successor of to-day, occupying a few rooms in that palace and taxed to death, must sigh with nostalgic regret for those days of pomp and circumstance as—almost unrecognized—he hurries through the crowded streets of his commercialized cathedral city. Dr. Hurd, too, was a very distinguished man, an eloquent preacher and a fine classical scholar. "Hurd, Sir, is a man whose acquaintance is a valuable acquisition," said Johnson. How difficult it is, by the way, to write about the eighteenth century without quoting him.

Now it had happened that some years before he died Warburton had written a rather scathing pamphlet, refuting the views of two dissenting ministers, Leland and Jortin, who had ventured to criticize him. Later on, he regretted having done so and suppressed it. In 1789, Parr, at his own expense, had the pamphlet reprinted, and added to it another pamphlet, "by a Warburtonian," the Warburtonian being Dr. Hurd. He wrote a venomous preface, in which he said that Leland had been "most petulantly insulted"; Jortin "most inhumanely vilified." Why did Parr revive the affair? Three of those involved in it were dead and the fourth was an old and greatly respected prelate. Well, Parr had a truly characteristic reason—he frankly avowed that he intended "*to lessen the numbers of those who speak too well of Dr. Hurd!*" Hurd had offended him. On his appointment to the curacy of Hatton, he had called on the bishop at Hartlebury, where he was "offered no refreshment and dismissed with scant ceremony." No doubt, too, he had been told of Dr. Hurd's remarks about his (Parr's) "preposterously long vernacular sermons," particularly referring to the Spital sermon. When Alderman Coombe became Lord Mayor of London in 1799 he asked Parr to preach this sermon and wished he hadn't. The thing he most disliked about it, he said, was "hearing the church clock (Christ Church, Newgate Street) strike the four quarters during its delivery." Parr was very proud of the sermon. Once, at a dinner party, he asked a lady what she thought of it. She answered: "My opinion, sir, is expressed

Samuel Parr, from a portrait by J. Opie, R.A.

John Lyon's School House (now Fourth Form room at Harrow) where Samuel Parr was for a time assistant master

in the first five words of the sermon: 'Enough and more than enough!' "

Parr sulked for the rest of the evening. To crown all, Bishop Hurd had actually hesitated in admitting to Holy Orders one of Parr's special friends and—needless to say—admirers, for otherwise there could be no friendship with the conceited little doctor. Even his biographer, Johnstone, has no excuse to offer for his action. "I regret my honoured friend's attack upon Hurd, the more, because I think the cause of letters had nothing to do with it," he wrote, and again: "Why should so learned a man as Dr. Parr attack so venerable and so respectable a man as Dr. Hurd in this bitter manner? What could be his motives? What motives could justify such an attack? Its venom, its sly aims, its dexterous thrusts, as well as its furious blows are unparalleled."

And still Dr. Parr wondered that preferment and the Bench of Bishops continued to elude him!

In 1783, Dr. Robert Lowth, Bishop of London, had conferred upon him on the request of his (Parr's) old patron, Lord Dartmouth, the Prebend of Wenlock's Barn in St. Paul's Cathedral. Dr. Lowth's letter shows how ecclesiastical patronage functioned in those days.

Dear Sir, [he writes]. *When Lord Dartmouth spoke to me in your favour I assure you I most readily and with great pleasure accepted his recommendation. Though it is now a great while ago, I never forget it, but have never had any opportunity of offering to you anything that would be agreeable. The Prebend of St. Paul's now vacant, though of little value, yet will be attended with no sort of trouble, but that of taking possession. If you come to town next week, time enough to be collated before the following Sunday you may read on that Sunday the service, and your whole business will be finished. You need not bring with you any testimonials: nor so much as your letter of orders: for I think I ordained you priest myself. The conditions of the Prebend are as follows; An estate of £200 a year is held by the Prebend by lease of twenty-one years, which, if renewed at four years, will give you a fine of £100: if at seven years, of £250. The late prebendary was proprietor of the lease, which he took care to renew every year to keep the term always full. So you can have no fine till four years hence. The reserved annual rent is £18 10s. Bread money—which I cannot explain to you—is £3 9s. First fruits are £21 6s. 8d. Tenths, £2 2s. 8d. The only duty is, I think, a sermon every year.*
    I am, dear sir,
      Your most humble obedient servant,
        R. London.

London House,
 8th March, 1783.

H

This was not the first time that Parr had been suggested for a prebend's stall. During his residence in Norwich, Lord Dartmouth had asked Lord Thurloe, the Lord Chancellor, to give him one in Norwich Cathedral, but Thurloe refused his request with an oath.

There was great competition for these prebend's stalls, for they frequently turned out to be exceedingly lucrative. Although the salary attached to them was trifling, they carried the right to a share in the cathedral property. In Parr's case, this property consisted of some Regent's Park Canal shares. The lease of these reverting to the cathedral about three or four years before his death, gave him an annual income of over three thousand pounds. This pleasant arrangement was abolished during the last century—a reform which was not appreciated by the holders of prebends' stalls.

One of the most unfortunate affairs in which Parr involved himself, concerned Dr. White, Professor of Arabic at Oxford University. White, an extremely popular don, had been invited to become Bampton Lecturer, and his lectures delighted all Oxford. Now the doctor had not found these lectures too easy to prepare—a profound knowledge of Near Eastern languages is, perhaps, not the best qualification for a Bampton Lecturer. He was, too, a very indolent man, so like Zion in the Scriptures he lifted his hands for aid. Who better able to afford it than his friend, that great scholar, Dr. Parr? Unfortunately, however, thinking it better to have two strings to his bow, he had also invoked the assistance of a learned ex-Dissenting minister, who had renounced the errors of dissent for those of the Church of England—the Reverend Samuel Badcock. Now there was more prestige than profit in giving the Bampton Lectures, the fee being, I believe, £300, out of which the lecturer had to pay for them to be published in book form. The money being of no object to Dr. White, he gave Badcock a bond for £500 for his help. Subsequently to the lectures, Badcock died, and rumours began to go round Oxford that he had had a considerable share in compiling them. These rumours were probably started by Badcock's sister; she had presented the bond for payment and White had very foolishly refused to honour it, on the ground that it was for work to *be* done, not for work done.

At this juncture, Dr. Parr arrived on the scene and, full of sound and fury, flung himself into the fray. Without consulting White, he pronounced Badcock's claim to be absolutely unjustified, because he *himself* had written at least a fifth part of the lectures and had corrected and supervised them all!

As may be imagined, the affair created an immense sensation. The newspapers took it up, and an inquiry was ordered, which, through leaving it doubtful *who* had had so considerable a share in the authorship of the lectures, made it quite clear that Dr. White's part in the writing of them had been comparatively small. The evidence tended to prove the truth of Parr's assertion, but he was universally execrated for betraying his friend. It was not the first time he had helped White. He had written two sermons for him to preach at St. Mary's, Oxford, and had great difficulty in getting them returned, indeed, he did not recover them until 1808. By that time their relations had become a little strained. Instead of "Most worthy and Learned Friend," it was "Dr. White presents his compliments to Dr. Parr," and Parr was only prevented from publishing a venomous attack on the ex-Bampton Lecturer by the advice of Edmund Burke, who more than once intervened to prevent his getting into hot water. What added to Parr's fury was that Dr. White's popularity at Oxford not only saved his reputation; he was given a canonry at Christ Church, a position which he (Parr) had vainly tried to obtain.

Dr. Parr prided himself greatly on his sermons and published many of them, but when he preached his lisp and his manner of speaking made him almost unintelligible. Lord Holland said of him: "When he speaks no one can understand what he says, and when he writes no one can read what he has written."

It is difficult to understand why he delighted in preaching the inordinately long sermons which used to be associated with the Evangelical party, whose principles he affected to despise. And it is equally difficult to discover which of the various shades of opinion within the Church of England *did* meet with his approval. As we have seen, he liked an elaborate service, but in his own church there was none of the dignity of the Catholic ritual. He hated dissent, but defended dissenters, professed great tolerance, but believed in hell! Unitarians he particularly disliked. They *might* possibly be saved, he said, "but they must be scorched first!" Like many people, he was given to conforming the gospel to his own mind rather than conforming his mind to the gospel. Probably when—if ever—the worthy doctor wrestled with his conscience, Conscience, convinced by his arguments, gave up the struggle. Thus, Conscience and Samuel were always on excellent terms.

IV

THERE can be few men whose appearance has so belied their personality as did that of Dr. Parr. Judging from his reputation as a flogging schoolmaster, his bombastic utterances and the constant quarrels in which he was involved, one would have imagined him to be a big, powerful, authoritative individual. It was quite the other way about. De Quincey[1] gives an amusing account of his first meeting with the doctor. It took place in 1812, in the drawing-room of a Mr. Basil Montagu, an eminent barrister and a friend of Parr's. A number of well-known people had been invited to meet him at tea. From a back drawing-room was heard the "clamorous laugh" of Dr. Parr, just arrived from the country. Presently the door opened and in he walked. On seeing him, De Quincey could not believe that it *was* Parr. "So much did he contradict all my rational perceptions," he says. "Dr. Parr's undeniable reputation as a sanguinary flagellator throughout his long career of pedagogue had prepared me—nay, entitled me—to expect a huge carcase of man, fourteen stone at the least. Even his style, pursy and bloated, and his sesquipedalian words, all warranted the same expectation. Hence, then, my surprise, and the perplexity I have recorded, when the door opened, and a little man in a most plebian wig (far indeed, from that wig of his which the *Edinburgh Review* of eight or nine years earlier had described as "the mighty astonishment,") cut his way through the company and made for a *fauteuil* standing opposite to the fire. Into this he *lunged*; and then forthwith without preface or apology, began to open his talk upon the room. Here arose a new marvel and a greater." "If I had been scandalized at Dr. Parr's want of thews and bulk, conditions as indispensable for enacting the part of Sam Johnson, much more, and with better reason, was I now petrified with his voice, utterances, gestures and demeanour. Conceive, reader, by way of counterpoise to the fine classical pronunciation of Dr. Johnson, an infantile lisp—the worst I ever heard—from the lips of a man above sixty, and accompanied with all sorts of ridiculous grimaces and little stage gesticulation. As he sat in his chair, turning alternately to the right and to the left, that he might distribute his edification in equal proportions among us, he seemed the very image of a little French gossiping abbé."

"Yet all that I have mentioned was, and seemed to be, a mere trifle by comparison with the infinite pettiness of his matter. Nothing did he

[1] *Whiggism in its Relations to Literature.*

116

utter but little shreds of calumnious tattle—the most ineffably silly and
frivolous of all that was then circulating in the Whig *salons* of London
against the Regent !" It was, by the way, just at the time that the Whigs
had hoped that the Regent would reward them for having stood by him,
and he, instead of doing so, had supported Pitt. Dr. Parr, continues De
Quincey, began in precisely these words:

Oh! I shall tell you [laying a stress upon the word *shall*, which still furthered
his resemblance to a Frenchman] a stohee [lispingly for story] about the Pince
Thegent [such was his nearest approximation to Prince Regent]. Oh, the
Pince Thegent! What a sad sad man he has turned out! But you *shall* hear.
Oh, what a Pince! What a Thegent!

and so the old babbler went on, sometimes wringing his hands in lamenta-
tion, sometimes flourishing them with French grimaces and shrugs of
the shoulders and contracting his fingers like a fan. After an hour's twaddle
of this scandalous description, suddenly he rose, and hopped out of the
room, exclaiming all the way, "Oh, what a Pince! Oh, what a Thegent!
Is it a Thegent, is it a Pince that you call this man? Oh, what a sad Pince!
Did anybody ever hear of such a sad Pince!—such a sad Thegent!—
such a sad, sad Pince Thegent!" etc., *da capo*. So this, thought De
Quincey, is the champion whom his admirers would propound as the
adequate antagonist of Samuel Johnson!

Parr had met the Prince Regent at a dinner party given by the
Duke of Norfolk at Norfolk House. He was not such a "sad Pince"
then! Among the guests were Fox, Sheridan and Lord Erskine. The
name of the Archbishop of York (Dr. Markham) being mentioned, the
Prince said:

"I consider Markham a much greater, wiser, and more learned man
than Hurd, and a better teacher, and you will allow me to be a judge,
for they were both my preceptors."

"Sir," answered Dr. Parr, "Is it your Royal Highness's pleasure that
I should enter upon the topic of their comparative merits as a subject
of discussion?" "Yes," said the Prince. "Then, sir," replied Dr. Parr,
"I differ from your Royal Highness entirely in opinion," and he proceeded to disagree with and contradict everything the Prince said.
Apart from the want of tact, breeding and *savoir-faire* he showed in argu-
ing with the Prince, it was the height of impertinence for him to take
the conversational lead in that very distinguished gathering. The Prince
took it all with great good humour—probably because he was a brilliant
mimic, and after this occasion his imitation of the pompous little doctor
was one of his star turns.

In striking contrast was the behaviour of Dr. Johnson at his interview with George III. It took place in the library at Queen's House—Dr. Johnson had helped towards the formation of this library.

In their separate styles of behaviour [says De Quincey] one might fancy each to have been governed by the presiding genius of the place. Johnson behaved with the dignity of a scholar and a loyal son of the Muses, under the inspiration of strong book-mindedness; Parr with the violence of a pedagogue under the irritations of wine and indigestion.

The King asked Johnson if he was then writing anything.[1] He answered, he was not, for he had pretty well told the world what he knew and must now read to acquire more knowledge. The King, as it should seem with a view to urge him to rely on his own stores as an original writer, and to continue his labours, then said: "I do not think you borrow much from anybody." Johnson said, he thought he had already done his part as a writer. "I should have thought so too," said the King, "if you had not written so well." Johnson observed to me, upon this that "no man could have paid a handsomer compliment; and it was fit for a king to pay. It was decisive." When asked by another friend at Sir Joshua Reynolds's, whether he had made any reply to this high compliment, he answered: "No, sir. When the King had said it, it was to be so. *It was not for me to bandy words with my Sovereign.*"

Dr. Parr was fond of boasting about his friendship with Johnson. The only reference in Boswell to their having met is, "Sir, I am obliged to you for having asked me this evening. Parr is a fair man. I do not know when I have had an occasion for such free controversy." Parr was evidently on his best behaviour that evening. The *Dictionary of National Biography* suggests that this was probably the only time they met. If such be the case it is difficult to understand how Parr had collected the material for his projected biography. He himself, however, claims a far more intimate acquaintance with the doctor: "I am rather a favourite with him and seldom go to town if I have any time to spare without calling upon him," he tells us. "Once, sir," he says, "Sam and I had a vehement dispute upon that most difficult of all subjects—the origin of evil. It called forth all the powers of *our* minds. No two tigers ever grappled with more fury, but we never lost sight of good manners. There was no Boswell present to detail our conversation. Sir, he would not have understood it. And then, sir, who do you think was the umpire between us? That fiend Horsley."

Now this, *pace* Dr. Johnstone, who in his biography is constantly harping on Parr's love of truth, is almost certainly a pure invention. No more than Parr, did Johnson like being contradicted and Parr was

[1]Boswell's *Johnson.*

constitutionally incapable of carrying on such a discussion without trying to shout his opponent down. Another anecdote Parr related concerning an interview with Johnson is that once when Johnson stamped his foot to emphasize a point, he also stamped, "as he could not think of allowing his antagonist to be a stamp ahead." Is it possible to imagine Dr. Johnson allowing any gesture of his to be parodied in, as De Quincey says, "a cool spirit of mockery? No man ever lived who was less likely to put up with an insult. If we also remember that Johnson loathed the Whigs—he considered them to be in direct descent from Satan—it is quite evident that either of the two interviews recorded would have ended by Johnson throwing Parr out of the house. He could have done it easily with one hand. Perhaps no human being was ever more humble-minded and exempt from any taint of malevolence, vanity, or falsehood, than Johnson. Parr—to whom subtlety was unknown—was incapable of glimpsing, however remotely, the self-doubtings which underlay Johnson's rough exterior. It is impossible that there can have been any intimacy between them.

Dr. Parr was a warm champion of Queen Caroline's cause. When, after the death of George III, she landed in England, he assured her publicly that he would render her every possible assistance that his hand and talents allowed. He was begged not to mix himself up with her affairs by a nobleman—one of the chief Court officials—but instead of taking the letter in good part, he resented it as an insult. The writer was "servile, impertinent, officious." So he immediately packed his trunk and took coach for London, to write his name in her visiting book. The new King merely remarked that "he did not understand Dr. Parr's taking so much trouble for nothing." When her name was ordered to be erased from the liturgy, he recorded his indignation in the Prayer Book of Hatton Church. He had prayed for her as Princess of Wales; she was now Queen, and when he prayed for the Royal Family, he included her. But, as was so often the case with him, the friendship did not last. For some reason which Dr. Johnstone does not clearly explain, he managed to offend her deeply. On his last visit, she asked him when he proposed returning to his parochial duties.

Parr was an indefatigable letter-writer; he corresponded, so Johnstone tells us, with two or three royalties, eight dukes, five marquesses, twenty-six earls, thirty-one barons, and with famous public men innumerable, not to speak of archbishops and bishops—rather odd, this, considering that he often said publicly that three out of every five of them were "perfect knaves." But most of his correspondence with high clerical dignitaries was in his later years, when age had mellowed him to some extent. One wonders whether he knew *personally* all these distinguished people; certainly with the exception, perhaps, of Fox, he was on *intimate* terms with very few of them. The eighteenth century was very ceremonious. People wrote one another immensely long letters, full of flowery compliments and urbane insincerities. That they cordially hated some of the friends (?) to whom these letters were addressed, meant nothing. This makes it rather difficult to judge on what terms they were with those to whom they wrote. A man would begin a letter to an intimate friend with "My dear sir," and end, "your humble and obedient servant." Parr had the letter-writing habit, and if a man was famous in any way, especially if he had written a book on politics or theology, he would almost certainly receive a letter from Hatton. There are many like him. They will write to men they have never met on the slightest pretext, and keep up a correspondence with them. Parr could very wel have written a book and called it "Friends I Have Never Met!"

With some of his distinguished acquaintances, however, he was at least on dining terms. Among these were his old patron, Lord Dartmouth, with whom he seemed never to have quarrelled. He liked the great in spite of his unfortunate knack of insulting them. In 1815 or 1816 he writes: "I visited Lord Tamworth at Stanaton, the Duke of Devonshire at Chatsworth and Lord Scarsdale at Derby. I have twice visited the Duke of Bedford at Woburn and again and again my honoured patron, Thomas William Coke of Holkham." He also dined with the Duke of Sussex. His Royal Highness's letters to him are mostly on literary or ecclesiastical subjects and, though extremely amiable, they are not very interesting. Up to the time of Edmund Burke's "treachery" as he called it, they had corresponded a good deal. In writing to Parr to thank him for including him in *Bellenden*, Burke said:

You are very generous in your condolence with me on the little estimation in which it is my fortune to be held. I am, however, myself not in the smallest degree affected with that circumstance. Whatever attention either is, or has at any time been paid to my opinions in the exercise of my public duty, is certainly more than I can lay any claim to : and I ought therefore to receive any measure of it, however small, as I do receive it, very thankfully. From a confidence in my own good intentions, I might wish my credit to be greater: as I might by that means become of more use to the part of affairs which I touch. But in this respect, perhaps I am mistaken.

Burke has the honour to be Parr's "most faithful and obliged humble servant." Such is the modesty of the great.

There is a letter from Mrs. Fox, thanking Parr for his letter of condolence on her husband's death. It throws a pleasant light on the home life of the famous Whig orator. Mrs. Fox speaks of him in much the same terms as Queen Victoria spoke of her "Ever Lamented", and writes:

I try to be resigned, God knows, but the magnitude of my loss is so weighty that it is, indeed, very, very difficult for me to bear up at all. The way in which my angel husband lived with me was so different to that of most men, it makes my loss so much the greater, as he was so much the kindest lover, husband and friend that woman ever had.

Mrs. Fox goes on to say that though her husband was not spared to enjoy the "glorious triumph of last Monday's majority," he was certainly rejoicing at it in the realms of the blest.

There is an interesting letter from Fox, saying:

I have been looking into some of Euripides' plays again, and am as usual delighted, but I do not know if you will support me in my opinion that he is far, very far, superior to the two other Greek tragedians. I daresay you will agree in feeling the truth of what Quintilian says of his utility to orators. If I had a boy whom I wished to make a figure in public speaking, I would recommend Euripides to him morning, noon, and night, perhaps preferably to Homer and Virgil themselves.

Yours ever,
C. J. Fox.

From early youth Parr had kept up a correspondence with his old schoolfellow, William Bennet—afterwards Bishop of Cloyne—but it ceased in 1796 and was not renewed till shortly before Parr died. Johnstone says that Bennet dreaded his "violence of temper and strong expression on subjects of intense public interest." In writing to him on the subject, Bennet says:

What can you mean by wrongs and insults? It is not my nature to insult anyone—I may have wronged you, that is, I may have attributed to you sentiments which you do not entertain. For I thought, and still think, I have proof that you have given every encouragement to [name omitted] and others, who are enemies to all the prospects of happiness I have in this world . . . May you retain some affectionate regard for one who, though your silent, is still your sincere friend,

William Cloyne.

Some years before Bennet had written to him, saying: "I am sorry you attack the Church for fear of consequence to your own advancement."

There are some letters from Sheridan who had been for a short time one of his pupils when he was an assistant master at Harrow. Oddly enough, one of the assistant masters described him as "a shrewd, artful, supercilious boy, without any shining accomplishments, or superior learning." Roderick, however, formed a very different opinion of his character, saying he was vivacious, ingenious, mischievous and good-humoured; that his exquisite talents for society made him the delight of his friends and companions, and that he studied behaviour rather than "notions" and to be accomplished rather than knowing. Sheridan, apparently, was on fairly intimate terms with the doctor. He writes to him from Crewe Hall, when preparing for the debate on Warren Hastings. "There is some argument or special speech which you pointed out to me at Crewe and advised me to read with a view to Hastings' trial. I have forgot what it was. Pray, if you recollect, favour me with a line while I am at this place. Have you seen a Latin poem abusing us all, which I see mentioned in the papers?" In another letter Sheridan speaks of "a furious wrangle in the House of Commons" and the perfidy of Pitt, and in yet another, written during one of the fits of depression from which he suffered:

My life is so irregular, and the present state of my mind so much so, that I pursue almost nothing that I ought: and among my omissions there is not one for which I reproach myself so much as my seeming neglect towards you.

I give way unpardonably at times to gloom and fancifulness, and put off from day to day things which I ought immediately to decide upon. I am uneasy at not having a line from Tom. I send a servant for fear of further mistakes. I know not how to thank you for your goodness to Tom, but I will write when I am not so pressed for time, and explain myself more on this subject and entreat your counsel.

Yours ever obliged,
R. B. Sheridan.

One of the few men with whom Parr seems never to have quarrelled was his Colchester friend, the Reverend Thomas Twining. He (Twining) wrote delightful letters,[1] polished and humorous, and written in a style so colloquial that they might have been written to-day. Unlike Parr, he was born with the social sense, fond of art and a good musician—Parr's ignorance of the arts was encyclopædic and he seems never to have travelled. Twining's letters leave one lost in envy of the unhurried life people led in those days and of the colour and gaiety of London. Dirty it certainly was, but how intensely alive. In spite of bad roads and the danger of highwaymen, travelling must have been great fun in the late eighteenth century. To go from Essex—where Twining lived—to Yorkshire must have had all the excitement of going to a new country, and he gives us a vivid description of the scenes and customs he

[1] See *A Country Clergyman of the Eighteenth Century*, R. B. Twining.

noticed. He found civility and comfort in all the inns at which he stayed *en route*, and was delighted with the humour and friendliness of inn-keepers, coachmen and ostlers. There is something to be said for not being in a hurry; the taciturn chauffeur has no interest in the beauties of the countryside and no time for the humanities. Well, as we were taught in childhood, rapid communications corrupt good manners!

V

To brutes humane, to kindred man a rod,
Proud to all mortals, humble to thy God—
In sects a bigot, and yet liked by none,
By those most feared, whom most you deem your own,
Lord o'er the greatest, to the least a slave,
Half weak, half strong, half timid and half brave;
To take a compliment of too much pride,
And yet most hurt when praises are denied,
In dress all negligence, or else all state,
In speech all gentleness, or else all hate,
There most a friend, where most you seem a foe.
So very knowing that you nothing know,
Thou art so deep—discerning, yet so blind,
So learn'd, so ignorant, cruel, yet so kind.
So good, so bad, so foolish and so wise.
By turn I love thee, and by turn despise.

THESE lines, written by Parr's friend, Philip Homer, sum him up cleverly. As may be imagined, Parr was furious. Their friendship was, for many years, broken, but eventually Parr forgave him, for, like many violent-tempered people, he was not vindictive. When his insults mortally offended men whose friendship he valued, he was genuinely surprised that they took offence. He had, too, when he was attacking someone, an exasperating habit of beginning by saying how greatly he esteemed and honoured his victim. He did this when scarifying Bishop Hurd, Heath and Burke. And merely to differ from him, to neglect his advice, or even not to consult him, was excuse enough for an attack.

That he had many good qualities, we have already noticed. Even De Quincey, who lashes him without mercy, admits this. To those in trouble and too far removed from his own sphere to be in any other relations with him than those of receiving favours, he could be kindness itself; their sufferings, as De Quincey says, awoke all that was best in him. Many poor scholars, too, had good reason to remember him with gratitude. When that incomparable master of Greek and inveterate drunkard, Richard Porson, was down and out, Parr rescued him and took him into his house. Porson was of quite humble birth and when a boy, he showed so much literary talent that some families in his neighbourhood combined to send him to Eton and Cambridge, and—as is needless to say—he subsequently became one of the greatest of all classical scholars.[1] And not only in Greek and Latin; he had an extra-ordinary knowledge of all good literature. When sober, his charm was irresistible. But he was not often really sober.

A friend said of him that "he would drink ink if he found nothing else". When he was visiting Hoppner, the artist, Mrs. Hoppner exclaimed:

"My God, he has drunk a bottle of lamp spirit!"

The combination of husband and guest proved too much for Mrs. Parr. One day she insulted Porson so grossly that he left the house and never returned. But Dr. Parr continued to befriend him, and took infinite trouble to collect subscriptions to buy him an annuity.

To another hard-up friend he lent—in his later and more affluent days—five hundred pounds.

"I shall never see the money again," he said, "but no matter. It is for a good man and a purpose."

Porson was unable to prevent Parr from being taken in by the Shakespeare forgeries of that remarkable young man, Samuel Ireland. From a boy Ireland had been a Shakespeare enthusiast, and his great ambition was to discover some hitherto unknown poems or plays by his hero. His search proving fruitless, he had a brilliant idea. Why not *invent* some himself, and *then* discover them? With vast ingenuity he collected old deeds and charters of the period; an obliging bookseller showed him how to manufacture ink that had every appearance of age; he detached thread from some ragged tapestry with which to tie up his sonnets, and set to work. His first achievement was a letter from Queen Elizabeth to Shakespeare, then he fabricated a legal document, and soon had quite a collection of papers. He explained his possession of them by inventing a rich old gentleman—a great collector of old docu-ments—who, in return for favours received, had told him to take what he wanted. The next thing was to show them to some well-known literary authorities. This he did, and, strange to say, many of them were taken in, including Boswell, who, fortified by brandy and water, fell on his knees and kissed them. Not so Porson; a careful examination con-vinced him that they were forgeries. Malone, probably the best authority of his time, agreed. But Dr. Parr had no qualms. He and several of his admirers—none of them with any experience of ancient documents—

[1]De Quincey, by the way, does not consider Parr to have been so great a classical scholar as he was reputed to be. He gives him credit for being a master of Latin prose and for the *accuracy* which, he says, comes from long experience as a teacher. But in Latin verse he considers that Johnson far surpassed him, and as Grecians, he places Richard Porson and Sir William Jones infinitely higher. But Parr had one valuable quality possessed by no other classical scholar—of his day; he was a supreme master in the art of self-advertise-ment.

went bail with enthusiasm for their authenticity, and signed a certificate to that effect.

Encouraged by the *furore* he had caused, Ireland then "discovered" a play in blank verse, *Vortigern and Rowena,* which he showed to Sheridan, who agreed to produce it at Drury Lane. Not that Sheridan believed it to be genuine. "Shakespeare must have been drunk when he wrote it," he said cynically. But it was worth doing as a speculation. The great night arrived and the theatre was packed with Ireland's friends and supporters, among them Boswell, Nollekens and his wife, and Parr. It was his Waterloo. With shouts of ribald laughter, derision and cat-calls, it was hissed off the stage, and exit Samuel Ireland. Samuel Parr from that day on hated any reference to the affair, and even the name of Shakespeare was coldly received.

Never, says De Quincey, was Parr seen to better advantage than when animating the hopes, supporting the fortitude, or ministering to the comfort of the poor dejected prisoner in his gloomy cell at a time when self-reproach had united with the frowns of the world to make the consolation of friendship somewhat more than normally trying to the giver, and a thousand times more precious to the receiver. But, as in everything else, he knew no restraint—his favourite criminals were "martyrs." When Mr. Percival was assassinated by Bellingham—a man whom he had never injured and whom he did not even know by sight— Parr's chief interest in the matter was to find excuses for the crime. Again, the Duc de Berri was brutally murdered, also by a stranger. The doctor's comment was that the Duke was "a vulgar ruffian." In no case, however, did he carry his indiscreet sympathies so far as in the case of Joseph Gerald.

Gerald, who was the son of a rich West Indian merchant, was sent by his father to Parr's school at Stanmore, from which he was expelled for misconduct and sent home. On his return to England some years later, he became a barrister and renewed his acquaintance with his old schoolmaster. Unfortunately, he was a man of violent political opinions, and got himself into trouble in Edinburgh by getting mixed up with subversive political societies. He was arrested, tried by a jury of Scots, and sentenced to fourteen years' transportation. All his friends, including the doctor, had advised him to get out of the way when trouble began to brew, but he was bent on being a martyr. Parr not only raised money for his defence, but wrote a rude, bullying letter to Windham, the Home Secretary, saying that Gerald was quite as good a man as Pitt and far more learned. Now, Windham was a kindly man and he knew Parr. Had he received a tactful, courteous letter he would, no doubt, have done his best to get Gerald off, but naturally he could not take any notice of an application written in such a spirit. Parr's letter received a formal acknowledgment from a secretary, and the sentence was allowed to take its course.

In all these benevolent activities, however, Dr. Parr displayed a touch of the showman, for he never hid his light under a bushel. He liked playing the *beau rôle*, and as he strutted home after visiting the afflicted in prison, he was not unaware that people were saying: "What a good man! What a Christian!"

But in spite of his warm-hearted kindness for some people, and his hospitality—"Here at Hatton," he wrote to a friend, "we have a good home, good port, good library, good spirits and good air"—one is forced to admit that Dr. Parr was not an amiable character. His caprices, writes De Quincey, were "the fitful outbreaks of steady, mulish wrong-headedness". On a moderate estimate" he threw away ten times the amount of fortune, rank, splendour and influence that he ever obtained, and with no counter-veiling indemnity from any moral reputation such as would have attended all consistent sacrifices to high-minded principle." He was intensely jealous of those friends who had passed him in the race for honours and preferment; this caused him to demand a deference and respect which they were not always inclined to pay. "No man ever knew so little how to apply his mighty (were they so mighty?) talents to a great purpose," says Johnstone, and again, "he was the least accommodating of men, when he imagined himself to be the most."

A famous barrister once said to a man who happened to speak of him:

"Have you ever met Parr?"

"Never."

"Well, then, thank your stars that you have met with someone able to furnish you with some hints about him. He has no manners; you must expect none. He is a bear; wherever he goes you are suffocated with his beastly tobacco. To be sure, he is a lump of learning, but when I have said that, I have said all. I repeat, you will find him a lump of learning—nothing more."

His old Cambridge tutor, Dr. Farmer, had not, in Parr's later life, much respect for that learning. "He seemed to have been at a feast of learning from which he had carried away all the scraps," he said.

At the time of the French Revolution he was so much disliked and feared on account of his indiscreet sympathies, that it was considered highly imprudent, even unpatriotic, to meet him in society, and the authorities watched him closely, ready and anxious to act if he went too far.

In 1806 Pitt died. His ministry was dissolved and Lord Grenville, who was summoned by the King, formed the famous government of "All the Talents," in which Fox was included. Surely now, at long last, Parr would hear the welcome call: Friend, go up higher. But no; it was a Coalition Government, with Grenville—who hated him—as Prime Minister, and again preferment passed him by. Writing in the following year to the Bishop of Down, he said:

If Mr. Fox had continued in power he would certainly have made me a bishop.

Would he? It is doubtful. Fox was both tired and ill; he wanted peace, and to insist on the promotion of Dr. Parr was not the way to ensure it. He had, however, meant to promote the Bishop of Llandaff, Dr. Watson, of whom Lord Holland said: "Had our party remained in office we should have raised the Bishop of Llandaff to be Archbishop of York, for he behaved very well, I can assure you, to us," meaning the Grenville and Fox coalition. During most of the time the coalition lasted, Fox was too ill to attend to business and, of the two bishoprics that became vacant, one was given to Dr. Cleaver, a former tutor in the Grenville family, and the other to Dr. Randolph of Christ Church, Oxford. The following year Fox died, and with him died Parr's last hope of preferment. There was nothing to do but to make the best of it and remain quietly at Hatton.

In domestic life, Parr's biographer tells us, he was too great a scholar to be a favourite in the drawing-room. "All was to yield to his wishes, all was to be regulated by his habits. The ladies were obliged to bear his shag tobacco, or to give up his company." His pipe was so necessary to his comfort that he always left the table for it, *and the house of the person he visited*, if it was not prepared. He would select the youngest lady present to light it for him, and he made her stand in his arms and perform various ridiculous ceremonies while doing so.[1] "When, however, in the society of people who looked up to him," writes Johnstone, "when his spirits were calm, his temper unruffled; when no one dictated, or contradicted him, *then* he would reveal the depth of his goodness. He was happy; he was gay; he was merry—his gaiety, indeed, was boisterous. But his merriment did not last long; he soon relapsed into the grave, the didactic, and if he discharged a witticism, it was sarcastic. His conversation, like his writings, had plenty of grains of salt and drops of bitter gall."

He had, too, a trying habit of opening the dining-room window wide on the coldest nights—for air, he said—thus exposing ladies to the

[1] At this period smoking had gone out of fashion among the upper classes. "Smoking has gone out," said Dr. Johnson in 1773.

Joshua Reynolds

Professor Richard Porson

icy draught. As a guest he was not ideal. "When thwarted he had the power of being exquisitely disagreeable, especially to ladies. Once at dinner at Hatton, a lady remarked, seeing him show signs of impatience:

"You must excuse us ladies, doctor, whose privilege it is to talk nonsense."

Dr. Parr answered: "Pray, madam, did you talk nonsense, it would be your infirmity, unless indeed, you deem it a privilege for a duck to waddle because it cannot walk."

To a young man who had ventured to chaff him good-humouredly, he said:

"Sir, you are a young man, you have read much, thought little and know nothing at all."

Bell-ringing was his great delight. He had acquired the art at Harrow, and would bore people for hours discussing campanology and the qualities of the peals on which he had displayed his skill. He was particularly interested in the bells of Hatton Church, as his friends knew to their cost. He liked, says De Quincey, to lure people into the belfry and there he would set to work with solemn formality, exhibiting the "raising," the full funeral bell, and the regular bell. When the performance was over he stalked about the belfry with much pomposity, saying:

"There! What do you think of that?"

De Quincey suggests that his arms had been kept in training by half a century of successful flagellation.

His table manners were deplorable and he was full of fads. For instance, he could not be induced to sit at a table if salmon or cheese were served. Johnstone tells us that he was often called a glutton. He would "appropriate the food in so voracious a manner and eat so much and so fast that a stranger would perhaps have called him greedy." But Johnstone makes it quite clear that he was neither greedy, nor a glutton. It was simply that he habitually over-ate! "Neither was he, as was so often said of him, a bear in society, though it is true that his moroseness, impracticability and severity were the terror of many weak and effeminate spirits

During the lifetime of his first wife, life at Hatton had been unbearable. She was a haughty, sarcastic woman and he hints that she was quite a match for her husband

Considering all Dr. Parr's amiable qualities, we are surprised to read that life for the second Mrs. Parr—he had remarried in 1816—was none too easy. He was determined that the existing arrangements at his house should not be in any way changed, even by a wife. But she bore it with equanimity; after all, he was nearly seventy and, when the lease of the Regent Canal Shares—which he held by right of his prebend's

I

stall—fell in, he would not leave her altogether comfortless.[1] And so he continued to be the "petty tyrant of his fireside" without opposition. Soon after his second marriage he was reconciled with his granddaughters—the children of a daughter by his first marriage—with whom he had quarrelled. The two girls came to live at Hatton, and this did not make things easier for Mrs. Parr, as they were about her own age.

To the end of his life he kept up a vast correspondence, especially with those of his old pupils who had got on in life. He used to recall that his most interesting tie with them was that he had flogged them at some distant period. The more he had approved of a boy and the more hopes he had of his future, the more frequently he thrashed him. And boys being generous creatures, and flogging a recognized feature of eighteenth-century school life, they did not remember against him the erstwhile soreness of their little buttocks.

Here is an amusing instance of Parr's sadistic passion for flogging. When Sheridan's son was one of his pupils, he said to him one day:

"Tom, I am going out, and during my absence I know you will do something that will deserve a flogging, but I shall be tired when I return. Had you not better be flogged now?"

And flogged he was.

He delighted in thrashing the most promising boys and chuckled as he did so. One day at Stanmore his assistant said to him that he was sure one of the lads had a touch of genius.

"Say you so?" roared Parr. "*Then begin to flog to-morrow morning!*"

But there were those who disliked these methods. At a public dinner in Liverpool a gentleman called out to him from the other end of the table: "I hope, Dr. Parr, that you have given up that abominable system of flogging you used to be so fond of." Parr pretended not to hear him, whereupon he repeated the question and asked the doctor's opinion if such scholastic discipline was a good thing.

Parr answered: "Yes, sir, I do think discipline a good thing; for it is discipline that makes the soldier; it is discipline that makes the scholar; it is discipline that makes the gentleman. And, sir, it is the want of discipline that has made you that you are."

During the last years of Parr's life, his Prebend brought him in over three thousand pounds a year, a magnificent income in those days. He was able at once to gratify one of his ambitions, and set up a coach and four. Behold him "flying over the land and scouring town and country with four clerical-looking long-tailed horses." But half his pleasure in them was spoilt, for the panels of his coach lacked their proper heraldic decoration. Where was the mitre? Where the chaplain?

[1] It fell in a few years before he died.

Where the cockaded footmen? Early in 1825 Dr. Parr's strength began
to fail, he lost his appetite and his spirits, and incidentally became considerably less aggressive. But still he delighted in his coach and four
and his "prelatical pomp." Arrayed in his doctor's robe, he drove in
state to what he called a music meeting at Worcester—probably an
oratorio—joining in the singing with "unhappy results to the harmony."
But he went to sleep in the middle of the performance. He continued
to lament the neglect and malevolence of the Government in not having
given him the preferment which was his due, though he pretended to
be indifferent. "I am not fond of speaking on the subject," he said to
a friend, "but were I in my proper place in the House of Lords, I should
——," etc., etc.

Had he in those last years *one* loyal, affectionate friend to cheer him
in his many hours of depression? Yes, there was one man who stuck
to him through thick and thin, and whose kindness and touching affection
only ceased when in March, 1825, after a long and painful illness, his hero
died. It was his biographer. Not that Johnstone did not know his character,
indeed, as we have seen, he was constantly deploring his selfishness, his
tactlessness and his violence, but he can never have ventured to criticize
him![1] One imagines him to have been a sort of Boswell, without
Boswell's humanity, discernment and literary talent; as grateful for kicks
as for halfpence, incapable of taking offence, not very intelligent and
utterly devoid of humour. Of Parr's two Harrow friends, one, Dr.
Bennet, evidently liked him better at a distance, and the other, Sir
William Jones, wrote in Greek this not too flattering description of his
old school-fellow, which he sent to the Duke of Sussex. It was found
among the Duke's papers after his death.

"Dr. Parr is a man not easy to define: he is quite unlike anyone else, and
in what he says he is a mass of contradictions. No doubt he may be wise and
moderate, yet remarkable for indulging in every sort of expensive luxury.
He drinks the most costly wines, eats the finest of foods, sleeps at his ease,
choosing a scarlet coloured bed rather than an iron one. Kindly in disposition,
he loves his joke and banter and likes to win in any argument. He regards
squabbles as making for good company, declares that foreigners should be
expelled like spiders with a besom;[2] thinks that every five years the president
of a country should be pole-axed—not because he is wicked, but just because
he *is* president. He can call to mind forty men who should be hanged. In
fact, a gallows provides a cure for all diseases.

[1] "I could compare his bursts of passion to nothing but the hurricane of the tropics;
so fierce, so appalling, and so sudden," he said.
[2] A Greek scholar, Mr. E. H. Blakeney, who kindly translated Sir William Jones's
appreciation (!) told me that it was not easy to translate. "A large percentage of the
words are unknown to me," he said, "and are not given in the great Greek-English Lexicon.
In fact, I was greatly puzzled." (P.C.)

"In conversation he uses his mind in quite a tragical style and talks pompously. When out riding he will argue vigorously, whipping his horse, which is bored stiff with his erudite talk. In short, he is capable of word play, good at pitching a quoit, could make a kill in the bull ring, can devour sweetmeats, cherish a cat, yet never be aware that he differs radically from the rest of mankind."

Judging from the manner in which Dr. Parr's best friends[1] spoke of him, he must have been extraordinarily difficult to get on with. He had none of the pleasant social qualities that cause us to like Boswell, impossible as it is to respect him. Nor had he that sympathy, pity and understanding, which make Boswell's *Johnson* one of the most *human* books ever written—the first *modern* biography and, one may perhaps say, the last, before Lytton Strachey appeared on the scene. Parr could not criticize *himself*. He looked at his *magnum opus*, Dr. Parr, and all that he thought and did, and behold it was very good. He had spent the greater part of his life teaching boys, which gave full play to his passion for exercising despotic authority—no greater despot than the old type of schoolmaster ever lived. As we have seen, when everyone around him bowed down to his authority and acknowledged him as the source of all wisdom and goodness, who more amiable than Dr. Parr? But his charity was not that which "suffereth long and is kind, envieth not, vaunteth not itself, is not puffed up."

Then, though his studies had been entirely devoted to Greek and Latin, the great Greek writers had not taught him philosophy; he failed to make Pope's discovery of what is the proper study of mankind.

Fortune came to Dr. Parr late in the day. Was he happy as light thickened and the evening shadows closed in upon him? Yes, if a coach and four and three thousand a year constitute happiness. But he had missed the main object of his life, his supreme ambition: the mitre. One of his old Harrow school friends was a bishop, the other had died a judge, while he, for all his great talents and famous friends, was still curate of Hatton. He had boundless industry and energy, and he had spent his strength tilting at windmills; vast learning, and he had wasted it in futile literary controversies, leaving not one valuable contribution, even to the subject he had made his own and of which he was an acknowledged master.

He had failed in life because he had not been careful how he chose his enemies. He had deliberately made the most dangerous foe a man can have to contend with—Himself!

---

[1] It was said of him that even his best friends could not avoid his determination to quarrel and that he was ready to listen to any tales about them. But he was an easy prey to flatterers.

BIBLIOGRAPHY

The Works of Samuel Parr, LL.D., with a Memoir
  of His Life and Writings   John Johnstone, D.D.
                                                London, 1828.
Parriana, or the Notices of the Reverend Samuel Parr,
  LL.D.   E. D. Barker, London,
                                                1829.
Whiggism in its Relation to Literature   Thomas De Quincey.
Charles Butler's Reminiscences
Diary and Reminiscences of Henry Crabb-Robinson
Boswell's Johnson
A Country Clergyman of the Eighteenth Century Richard Twining.

JOSEPH NOLLEKENS

(*A Study in Avarice*)

"How now, who is here?
I, Robin of Doncastere,
And Margaret my feere.
That I spent, I had,
That I gave, I have,
That I left, I lost."

(Epitaph of the Earl of Courtenay, in St. George's Church, Doncaster.

THE late eighteenth century was the golden age for English sculptors; never before, nor since, has sculpture been so popular and so highly paid. Up to the beginning of the Georgian period, sculpture and masonry had, for most people, signified the same thing. In 1757, Roquet, Hogarth's friend, wrote: "Sculpture in England has hitherto been entirely funerary; it is only recently that it has been used for other purposes." But from then on it became fashionable. Not only were the great churches and many public buildings crowded with "storied urn and animated bust"; rich patrons of art began to form private sculpture galleries, and adorn their libraries with busts, and the gardens of their country houses with marble fauns and fountains. Busts especially were the thing, and most of the celebrities of the day sat to one or other of the sculptors in vogue; Flaxman, Chantrey, Roubillac —whom Lord Chesterfield called "the Pheidias of his day"—or, the extremely prolific Joseph Nollekens.

Nollekens was not a great artist; he never emerged from the ranks of the first-rate second-rate, and—except for a few of his busts—would to-day be almost forgotten had he not been the subject of what the late Edmund Gosse called, "the most candid biography, perhaps, in the English language." The author of this work was one John Thomas Smith, subsequently Keeper of the Prints and Drawings in the British Museum. He was born in 1766, and his home town, if not so distinguished as that of John Worthing—the first-class waiting-room at Victoria Station!—was unusual enough, for his birth took place in a hackney-coach, in which his mother was returning in all haste from a visit to her brother in East Street, Seven Dials. Smith does not include his very unceremonious entry on the stage among the seven most interesting events of his career, which were, he tells us:

"I received a kiss when a boy from the beautiful Mrs. Robinson."

"Was patted on the head by Dr. Johnson."

"Have frequently held Sir Joshua Reynolds's spectacles."

"Partook of a pint of porter with an elephant."

"Saved Lady Hamilton from falling, when the melancholy news arrived of Lord Nelson's death."

"Three times conversed with King George the Third."

"And was shut up in a room with Mr. Kean's lion."

Throughout his life Smith was intensely interested in London and its antiquities, and he paints a vivid picture of it as it was in his day. His mother's health began to fail soon after he was born, and he tells us how her doctor ordered her to rise early and drink milk at a cow-house at Williams's Farm, which was situated on the site of the future Coliseum. To reach it, she had only to walk up Great Portland Street into the fields which, after Portland Chapel was passed, spread on either side of the way. London in those days was a very small town compared with the huge, ugly, sprawling London of to-day; but it was infinitely more interesting, vital and colourful. A city of contrasts—of splendid mansions and squalid hovels; of the height of luxury and the depth of poverty; of exquisite culture and abysmal ignorance; a drunken, criminal London, in which smallpox and venereal disease were endemic, and an appallingly noisy London. Hawkers shouted their wares, unwieldy coaches and wagons rattled and bumped over the cobbled streets, their drivers yelling obscenities at one another, and ballad-mongers cried the latest broadsheets.

Smith's mother died when he was thirteen, and his father, who was Nollekens's chief assistant, got him (Nollekens) to employ little Thomas in his studio. As studio boy, he came into contact with half the celebrities of the day and began to acquire the vast knowledge of London life which he afterwards used to such good effect. He was a nice-looking, obliging little chap, and was made a good deal of fuss of by some of Nollekens's famous sitters. In that civilized period the studios of artists were not unlike those in Florence during the Renaissance, which were called *botteghe* (shops), and were open to the street. The artist's friends would drop in to see what he was doing and chat with the sitters. There is a print in the British Museum of a studio in which we see Horace Walpole, Dr. Johnson, Fielding and Nollekens, and another of that cultured patron of the arts, Mr. Townley, receiving friends in his private gallery.

Nollekens in his rough way was very kind to little Smith, though the only present he ever gave the boy was a box of chalks, which had crumbled and turned black with age ! They often went for walks together, and Nollekens, who knew and loved London, would show him its old houses and tell him anecdotes about the people who had lived in them. Once, in Dean Street, he pointed out the house in which Baptiste, the famous flower-painter, had lived, and also that in which he (Nollekens) was born. At that time Soho was very fashionable, and four ambassadors lived in Soho Square. The water of its fountain only ran when a windmill, which then stood in Rathbone Place, was going round.

On another occasion Nollekens took him to see Gainsborough, who was then living at Schomberg House, Pall Mall, which was divided into three houses. It was there that Gainsborough died in 1778. When they arrived his (Gainsborough's) friend, Colonel Hamilton, was playing the violin so beautifully that the artist, who loved music, said:

"Now, my dear colonel, if you will but go on, I will give you that picture of the boy at the stile, which you have so often wished to purchase of me."

Gainsborough, in order to keep Nollekens quiet, gave him a book of sketches to choose two from, and he gave little Smith a model in clay. Colonel Hamilton was not only one of the best amateur violinists of the day; he was a famous amateur boxer and frequently sparred with professionals.

Nollekens's father was an artist—a painter. He had studied under Watteau, and came to England from Antwerp. He was a sordidly avaricious man; during the rebellion of '45 his house was marked by the mob as being that of a Catholic, and the possibility of being robbed affected him so seriously that he practically died of fright. His son, Joseph, was born in 1737, and baptized at the Catholic Chapel in Duke Street, Lincoln's Inn Fields.

Joseph Nollekens, as a boy, was apprenticed to Peter Sheemaker, a well-known sculptor living in Vine Street, Piccadilly. He was a civil, inoffensive lad, but not particularly bright. Like Dr. Parr, he had a passion for bell-ringing. He would run to St. James's Church, Piccadilly, to see if there happened to be a funeral, and the sexton, who made rather a pet of him, would call out: "What, my little Joey, are you come? Well, you must toll to-day." In after years Nollekens said to the Lord Chancellor, Lord Bathurst, who was sitting to him: "Ah! there goes the bell tolling; no—it's only my clock on the stairs. When I was a boy you would have liked to have seen me toll the bell; it's no very easy thing, I can tell you (*look a little that way*). You must toll, that is to say I did, one hour for a man, three times three, and three times two for a woman (*now your lordship must mind*). There's a moving-bell and a passing-bell. They call that the moving-bell which goes when they move a body from one parish to the next. The passing-bell is when you are dying and going from this world to another place."

Nollekens's father died in 1747, and his mother married again—a Welshman, who persuaded her to leave London and go with him to his own country. The boy served his master faithfully for more than seven long years, and then, in 1760, wishing to gain a knowledge of Italian sculpture, he gathered together all his small belongings and went to Rome. His proverbial luck began at once, for soon after his arrival he met David Garrick, who, with his wife, was spending a fortnight there. "What!" said the famous actor. "Let me look at you. Are you the little fellow we gave the prizes to at the Society of Arts?" "Yes, sir," answered Joseph, whereupon Garrick invited him to breakfast, and sat to him for a bust, for which he paid twelve guineas. Then he met Lawrence Sterne, who also sat to him, and he competed for and won the Pope's gold medal for a *basso-relievo*.

His passion for money had already declared itself, and he was none too scrupulous as to how he got it. He began, quite legitimately, by taking advantage of the growing taste in England for Roman antiquities, and bought for a trifle—from the workmen who were employed in digging gravel at Porta Latina—a number of pieces of Roman terra-cotta. Most of these were found at the bottom of a dry well, where they had evidently been hidden for security. These he afterwards sold to Mr. Townley, and they are now in the British Museum. But some of his methods were more questionable. A certain dealer in Rome, named Jenkins, who was a notorious "botcher" of antiques, had been commissioned by Mr. Locke, of Norbury Park, to send him any pieces of sculpture he thought suitable. Jenkins having sent him a head of Minerva of very doubtful authenticity, Locke had sent it back. Nollekens, in the meantime, having bought a trunk of the same goddess for fifty pounds, agreed to buy the head which Locke had returned, and share any profits on the transaction. He then proceeded to botch it up, or in the language of dealers, "restore" it, and subsequently sold it for a thousand pounds! He made a speciality of terra-cottas, and managed to acquire specimens by Gian di Bologna, Michelangelo, and other famous sculptors. Damaged or not, they arrived in England in perfect condition!

Another pleasant little way of making money was smuggling silk stockings, gloves and lace. With real ingenuity he stuffed his plaster busts with them, and then spread an outside coat of plaster across the shoulders of each, so that they appeared to be solid casts. When, later on, Lord Mansfield was sitting to him, he pointed to the cast of Lawrence Sterne which he had made in Rome, saying: "There, do you know, my lord, that busto held my lace ruffles that I went to Court in when I came from Rome?"

Sometimes, however, he overreached himself. He bought a large picture which he knew he could sell in London for a considerable sum, and to avoid paying duty on it when he returned to England he cut it up into several pieces, thinking they would be regarded merely as scraps of canvas. But unfortunately for him the customs officer detected the intended deception, fitted the pieces together, and reported the matter to the authorities. Poor Joseph was made to pay duty on each piece separately!

During his residence in Italy he accumulated a collection of gold and silver coins, of the currency of the countries he passed through. He had no particular object in doing so, beyond the passion of the miser for hoarding. Had he sold them and invested the money he could have done very well out of them, and saved himself years of worry over their loss, for alas, they were stolen by thieves who broke into his house and took not only the foreign coins, but a hoard of English money, silver plate left to Mrs. Nollekens by her father, and many other valuable objects. The thieves entered the house through the back window in the staircase, went at once to the place in which the valuables were deposited, which was a room next to that in which Nollekens and his wife slept, and got away without disturbing anyone in the house. In leaving they dropped a dirty old wallet in which there were banknotes to a considerable amount. Probably the robbery was committed by friends of one of the numerous models who posed for his Venuses.

His way of living in Rome was squalid in the extreme. He employed an old woman to "do for him," and often managed to dine for threepence. "Nearly opposite my lodgings," he said, "there lived a pork butcher, who put out at his door at the end of the week a plateful of what he called "cuttings"; bits of skin, bits of gristle and bits of fat, which he sold for twopence, and my old lady dished them up with a little pepper, a little salt, and with a slice of bread, and sometimes a bit of vegetable. It made a very nice dinner."

On his return to England in 1770 Nollekens took a house, 9 Mortimer Street, and set up as a sculptor of busts and monumets.

He left Rome as ignorant as he arrived there. He had not learned to speak Italian, and of the history of Italian art—or of any other—he knew nothing and cared less. The enchanting Greek mythology, which had inspired most of the sculpture he had gone to study, had had no interest for him; indeed, it is doubtful if the various Greek deities signified anything at all to his prosaic mind. It was the same with literature. "To the beauties of the immortal Shakespeare," says Smith, "he was absolutely insensible, nor would he ever visit the theatre when his plays were performed, even to see his friend Garrick. But he liked pantomimes and Punch and Judy shows, and it gave him intense pleasure to see Mr. Rich scratch his ear with his foot, like a dog. He wrote and spelt about as well as a charity schoolboy of twelve. His table manners were so bad that in most houses where he was professionally engaged he was given his meals apart from the family."

In the years 1771-2 three great events happened to Joseph. He was elected an Associate of the Royal Academy. King George III sat to him for his bust; and he fell in love. He was now worth over twenty thousand pounds. The lady of his choice was Mary, the second daughter of Saunders

Welch. Welch, who was brought up in Aylesbury Workhouse, subsequently became one of the most successful businessmen in the City.
He was an intimate friend of Dr. Johnson, and also of Fielding, whom
he succeeded as a Justice of the Peace for Westminster. His kindness and
generosity were boundless, and he devoted himself particularly to helping the many poor abandoned women who so often appeared before
him. How Joseph, rough, ignorant, and quite devoid of any personal
attractions, managed to win the affections of the prim and precise Mary
Welch, it is hard to say; perhaps she admired his natural genius for
making money. He could hardly have chosen a wife more after his
own heart, as she was, if possible, even more avaricious than he was!
They were married at Mary-le-bone Church; probably there were two
ceremonies, as the bridegroom was a Catholic, not from conviction,
but because he had been brought up in that faith. He was never known
to subscribe to any Catholic charities, nor did he ever choose a subject
for his art from the Bible legends.

Mrs. Nollekens was a tall, graceful woman, with an excellent complexion and long fair ringlets that reached to her waist. She and her
husband formed an odd contrast when they walked abroad. She, with
legs tall, thin and straight; he, with legs short and bowed; she with
well-formed features; he short-necked, with narrow shoulders and body
too large; her nose was aquiline, his nose large and hooked; she carefully
dressed; he in drab clothes, and rather dirty ruffles which he wore long
after they had gone out of fashion. Welch gave his daughter an elaborate
trousseau; it cost over two hundred pounds. Smith describes her wedding
dress: "She was attired in a sacque and petticoat of the most expensive
white silk, resembling network, enriched with small flowers, which
displayed in the variation of folds a most delicate shade of pink, the
uncommon beauty of which was greatly admired. The deep and pointed
stomacher was exquisitely gimped and pinked, and at the lower part
was a large pin, consisting of several diamonds, confining an elegant
point-lace apron: certainly at that period rather unfashionable, but on
this happy event affectionately worn in memory of her dear mother,
who had presented it to her, indeed, Mrs. Nollekens was frequently
heard to declare that she was above "the fleeting whimsies of depraved
elegance." The sleeves of this dress fitted the arms closely to a little
below the elbow, from which hung three point-lace ruffles of great
depth; a handkerchief of the same costly texture partly concealed the
beauty of her bosom; wherein, confined by a large bow, was a bouquet
of rosebuds, the delicate tints of which were imperceptibly blended with
the transparency of her complexion, and not a little increased the beauty
of a triple row of pearls, tied behind with a narrow, white satin ribbon."

Her hair she wore unpowdered, arranged over a cushion to a considerable height with large round curls on either side, the whole topped by a cap of point lace. Shoes made of the same material as her dress, with square Bristol buckles, and heels three and a half inches high, completed her costume. Poor little Joseph, even with his hat on, hardly reached to her shoulder. But he too, was wonderfully arrayed in purple, white silk stockings, and the famous lace frills and ruffles he had bought in Rome.

Their household was run on the most economical lines. Sometimes in the evening they would indulge in a little excursion to the French Gardens in Marylebone Lane. To avoid expense, they took with them some rolls, or rusks, tea and sugar, so all they had to pay was a penny each for hot water and the use of tea-cups. They kept two servants, and on alternate Sundays each of them had the evening out, as Nollekens was convinced that "if they were not allowed to visit the 'Jew's Harp,' or some other resort, they would never wash themselves." Mrs. Nollekens displayed infinite ingenuity in beating down her tradesmen.

"What is the price of a good mop?" she asked of a Mrs. Bland, who kept a general shop. Mrs. Bland took one down and, striking it on the floor to show off its bushiness, said:

"There, ma'am, *there's* a mop! Half a crown."

"What! Half a crown! My good woman, why, I gave only two shillings and threepence for the last."

"Yes, ma'am," said Mrs. Bland, "but that was ten years ago."

"Come, come, Mrs. Bland, don't be rude. I know perfectly well when it was: but what will you allow me now for an old stick?"

"Three halfpence, ma'am."

"No, Mrs.—what's your name; allow me threepence, and I will give you two shillings and you may send me in your mop."

As Mrs. Bland refused, Mrs. Nollekens shut the door and went off in a temper.

To a poor old woman who sold apples, she was heard to say:

"Pray, Goody, how many apples can you let me have for a penny?"

"Bless your kindness! You shall have three."

"Three!" exclaimed Mrs. Nollekens, "No, you must let *me* have four, for there's my husband, myself and two servants and we must have one apiece."

"Well, I suppose you must take them," said the poor woman.

When eighteenpence was the price of half a calf's head, it was a dish of which she was "passionately fond." When it exceeded that price, she was "tired of it." "People who were not connected with the Court," she said, "had no need of a superfluity at their tables!" She would search Oxford Street for the cheapest shops, taking her dog, Cerberus, in order that it might snatch scraps from the butchers' stalls and save her the expense of buying it bones. Rude butchers would call as she passed, "Here comes Mrs. Nollekens with her bull-bitch."

Sometimes, with great heart-searchings, they would feel obliged to ask friends to dinner. Smith describes one of these feasts at which he was present. The house having been furnished with great economy, chiefly from second-hand furniture dealers, they had not a proper dinner-table, so two tables were joined, the legs of one being much shorter than those of the other. Knives and forks matched fairly well, but the plates were cracked and burnt from having stood on the hob, and the dishes were flat and held little gravy. The dinner consisted of a leg of pork with celery and mashed potatoes; this was followed by a lobster, and there was also a chicken and a reindeer's tongue with parsley and butter, but the boat was minus a ladle. Wine was not mentioned until the servants were ordered to "take off." "Much about this time," says Smith, "there was a great bustle, in which I heard Mrs. Nollekens's voice vociferate, "I will have it found." At last one of the servants, Bronze, entered, to whom she had given commands to fetch it.

Mr. Nollekens: ". . . and after all, pray, where did you find it?"
Bronze: "Why, sir, under the pillow of your bed."
Mrs. Nollekens: "There, Mr. N, I knew you had used it last night."
The missing object was a back-scratcher!

Mrs. Nollekens then observed: "My dear Nolly, you had no need to have wasted the writing-paper for the claret, for as it is the only bottle with a tall neck, we should have known it," and, turning to a guest— "My dear Mrs. Paradise, you may safely take a glass of it as it is the last of twelve which Mr. Caleb Whitefoord sent us as a present." The company then went to the drawing-room for tea, Nollekens staying behind to see that the remains of the meal were put away for next day's dinner.

Mrs. Nollekens, knowing that her father liked Yorkshire ale, sometimes tried to get some—without paying—but was very rarely successful. She was extremely annoyed with her wine merchant for refusing to allow her anything for empty bottles; true, they were nearly all of different shapes and sizes, but then, how could she help it? They were all presents. When, too, his son was missing, had she not allowed him to stick one of his bills, advertising for information about the boy, on her yard gate? He was afterwards discovered to have been drowned while bathing in Marylebone Basin. This large and deep pond was situated in the fields which covered the site of what is now Portland Place and Mansfield Street. It was very dangerous for inexperienced bathers, and many lads were drowned in it. There was a smaller pond, fed

Joseph Nollekens

"Cupid and Psyche" by Nollekens

from it by an arm, which looked like a ladle. This pond was called Cockney Ladle, and the parish beadle lay in wait to seize the clothes of small boys while they were bathing. It is difficult to realize how countrified was much of London in those days. Lord Eldon often spoke of the fine fruit he grew in his garden in Gower Street, and Knightsbridge was still a village.

Mrs. Nollekens—who considered herself, socially, a good many cuts above her husband—was very useful to him professionally. At her father's house she had met many of the celebrities of the day, and they came to see *her*, not Nollekens. Among her friends was Dr. Johnson. At this time, says Smith, he (Johnson) "was tall and must have been, when young, a powerful man: he stooped, with his head inclined to the right shoulder; heavy brows, sleepy eyes; nose very narrow between the eyebrows, but broad at the bottom; lips enormously thick; chin wide and double. He wore a stock and wristbands; his wig was what is called "a busby," but often wanted powder. His hat, a three-cornered one; coats, one a dark mulberry, the other brown, inclining to the colour of Scotch snuff; large brass or gilt buttons; black waistcoat and small clothes—sometimes the latter were corduroy; black stockings, large, easy shoes with buckles; his gait was wide and awkwardly sprawling; latterly he used a hooked walking-stick in consequence of having saved the life of a young man as he was crossing from Queenshithe to Bankside." Johnson had always admired Mrs. Nollekens, indeed, at one time he had half wished to marry her. "I think Mary would have been mine if Little Joe had not stepped in," he once said to Smith. It was just as well for both of them that "Little Joe" *did* step in. Johnson's generosity and his sympathy with the poor would have horrified her mean soul. Dr. Johnson, she afterwards said, "has done our servants more injury by that constant habit of his, of giving charity, as it is called, than he is aware of—and I shall take an opportunity of telling him so when I next sit next to him at dinner at Sir John Hawkins's."

The doctor admired Nollekens too—"Well, sir, I think my friend Joe Nollekens can chop out a bust with any of them"—but all the same he was not very pleased with the way *he* had been chopped out; in the bust he is not wearing his wig, but is shown with thick, heavy locks. This annoyed him vastly. "People should be portrayed as they are seen in company," he said, and added: "Though a man for his ease may wear a nightcap in his chamber, he ought not to look as if he had taken physic."

Mrs. Nollekens's parsimonious habits were sometimes trying to her

K

husband's sitters. One bitterly cold day Lord Londonderry took advantage of Nollekens having left the studio for a minute or two, and emptied the coal-scuttle on to the tiny fire. Mrs. Nollekens, coming in, exclaimed at his extravagance. "Never mind," said he, "you can put it on my bill." Her husband, when Jackson was painting his portrait in the drawing-room, said, "I'm afraid the room is rather cold, but there hasn't been a fire in it for forty years." Their manœuvres to save money were endless. They would sit in the dark to save lighting candles, and at the Royal Academy Club dinners Nollekens would pocket the nutmegs provided to make the red-wine negus. Economy in food being carried almost to starvation point in his own house, he would make up for it when dining out. At one house he managed, as he said, to get through "a nice roast chicken with two nice tarts and some nice jellies," and at another house he ate two pounds of venison, the fat of which "was at least two inches thick."

Mrs. Nollekens was even more ingenious. "My worthy friend, Dr. Hill," Smith writes, "who gave free advice to the poor twice a week at his house in Bond Street, was visited by a woman dressed shabbily-genteel, whom he treated, until one of the patients informed him that she was no less a person than Mrs. Nollekens, the wife of the famous sculptor. He therefore determined to expose her the next time she came by getting all the poor into the room before she was admitted. When she was seated he made her a profound bow. "I wonder, madame," he said, "that a lady of your fortune and the wife of a Royal Academician, could think of passing yourself off as a pauper; *you*, who ought to help me to relieve these poor people. You are welcome, madame, to the assistance I have given you, but I hope that you will now distribute the amount of my fees from persons in your position to your distressed fellow-creatures around you in this room." Mrs. Nollekens, for once thoroughly abashed, gave him the few shillings her purse contained and, promising to send more, made a hasty and undignified exit.

To do Nollekens justice, he was not so avaricious as his wife; when his sympathies were aroused he could be generous; *she* never. There was an old writer on art and architecture who had fallen on evil days, and who sometimes visited him. One day Nollekens asked him what made him so depressed. "I am low-spirited," was the answer. "Then go to the pump and take a drink of water," said Nollekens. The poor old man looked sadly round, burst into tears, and went away. Later on, Nollekens said to Smith's father: "What is the matter with Richardson, he looks so glumpish?" "Ah, sir," said Smith, "he is distressed, poor fellow! And you have hurt his feelings by desiring him to go to the pump for relief. He was in tears when he left us." "Bless me! I hurt him," said Nollekens, full of remorse, and that evening he went to see the old man; gave him twenty guineas and promised him to give him the same sum every year as long as he lived. On another occasion when Turner, the Royal Academician, asked him for a subscription to the Royal Academy Artists' Fund, he said, "How much do you want?" "A guinea," answered Turner. Nollekens went to a table-drawer, took out thirty guineas and gave it to him. And yet this same man was continually studying how cheaply he could eat, and was seen disputing with a half-starved cobbler because he refused to put a few more nails into a pair of shoes, for the mending of which he was paying twopence!

Another good trait in his character was that, though constantly adding to his admirable collection of prints and engravings, he never asked the engravers to *give* him first impressions, but always paid the full price. Naturally a great many valuable prints in the collection, especially those from the owners of private plates, had been presented to him by his admirers. His acts of kindness, said Smith, depended entirely on his humour at the moment; he had no "fixed principle" of generosity. "We must not judge of our charity by single acts and particular instances, for they are not always good men who do good things," said Hannah More. Sometimes Nollekens would be liberal simply to annoy his wife. One day she was rating him for paying a man full wages just for doing odd jobs. Sidling up to him, Nollekens said in a stage-whisper that he would give him two shillings a week more, just to spite her.

He was exceedingly mean to the unfortunate models who posed for him. Sometimes, however, he met his match. Smith tells us that "One May morning during Mrs. Nollekens's absence from town, Mrs. Lobb, an elderly lady in a green calash, from the sign of the "Fan" in Dyot Street, St. Giles's, was announced by Kit Finney, the mason's son, as wishing to see Mr. Nollekens.

"Tell her to come in," said Nollekens, concluding that she had brought him a fresh subject for a model, just arrived from the country, but upon the lady's entering the studio, she vociferated before all his people:

"I am determined to expose you! I am, you little grub!"

"Kit!" cried Nollekens, "Call the yard-bitch"; adding, with a clenched and extended fist, that if she kicked up any *bobbery* there, he would send Lloyd for Lefuse, the constable.

"Ay, ay, honey!" exclaimed the dame, "That won't do. It's all mighty fine talking in your own shop, I'll tell his worship, Collins, in another place, what a scurvy way you behaved to young Bet Belmanno yesterday! Why, the girl is hardly able to move a limb to-day. To think of keeping a young creature eight hours in that room, without a thread

upon her, or a morsel of anything to eat, or a drop to drink, and then
to give her only two shillings to bring home! Neither Mr. Fuseli nor
Mr. Tresham would have served me so. How do you think I can live
and pay the income tax? Never let me catch you or your dog beating
our rounds again; if you do I'll have you both skinned and hung up in
Rat's Castle—Who do you laugh at?" she continued, at the same time
advancing towards him; "I have a great mind to break all your *gashly*
images about the head of your fine Miss, in her silks and satins"—mis-
taking his lay-figure for a living model of the highest sort—"I suppose
you pay my lady well enough, and pamper her besides?"

Nollekens, perceiving Mrs. Lobb's rage to increase, for the first time,
perhaps, drew his purse-strings willingly; putting shilling after shilling
into her hand, he counted four and then stopped.

"No, no," said she, "if you don't give me t'other shilling, I don't
budge an inch."

This he did, and Kit, after closing the gates, received orders to keep
them locked for three or four days at least for fear of a second attack.

Avarice has been called the rich man's vice. Be that as it may be,
rich people are generally far more careful of their money than poor
people, especially in small things. The late Lord Clanricarde would go
about wearing patched clothes and boots in the last stages of decay,
nor would he ever take a cab unless obliged to do so. Yet he would stroll
into Christie's and bid twenty thousand pounds for a picture. Another
well-known Victorian peer had a passion for saving pieces of string.
Very rich people are sometimes incredibly mean about food. The present
writer remembers lunching many years ago at a great London house.
It was a party of six, and a butler and two powdered footmen waited.
An imposing crested silver dish was uncovered, which contained exactly
six small cutlets; the vegetables were on the inside of enough. This was
followed by six little tartlets, and the feast ended with small pieces of
ordinary cheese and minute pats of butter. One bottle of wine was
allowed for the party. Turner, who left a fortune, was avaricious in the
extreme. Nollekens was by nature friendly and good-natured, and it is
quite possible that had he married a kind, hospitable woman, he would
have been a very different man, for despite his avarice he was oddly
sympathetic in many ways. *She* was never moved to pity. Nollekens
never had to seek for commissions; he was overwhelmed with them.
And as he had neither self-respect, respect for others, nor good manners,
his fashionable clients had to take him as they found him. Once, after
keeping Lady Arden waiting for a long time, he excused himself, saying:
"I couldn't come up before as I was downstairs washing my feet. They
are now quite comfortable." Even King George III was treated quite

unceremoniously, though Nollekens was the most loyal of men. It is said that when His Majesty was sitting for his bust he (Nollekens) missed a day, and on the following day attended the King to receive his commands for the next sitting. The King, with his usual indulgence for uneducated and ignorant people, said:

"So, Nollekens, where were you yesterday?"

Nollekens: "Why, as it was a saint's day, I thought you would not have me, so I went to see the beasts fed in the Tower."

The King: "Why did you not go to Duke Street?"[1]

Nollekens: "Well, I went to the Tower, and do you know, they have got two *such* lions there! and the biggest did roar so; my heart! How he did roar!"

"And then Nollekens mimicked the roaring of the lion so *loud* and so close to the King's ear, that His Majesty moved to a considerable distance to escape the imitation, without saying like Bottom: 'Let him roar again, let him roar again!' "

A modeller, says Smith, "keeps his clay moist by spirting water over it, and this he does by standing at a little distance with his mouth filled with water, which he spirts upon it, so that all the water is sent into all the recesses of the model before he covers it up. This, Nollekens did in the King's presence, without declaring what he was about to do." King George had very gracious manners. Once, Smith tells us, as he (the King) "was passing through an avenue of Windsor Park leading to the Royal Lodge, he was assailed by a rude, boisterous fellow, standing astride with folded arms, who declared he would not pull off his hat to any king. His Majesty stopped his curricle, took off his hat, and with a smile said: 'I will take off mine to the meanest of my subjects.' This so crushed the gentleman that he could think of nothing more to say."

In his personal relations with the Court circle, King George was both friendly and human, and he had a considerable sense of humour. In the official *History of White's*, edited by the Hon. Algernon Burke, there is an amusing anecdote of an address, supposed to have been presented to His Majesty on his return from Hanover. White's Chocolate House, St. James's, was then a famous gaming house.

The Gamesters' Address to the King

Most Righteous Sovereign,
May it please your Majesty, we, the lords, knights, etc. of the Society of White's, beg leave to throw ourselves at your Majesty's feet (our honours

[1]Referring to the Catholic Chapel in Lincoln's Inn Fields.

and consciences lying under the table, *and our fortunes being ever at stake)
and congratulate your Majesty's happy return to these kingdoms, which assembles
us together, to the great advantage of some, the ruin of others, and the unspeakable
satisfaction of all, both us, our wives, and children. We beg leave to acknowledge
your Majesty's great goodness and lenity, in allowing us to break those laws,
which we ourselves have made, and you have sanctified and confirmed: while
your Majesty alone religiously observes and regards them. And we beg leave
to assure your Majesty of our most unfeigned loyalty and attachment to your
sacred person: and that next to the King of Diamonds, Clubs, Spades and
Hearts, we love, honour and adore you.*

His Majesty returned a most gracious answer.

My Lords and Gentlemen,
    *I return you my thanks for your loyal address: but whilst I have such
rivals in your affection as you tell me of, I can neither think it worth preserving
or regarding. I look upon you yourselves as a* pack of cards *and shall* deal
with you accordingly.

In 1784 Mrs. Nollekens lost her father, Saunders Welch. A man
of humble birth, brought up and educated in a workhouse, he died rich,
loved, and universally respected, a Justice of the Peace, and a member
of the famous Beef-Steak Club. Its membership was restricted to twenty-
four, and included the Duke of Sussex, the Earl of Peterborough, John
Rich, of *Beggar's Opera* fame, John Wilkes and Hogarth. This shows
how high was the value placed on personal qualities and talent in that
aristocratic and civilized period. Dr. Johnson was another case in point.
Had he lived in the prosperous Victorian era—of nostalgic memory!—
he could never have wielded the influence, or attained the commanding
position he occupied in the London of George III. It was the same, at
the end of the century, with the delightful Mr. Creevey who, though
not *born* an aristocrat, was *made* one by his personality, and who
gossiped himself into every great house in the country.
    Welch was a big man and, in his prime, robust, powerful and very
courageous. Mrs. Nollekens often told the story of how he went to
Cranbourne Alley to deal with the journeymen shoemakers who had
struck for higher wages. Immediately he appeared they cheered him,
shouting, "Welch, Welch for ever," and the leader cried, "Let us get
a beer barrel and mount him." He reasoned with both parties so success-
fully that a meeting was held and an increase of pay was arranged.
The men then carried him on their shoulders to his office, gave him three
cheers more, and went away.

It once happened that Welch was informed that a notorious thief and bully, who had for some time been a nuisance to Londoners in the green lanes round Mary-le-bone, and who had eluded the Bow Street runners, was in a first-floor room in a house in Rose Street, Long Acre. At that time the streets were entirely paved with cobble-stones, so coachmen could drive very close to the houses. Welch hired the tallest hackney-coach he could find, and mounted the box with the coachman. When they arrived at the house, he got on the roof of the coach, threw open the sash of a window, entered the man's room and dragged him naked on to the coach. After he succeeded Sir Harry Fielding at Westminster, his court was often crowded by gentlemen who had been to see the executions at Tyburn and had been robbed of their watches or pocket books, and by ladies—who, strangely enough, took great pleasure in these hangings—who had lost their velvet cardinals or purses.

Nollekens shared this odd passion for seeing executions. When Smith was eight years old, Nollekens took him to see the notorious highwayman, Jack Rann, pass on his way to be hanged at Tyburn. He was known as "Sixteen-string Jack," because he had been a coachman and had worn livery breeches with eight strings at each knee. Stooping down to the little boy, Nollekens said: "If my father-in-law, Mr. Justice Welch, had been High Constable, we would have walked by the side of the cart all the way to Tyburn."

"Dr. Johnson," says Boswell, "told me that he attended Mr. Welch in his office for a whole winter, to hear the examinations of the culprits, but that he found an almost uniform tenor of misfortune, wretchedness and profligacy." The friendship between Welch and Johnson was unbroken till the death of Welch. In his will he left the doctor five guineas, which, says Boswell, "Johnson received with tenderness as a kind memorial."

Henry Fielding, writing in 1774, and speaking of the great difficulty he had in moving about owing to dropsy, said:

"By the assistance of my friend, Mr. Welch, whom I can never think or speak of but with love and affection, I conquered this difficulty."

When John Wilkes went to Fielding's court to apply for a warrant "to arrest the persons of the Secretaries of State, by whose order my bureau desk, and escritoire have been broken open, and all my papers seized," the sitting magistrate, Mr. Spinnage (Fielding being absent)' refused to grant the warrant. Wilkes then applied to Welch, who smiled at his threats and also refused.

Welch left his landed property to his two daughters, Anne and Mary (Mrs. Nollekens) but except for a few legacies, everything else to Anne—much to Mrs. Nollekens's annoyance—for her kindness and affection to him. Among the innumerable people whom Welch helped

was Richard Wilson, the landscape painter. Wilson was often very hard
up and once, when he had not sold a picture for some time, he met
Welch, who said, "You never come to dine with me now." Poor Wilson
explained his situation and regretted that Welch did not collect pictures.
"I certainly do not understand them," answered Welch, "but if you will
dine with me on Monday week I will bespeak a fifteen-guinea picture
of you."

"Heaven knows what will have become of me by that time," said
Wilson.

"Well, then," answered Welch, "if you are not engaged to-morrow,
send a picture to my house and join me at dinner. I will pay you the
money."

Among the celebrated people who visited Nollekens's house was
Angelica Kauffmann, of whom Smith tells an amusing story. Before
she married the artist Zucchi, she had a passionate intrigue with a dis-
carded valet of Count Horn, who was masquerading as his ex-master.
He was a handsome young man, and Angelica at once fell a victim to
his charms and married him. Soon after, when attending the Queen at
Buckingham House, she told Her Majesty that she had married Count
Horn; was warmly congratulated and invited to come to Court with
her husband. The *soi-disant* count, however, who was keeping well
out of the way of everyone likely to know the real count by sight,
excused himself on the pretext that his baggage had not arrived. But
alas for him, Count Horn came unexpectedly to London, and at a
levée was much surprised on receiving the King's congratulations on his
marriage. Explanations followed, and Angelica, who was disillusioned
by the Queen herself, was inconsolable. The false count was persuaded
to leave London on being given a pension; Angelica resumed the name
of Kauffmann and, fortunately, was never troubled by him again.

Nollekens did not care much for the fair Angelica, and often made
fun of her passion for young men. When she was at Rome, before
her marriage to Count Horn's valet, she was ridiculously fond of display-
ing her person and being admired. For this purpose she took her place
one evening in one of the most conspicuous boxes of the theatre, accompanied by Nathaniel Dance and another artist, both of whom, as well
as many others, were desperately enamoured of her. Angelica, says
Smith, might perhaps have recollected the words of Mrs. Peachum in
The Beggar's Opera:

> Oh, Polly! you might have toy'd and kissed.
> By keeping men off, you keep them on.

"While she was standing between her two beaux, and finding an arm of each lovingly embracing her waist, she contrived, whilst her arms were folded before her on the front of the box over which she was leaning, to squeeze the hand of both, so that each lover concluded himself beyond all doubt, the man of her choice."

Angelica Kauffmann died in 1810, and two years after her death Mrs. Nollekens lost her sister, Anne Welch, of whom she was very fond, always, Smith tells us, "paying the strictest attention to every observation or wish she uttered, according to the early advice given her by their friend, Dr. Johnson, who generally called Anne Welch "Miss Nancy." The fact that Anne loathed Nollekens, sometimes made relations difficult. She was buried in Bath Abbey, and Mrs. Nollekens had a fulsome and typically eighteenth-century inscription engraved on her tomb.

Admired by her friends, beloved by her acquaintances, blessed with distinguished abilities, she was so improved by the knowledge of various languages and science, that elegance of diction, beauty of sentiment, the majesty of wisdom, and the grace of persuasion, ever hung upon her lips. The bonds of life being gradually dissolved, she winged her flight from this world in expectation of a better, on the 15th of January, 1810. Her afflicted and affectionate sister, Maria Nollekens, in full assurance of their happy reunion, caused this monument to be erected.

The epitaph only needed the final sentence of another famous epitaph of the period, to make it perfect.

She painted in water-colours and of such is the Kingdom of Heaven!

Considering poor Mrs. Nollekens's chagrin on finding that her sister's house at Aylesbury and its valuable furniture had been left to someone else, her feelings do her vast credit!

One of the Nollekens's most distinguished visitors was Mrs. Thrale, who came with Dr. Johnson to see Lord Mansfield's bust. The sculptor, who did not know her, called out to Johnson: "I like your picture by Sir Joshua Reynolds very much. He tells me it's for Thrale, a brewer, over the water: his wife's a sharp woman, one of the blue-stocking people——" "Nolly, Nolly," said the doctor, "I wish your maid would stop your foolish mouth with a blue-bag." Mrs. Thrale smiled and whispered to Johnson: "My dear sir, you'll get nothing by blunting your arrows upon a block."

Garrick does not appear to have been one of their friends, although Nollekens's early bust of the actor was one of his best. Possibly Garrick, elegant and very popular socially, did not like the squalor in which the Nollekens lived, and, having all the actor's vanity, the sculptor's indifference to his fame annoyed him. Reynolds and Nollekens, howeevr, had a sincere liking for each other, and when Hone, the fashionable miniature painter—who was jealous of Reynolds's immense success and prestige—attacked Sir Joshua on some trumped-up story regarding his relations with Angelica Kauffmann, Nollekens was furious. One morning Hone called on him and said, "Joseph Nollekens, Esquire, R.A., how do you do?" Nollekens answered: "Well now, I suppose you've come to get me to join you in the Academy to-night against Sir Joshua, but you're very much mistaken and I can tell you more; I will never join you in anything you propose." He then rated him soundly about his attempts to slander and ridicule Reynolds.

"Why now, how can you be so ill-tempered this morning? I have brought you two prints, which I bought at Old Gerards."

"Well, I don't care," answered Nollekens. "You don't bribe me that way. I know what you are going to do to-night, and I'll vote against you, so you may take your prints back again."

Nollekens, for some reason or other, detested Romney, and the dislike was mutual. The famous painter despised the sculptor for his avarice, his rough ways and love of "low life", and would never allow him to model from his portraits. With Flaxman, Romney was on the best of terms, indeed, they almost idolized each other.

Nothing pleased Nollekens more than the milk-maids' dances on May Day. His opposite neighbour assured Smith that one May Day she had seen no less than five garlands and their lasses, who had danced at his parlour window, to each of whom he had given half a crown. The milkmaids' garland was a pyramidical frame covered on each side with polished silver plate and adorned with knots of gay-coloured ribbons and posies of fresh flowers, surmounted by a silver urn or tankard. The silver was hired from the pawnbrokers at so much an hour. Mrs. Nollekens was furious at her husband's extravagance, and she[1] was still more angry when she discovered that the "abandoned women" who sat to him for his Venuses, hired themselves out on May Day as dancers. "A man like you," she exclaimed, "who could obtain orders any time for the Opera House, where you could see Vestris. How can you agitate your feet as you do at such strumming is to me perfectly astonishing! See! look over the way at the first-floor window of the 'Sun and Horse-shoe.' The landlord and his wife are laughing at you. How can you so expose yourself, Mr. Nollekens? I wish from my heart Dr. Burney would come in just now! And I am quite sure that Miss Hawkins,[2] poor as her ear is for music, and whose playing, as the doctor says, distracts one to hear—even she, as I say, could never be pleased with such trash." But

[1] *Hone's Every-day Book.*
[2] Daughter of Sir John Hawkins.

Nollekens took no notice of her, and continued to "agitate his feet" to the dance music; indeed, says Smith, he preferred it to the "magic sweetness of church voluntaries."

As Joseph left the room to get his half-crown, she caught a hussy's decoying leer at her husband, just as the blind fiddler was striking up "Come, thou rosy-dimpled boy." This was the last straw. Bursting with passion, she vowed she would tell her sister. "So do," said Joseph, "and then she'll tell you what a great fool you *was* for having took me, as she always does."

"You filthy thing," screamed madame, "your grovelling birth protects you from my chastisement."

"Come, I like that vastly," he answered. "True it is, your father preserved a *plum*;[1] but it was only a grocer's one. Why, I had five times the money he died worth when I made you my wife and you know what you whispered to me in bed about your mother." At that moment a servant entered to tell Nollekens that the woman whom Richard Cosway had recommended to him was dancing at the yard gate and wanted to see him! A sitter arriving, the quarrel ceased for the time being, but it was resumed, according to Bronze, the servant, when the charming couple had retired for the night. Their disputes about money and household accounts were endless—they would quarrel a whole day over a few pence, which one of them had expended for the other.

Smith relates an interesting conversation between Nollekens and John Catling, the chief verger of Westminster Abbey, in which they speak of old customs that have passed away. It took place when Nollekens was working there on a monument.

Nollekens: "Why, Mr. Catling, you seem to be as fond of the abbey as I am of my models by Michelangelo. My man tells me you was born in it."

Catling: "No, not in the abbey. I was born in the tower; on the right hand, just as you enter the cloisters."

Nollekens: "Oh, I know. Now I wonder you don't lose that silver thing you carry before the Dean when you are going through the cloisters. And why do you suffer the schoolboys to chalk the stones all over? I have seen spilt pudding, grease, lard, butter and I don't know what all."

Here the verger gave Nollekens an admonitory touch on the arm, for the bishop was passing through Poet's Corner on his way to the House of Lords. It was Dr. Samuel Horsley—"that fiend Horsley," according to Dr. Parr.

[1]A "plum" was slang for a substantial sum of money. Nollekens was worth £20,000 when he married, so Welch's fortune cannot have been large, *if* one can believe Nollekens.

Nollekens: "What does he carry that blue bag with him for?"
Catling: "It contains his papers on the business of the day."

Nollekens then said that his wife wanted to know what had become of the wooden figures with wax masks, all in silk tatters, that the Westminster boys called the "Ragged Regiment." These figures were effigies of famous men who were buried in the abbey. They were carried in state at their funerals and afterwards preserved. There are a few of them still remaining.

"Why," answered Catling, "we had them all out the other day for John Carter and young Smith to draw from. They are put up in those very narrow closets between our wax figures of Queen Elizabeth and Lord Chatham in his robes in Bishop Islip's Chapel, where you have seen the stained glass of a boy slipping down a tree, and the eye slipping out of its socket."

Nollekens: "What! Where the poll-parrot is? I wonder you keep such stuff. Why, at Antwerp they put such things in silk outside in the streets. I don't mind going to Mrs. Salmon's Waxwork in Fleet Street, where old Mother Shipton gives you a kick as you are going out. Oh dear! You should not have such rubbish in the abbey; and then for you to take money for this foolish thing and that foolish thing, so that nobody can come in to see the fine works of art without being bothered with Queen Catherine's bones, the Spanish Ambassador's coffin, the lady who died by pricking her finger and that nasty cap of General Monk's you beg of people to put into."

This cap is mentioned in the *Ingoldsby Legends*:

> I thought on Naseby, Marston Moor,
> And Worcester's crowning fight.
> When on my ear a sound there fell,
> It filled me with affright.
> As thus, in low unearthly tones,
> I heard a voice begin—
> "This here's the cap of General Monk!
> Sir, please put summat in."

Nollekens then told the verger that the dean ought to see to it that the monuments were dusted. He complained of those who wanted to draw in the abbey having first to write, and then to be brought up before the dean and required to pay fees. He returned always to his grievance against "them Westminster boys."

Nollekens, who loved going to the opera for the sake of the dancing, was delighted when the Opera House in the Haymarket was burnt down, and the managers hired the Pantheon. At the Haymarket gentlemen were obliged to go in full dress; at the Pantheon the custom was dropped, and he could go dressed as he liked. Boswell, meeting him there one evening, exclaimed: "Why, Nollekens, how dirty you go now! I recollect when you were the gayest dressed of any in the house." Nollekens replied: "That's more than I could ever say of you." Boswell never looked well dressed, for as he very seldom washed himself, his clean ruffles were in striking contrast to his dirty hands.

Nollekens was made by the mode of his period, as were the popular painters of the mid-nineteenth century, Millais, Marcus Stone, Burne-Jones, Boughton, Leader and the rest, and he was as good a business man as they were. One looks in vain for any trace of spirituality in his art: any hint of the *mind* behind the features. As portraits his busts were often admirable, for although he was not a good draughtsman, his work was alive; he imbued it with his own bursting vitality. It is curious that during his long stay in Italy he learned nothing from the exquisite art of Donatello and his school, from Jacopo della Quercia, from Cellini, or indeed, from any of the early Renaissance sculptors. He professed a great *culte* for Michelangelo, but never achieved his dignity. An artist in any medium must be, at least, *aware* of the arts he does not himself practise; he must have intellectual interests. Nollekens had none; neither had he a trace of idealism, or of sympathy with the joys and sorrows of common humanity. His talent began and ended with the ability to "chop out a bust." Had he been born in the days when the Church was the great—and only—patron of the arts, his spiritual nature might have developed, for he would have been obliged to use his imagination. There are a good many specimens of his monumental work to be seen in various churches about the country. When anything gets into a church it generally stays put; Art and the Church of England never having been on even bowing terms. Still, he was certainly one of the best sculptors of a period which produced no sculpture worthy to rank with its painting, or its exquisite craftsmanship in the making of furniture and china.

When Lord Elgin's marbles arrived in England, a committee was appointed to consider their purchase for the nation, and sat in the House of Commons. Nollekens was one of the artists who were asked to give their opinion of them, and it is interesting to compare his answers, to the chairman of the committee, with those of Flaxman, which showed a thorough knowledge of sculpture in general and of Greek sculpture in particular. Perhaps one of the most striking tributes to their greatness was that of a riding-master, who took his pupils to see them. "See, gentlemen," he said, "look at the riders all round the room; see how they sit; see with what ease and elegance they ride; I never saw such men in my life; they have no saddles, no stirrups, they must have leaped upon their horses in a grand style. You will do well to consider the position of those noble fellows; stay here this morning instead of riding with me, and I am sure you will seat yourselves better to-morrow."

Nollekens made two busts of Fox: one from life in 1802, and one death mask in 1806. The former was one of his most successful works and added greatly to his reputation. It shows Fox with toupet and curls, as Sir Joshua Reynolds painted him. Of this there are several engravings. The death mask was less satisfactory, though, says Smith, "ghastly as it is and totally unlike as the features are to those of Mr. Fox when living, still the shape of the forehead is truly remarkable and interesting."

Nollekens never managed to get Pitt to sit to him. When he (Nollekens) had finished the monument to the three captains (William Boyne, William Blair and Lord Robert Manners) who fell in Rodney's battle with the French off the West Indies in 1782, which had been commissioned by the Government for Westminster Abbey, it waited its inscription there for seven years, during which period it was "shut up," according to Dean Stanley. It had previously waited four years in Nollekens's studio. The sculptor, at last losing his patience, petitioned the King to take the matter into his royal consideration. The haughty Pitt was so annoyed with him for daring to interfere, that he refused either to sit to him, or to recommend him in any way. Nollekens got his revenge. Not having succeeded in making a bust of Pitt in life, he took his death mask, and in various ways made no less than fifteen thousand pounds out of the famous statesman: the statue and pedestal for Trinity College, Cambridge, seventy-four busts in marble at a hundred and twenty guineas each, six hundred casts at six guineas, and so on. The marble had cost him only twenty pounds and, as it was not large enough for Pitt's head, he drilled a lump from between the legs and pieced it together in a way no Italian sculptor would have dreamed of doing. All this to Smith's profound disgust. Nollekens, however, economized in marble as he did in everything else. He took immense pride in "manœuvring the marble," as he called it, and making it up of bits.

Notwithstanding his great natural talent, his excellent technique, remarkable facility, and his interest in his work, sculpture was with him a trade; not an art. He was a born sculptor; not a born artist. Nollekens, Smith writes, "now and then amused himself and a friend or two with his prints, but seldom spoke of the beauties of ancient bronzes; and as for expatiating upon the boldness and vigour of a Roman medal, that with him was quite out of the question. It is true that he had a collection of gems—impressions mostly taken from the antique—

though certainly made with very little discrimination as to their superior excellence in point of art in comparison with those by his contemporaries, Burch, Merchant and Tassie, for he would be as highly pleased with an inferior imitation of an antique as with an original of the choicest excellence. In placing the various subjects in boxes, he never attended to any kind of classification whatever, since it was the same thing to him whether they were sacred or profane, and a figure of Eve or a Susannah was placed with that of a Lucretia or a Leda. His heads, though they were kept by themselves, could boast of no better arrangement, as that of Hannibal was placed next to one of Flora and his mode of jumbling of eminent characters together, reminded one of Lingo the schoolmaster[1] who, in the *Agreeable Surprise* asks Cowslip, the dairy-maid, if she has ever heard of Homer, Moses, Heracles or Wat Tyler!"

Among the many famous people of the eighteenth century, who, besides Nollekens, figure in Smith's fascinating book, is William Blake. Smith did not know him personally, but he was an intimate friend of Flaxman, for whom Blake had the same admiration and affection as had Romney. Flaxman, indeed, was loved and respected as few men have been. He had all the qualities which Nollekens lacked; imagination, spirituality, dignity, and he was also possessed of the social graces. Blake, says Smith, had a singular gift for prophecy. An instance of this occurred in connection with the tragic death of that extremely talented engraver, William Ryland, who was hanged for forging—in a singularly stupid manner—a bond for several thousand pounds. Blake's father intended to apprentice him to Ryland, and took him to Ryland's shop to talk things over. On their way home the boy said, "Father, I do not like that man's face. I feel sure he will live to be hanged." At that time Ryland was a popular and highly successful engraver. Frederick Tatham, the collector and a patron of Nollekens, said to him that to take a stroll with Blake was like "walking with the prophet Isaiah." Smith was never for an instant in doubt of Blake's genius. "The time will come," he said, "when Blake's works will be sought after with the most intense avidity." This was proved when, in 1903, Quaritch paid five thousand six hundred pounds for his illustrations to the Book of Job. Nowadays dealers and collectors compete eagerly for everything of his that comes into the market. There is no doubt that Blake, like Lord George Gordon, was mentally unbalanced, but in a very different way. He was a religious visionary: a mystic of the type of St. Jean de la Croix. "I am more famed in Heaven for my works than I could well conceive," he wrote to Flaxman—also a profoundly religious man. "In my brain are studies and chambers filled with books and pictures of old, which I wrote and

[1]Lingo was a pedantic schoolmaster in a popular musical farce of the day by O'Keefe.

painted in ages of eternity, before my mortal life, and those works are the delight and study of archangels." He believed in every kind of supernatural phenomena, and was convinced that he saw a fairy's funeral in his garden. His married life was ideally happy; he and his wife might well have competed for the Dunmow Flitch!

In 1817 Mrs. Nollekens died. She had been a complete invalid for three years, with a deformed spine and paralysis. Nollekens behaved with all due propriety, but showed few signs of inconsolable grief. He himself was avaricious enough, but towards the end of her life economy became a mania with *her*, and obsessed her mind to the exclusion of every other interest. It had long alienated her from all their old friends, and from the leaders of the art world, and she had depended for society on people of a lower class whom, in her heart, she cordially despised. Perhaps Nollekens felt a little relieved? He soon began to use two candles instead of one, drank more wine, went to bed later, and often invited visitors to dine with him. Few, however, could endure his coarse manner of feeding, the dirty cooking, the half-melted butter mixed with flour, which he loved, and his filthy way of eating. Moreover, his own health was failing; he was terribly afflicted with scurvy, which made him an unpleasant companion, and he had had two paralytic seizures.

After he was no longer able to go out, one of the priests from the Catholic chapel in Lincoln's Inn Fields visited him to hear his confession. One rainy morning, says Smith, "Nollekens, after confession, invited his holy father to stay till the weather cleared up. The wet, however, continued till dinner was ready, and Nollekens felt obliged to ask the priest to partake of a bird, a present from the Duke of Newcastle. Down they sat; the reverend man helped his host to a wing, and then carved for himself, assuring Nollekens that he never indulged in much food; though he soon picked the rest of the bones. "I have no pudding," said Nollekens, "but won't you have a glass of wine?—oh, you have got some ale." However, Bronze brought in a bottle of wine, and on the remove, Nollekens, after taking a glass, went, as usual, to sleep. The priest, after enjoying himself, was desired by Nollekens, while removing the handkerchief from his head, to take another glass. "Tank you, sare, I have a finish the bottel." "The devil you have!" muttered Nollekens. "Now, sare, as the rain is ovare, I will take my leaf." "Well, do so," said Nollekens, who was determined to let him go without his coffee. He gave strict orders to Bronze not to let the old rascal in again. "Why, do you know," he continued, "that he ate up all that large bird, for he only gave me one wing, and he swallowed all the ale, and out of a whole bottle of wine I had only one glass!"

After this, being without a confessor, his attendant, Mrs. Holt, read

Dr. Johnson

Dr. Johnson at "The Mitre"—a picture by Rossetti. The two
young women had come from Staffordshire to consult Dr.
Johnson on Methodism

the prayers to him. She was a kind, good woman and made Nollekens, during his last years, more comfortable than he had ever been. She insisted on cleanliness and would not allow him to economize in clean bed linen and candles. She slept on a sofa beside his bed, and when he could not sleep he would talk to her.

"Sit up, I can't sleep, I can't rest. Is there anybody I know that wants a little money to do 'em good?" he asked her one night.

"Yes, sir, there is Mrs.——" she answered.

"Well, in the morning I'll send her ten pounds," said Nollekens.

Mrs. Holt told Smith that she never knew him to forget a promise.

For all his meanness, he was kind enough to his servants, always giving them presents of money on his birthday. After his wife's death he increased these gifts, giving them ten or twenty pounds each. When Mrs Holt entered his service she declared that she would not stay unless he bought himself a new coat and waistcoat. His entire wardrobe then consisted of one night-cap, two shirts, three pairs of much-darned stockings, two old coats and two waistcoats. His shoes had been constantly mended and nailed, and they were odd ones. There were no kitchen towels, no soap, and nothing to clean the grate with; indeed, the whole furnishing was poverty-stricken to the last degree. Towards the end of his life Nollekens fell into a state of almost complete imbecility, and had it not been for the devotion of Mrs. Holt his state would have been wretched in the extreme, for Bronze and the other servant were too old and feeble to look after him.

He continued at times to amuse himself with modelling in clay, and liked having some of his old models to tea. They generally went away richer than they came. So childish was he that one ancient Venus managed to get ten pounds out of him to make a plum pudding! But the sands were running out. On 23rd April, 1823, a third paralytic stroke made an end of him.

He left a fortune of over two hundred thousand pounds. Smith, whom he had known as a little boy, and to whom, to atone for never having given him anything, he had repeatedly promised a handsome legacy, was left a hundred pounds. Perhaps Smith, though he had been consistently loyal to him and had borne with all his unpleasant ways, had been as candid in his personal relations with Nollekens as he was in his biography! But Smith did not need money. Happy in his position of Keeper of the Prints, in the old Print Room of the British Museum; happy, too, in the possession of innumerable friends, who delighted in his inexhaustible fund of anecdotes and recollections, his irrepressible humour and his brilliant gift of mimicry, he passed his time very pleasantly until his death in 1833.

L

Smith was not the only expectant legatee to be disappointed. Many old friends who had every reason to expect handsome legacies, were left only small sums, or nothing at all. Of all the distinguished artists with whom he had had relations, only Richard Cosway, Sir William Beechey, Benjamin West, and the widow of Zoffany were remembered; and to none of these did the legacy exceed three hundred pounds. With Francis Douce and Mr. Palmer, who inherited the residue of his large fortune, he seems never to have been on particularly intimate terms. The will is written in his usual illiterate English—spelling was always a sore point with him, and the efforts of Anne Welch to improve it had earned his undying hatred.

And so died this poor rich man—poor indeed, for what use had he made of his fortune? What enjoyment had it brought him? The money he had accumulated at his bankers was out of his reach and contemplation; he was spending only what he had in hand, and lived like a beggar in fear of actual want.

Perhaps—let us hope for the best—what he *gave* was enough for his journey money to the "undiscovered country." But he must have travelled third class!

BIBLIOGRAPHY

Nollekens and His Times   John Thomas Smith.
                                              Edited by Fred Whitten, London.
                                              John Lane. MCMXX.

A Book for a Rainy Day   John Thomas Smith.

THE YOUNG DISRAELI
(*A Study in Ambition*)

I

EVERY country, it has been said, gets the Jews it deserves. If this be the case, England must have fallen sadly from grace during the last hundred years, for Isaac Disraeli, the father of Benjamin, was a very good Jew indeed. He was the son of one Benjamin Israeli, who came to England from Italy. When he was naturalized in 1748 he described himself as "of Certo (Ferrara) in Italy," and it was after this that he began to write his name as D'Israeli—Israeli being an Arab word meaning Israelite. His grandson,[1] after he had become famous, claimed for his family a far less humble origin.

"My grandfather," he wrote, "who became an English denizen in 1748, was an Italian descendant of one of those Hebrew families whom the Inquisition forced to emigrate from the Spanish Peninsula at the end of the fifteenth century, and who found a refuge in the more tolerant territories of the Venetian Republic." He goes on to tell us that they flourished exceedingly in Venice for over two hundred years, and assumed the name of Disraeli—a name never borne by any other family—in order that their race might be for ever recognized. Why, since they were so prosperous, they quitted the sunshine of Italy for the fogs of London, he does not tell us.

Unfortunately no evidence of their Spanish ancestry has ever been discovered, and the story of their connection with Venice is equally apocryphal; no trace of the family exists in Venetian archives. In all probability, grandfather D'Israeli sprang from a Levantine family, and in any case his circumstances when he arrived in England were humble enough. But Benjamin all his life was obsessed with a love of the grandiose; of old families and long traditions; and what more natural than that he should illuminate the dull, prosaic facts with the warm light of his Oriental imagination?

But whatever the old man's origin, he certainly had a hard time before success came to him. One of his actions earned his grandson's entire approval; he took for his second wife Sarah Siprut de Gaby, who, through her grandmother, was of the Villa Real family. Not only was she well born; she was well endowed, and the capital she brought her husband started him on the road to fortune. All his life he remained a good practising Jew, a member of the Bevis Marks Synagogue, and, though rather lax in his attendance, he contributed handsomely to its

[1] It was Isaac who dropped the apostrophe, and wrote his name as Disraeli.

support. To this couple was born a son in 1766—Isaac D'Israeli, father of the future Prime Minister of England.

Isaac's mother had to a high degree that sense of inferiority in belonging to a despised race, which is felt by so many Jews. She was a clever woman, and her social position mortified her intensely. Isaac was a pale, thoughtful child, fond of books and poetry, and she had nothing but contempt for him. A poet *and* a Jew! What could he look forward to but a future of degradation? She lived to be eighty-two, and to the end of her long life was never known to show him any affection. The poor woman died as she had lived, full of bitter contempt for her race and for a world which despised it. Nominally a Christian, she was buried at Willesden Church. Her grandson called her "a demon." Only once had he seen her in an amiable mood. "She came to stay with my father and mother at Hyde House, Chesham, in the year 1825, and was kind and suave to all, upon seeing which, I recollect that my mother remarked, 'Depend upon it she is going to die.' I remember with horror the journeys on Sundays from Bloomsbury Square to Kensington when I was a boy. No public conveyances, no kindness, no tea, no tips—nothing."

To his father's dismay, Isaac showed not the faintest interest in business, and one day seriously alarmed old Benjamin by producing a poem! Firm discipline was called for and adopted. Isaac was packed up, sent to Amsterdam, and placed in a college under the care of a tutor. But, alas, the tutor had an excellent library, and gave Isaac the run of it, and before he was fifteen he had read most of Voltaire's works and started on Bayle. At eighteen he returned to England steeped in Rousseau, and no better equipped for the battle of life than when he left England. Worse still, he was wearing appalling clothes, and his hair was long. He threw himself into his mother's arms, only to be repulsed with a contemptuous laugh. What was to be done? His father suggested sending him to work with a merchant at Bordeaux. Isaac replied that he had written a long poem exposing the evils of commerce, which was the corruption of man. Finally he was sent to Paris, where he revelled in the libraries and in the society of literary men, returning to England in 1788, with a considerable knowledge of life and a quantity of books. Seeing that he was utterly unfitted for the business world, old Benjamin left him to his own devices, and for some years he studied and wrote, though with little success. In his twenty-fifth year, however, he published anonymously a collection of anecdotes, sketches, and tit-bits of information, under the title of *The Curiosities of Literature*, which caused a sensation in the literary world and decided him to devote the rest of his life to study and literature. His maternal grandmother had left him enough to live on and he would eventually succeed to his father's modest fortune.

The Curiosities of Literature—the only one of his books which is still remembered, though his pen was never idle—is an extraordinary work and, together with his kindly, hospitable and generous nature, brought him hosts of friends, among whom were Byron, Scott, and Rogers. It was dedicated to Nollekens's friend, Francis Douce. Nothing seems to have escaped Isaac's interested, inquisitive, and encyclopædic mind. He tells us what the contemporary critics of famous writers of antiquity thought of them. They said that Socrates was brought to trial by his children as a lunatic; that Plato was extremely avaricious, impious and a liar; that Virgil had no invention, and that Cicero was a usurer. We learn what were the relaxations of great men, among them being those strangely contrasted clerics, Cardinal Richelieu and Dean Swift; he tells us with what enthusiasm Romans, Jews, and Christians burnt one another's libraries in the name of the Lord, and there are scandalous anecdotes of Queen Elizabeth and Queen Henrietta. He is very informative about St. Thomas Aquinas, who, he says, talks about angels as though he himself had been an old and experienced one! The saint's treatises on the angelic host led another writer of antiquity to speculate as to how many angels could dance on the point of a needle without overcrowding! St. Thomas argued learnedly as to whether Christ was not an hermaphrodite, whether there were excrements in Paradise, on the colour of the Virgin Mary's hair, and other matters of grave import.

The book is, in fact, a mine of information in every conceivable subject, and is, in itself, a miniature cyclopædia. Byron admired Isaac greatly, and said of his books (speaking to Colburn) "I don't know a living man's books that I take up more often—or lay down so reluctantly —as Israeli's. If there is anything new of Israeli's, send it me. He puts together more amusing information than anybody."

Isaac, on his part, liked Byron. But his was not a romantic mind. Throughout his life he remained essentially eighteenth-century, and Pope was his favourite poet. He never wanted to travel, hated violence of any kind, could not understand people quarrelling about religion, and asked nothing but to be left alone in his beloved library. How little the outside world interested Isaac is seen in the fact that though he lived through one of the most exciting periods of English history, there is not the slightest allusion to passing events in either his letters or his books. In this he was like Jane Austen, his great contemporary.

In 1802 he married Maria Basevi, the daughter of an Italian Jew. She was not a particularly intelligent woman. Her sole merit—and that no small one—was that she appears to have been an excellent wife and mother, who gained and kept the affection of her husband and children. She was, indeed, a thoroughly virtuous woman, and virtue is its own reward; were it not so, it would often be very badly paid. In the memoir of Isaac which his son wrote after his death, she is not even mentioned. His sister, Sarah, writing to congratulate him on it, said, "I do wish one felicitous stroke and tender word had brought our dear mother into the picture."

When Isaac married he moved from his bachelor chambers in James Street, Adelphi, to 6 King's Road, Bedford Row (now 22 Theobald's Road) and there on the morning of Friday, 21st December, 1804, or according to the Jewish calendar, Tebet 5535, was born his eldest son, Benjamin. On the eighth day he was duly initiated into the Covenant of Abraham, and circumcised by a relation of his mother, one David Lindo. He was not the eldest *child*—the daughter, Sarah, had been born two years previously. Three sons were to follow.

It was a strange London, the London in which little Benjamin first saw the light. Let us take a bird's-eye glimpse at it. For many years it was to continue eighteenth-century; the century summed up by Newman as that in which "Hoadly was the bishop, Pope the poet, Chesterfield the wit and Tillotson the doctor." Unfair, of course, and rather silly; you cannot epitomize an age in an epigram. Men still wore buckskin breeches, large-brimmed round hats, and long-tailed deep-collared coats. As for the women, a glance at some of our illustrations will show how *they* dressed. The old turnpikes at Hyde Park Corner close to Apsley House, at the Oxford Street end of Park Lane—almost rural—and in several other places, continued to mark the boundaries between town and country. There was no Belgravia during the first twenty years of the century. Behind what is now Grosvenor Place were five fields. Chelsea was a country village; so was Paddington with its village green, and South Kensington, save for a few country houses, was given over to market gardens. The London of the fashionable world was very small. It centred round St. James's, Piccadilly, and Mayfair. Many rich merchants, like Thackeray's Mr. Sedley, lived in and round Bloomsbury Square. Beau Brummell once adventured to Charing Cross, and, meeting Sheridan, apologized for being so far east. Clapham, Clapton, Stoke Newington and the suburbs then in existence were quite rural. The more prosperous city men who resided in them drove or rode to London; the others still lived over their places of business.

There were very few clubs, and they were extremely exclusive. The principal ones were "White's," "Brooks's," "Boodle's," "Arthur's," and the "Cocoa Tree", all in St. James's Street, the "United Service," in Albemarle Street, and the "Union" in St. James's Square. Society went to church—when it *did* go to church—at St. James's, Piccadilly, St. George's, Hanover Square, and St. Anne's, Soho. St. Margaret's, Westminster, though well attended, was rather outside the known world. The streets, patrolled by the night watchmen, many of them incompetent and decrepit, were very badly policed, and the purlieus of Westminster were notoriously unsafe. Outside London, highwaymen still flourished. Roman Catholics were tolerated on account of the number of old aristocratic families who belonged to the Catholic Church, Nonconformists were socially taboo, and Jews, of course, were beyond the pale.

There were a number of coffee houses, and very pleasant places they must have been. Some of them were fashionable; some exclusively literary, and others served as clubs for the professional and middle classes. Drunkenness was universal in all classes; so was gambling. The rich gambled at their clubs, at Crockford's, and in their own houses: the masses anywhere and on anything, especially horses, cock-fights and prize-fights. Tea gardens, too, were much frequented. Though Ranelagh closed in 1803, Vauxhall continued to flourish until 1859. On Sundays the middle classes journeyed to Hornsey Wood, Kilburn, Hoxton, or the City Road, to take the air and drink tea.

The most popular theatres were the Royal Opera House in the Haymarket, Covent Garden, the Theatre Royal, the Olympic, and Sadler's Wells—rather a journey—and you went to Drury Lane to see Mr. Sheridan's plays. Dancing, especially at Almack's, was vastly popular in the fashionable world. Almack's was the most exclusive *mixed* club in London. Three-fifths of the nobility knocked at its doors in vain, and to have the *entrée* conferred greater social distinction than to belong to the Court circle. It was ruled with a rod of iron by a few great ladies, among whom were Princess Lieven and Lady Jersey. In 1815 Lady Jersey brought the quadrille from Paris; it became the rage, and soon afterwards the waltz mania set in. Lord Palmerston might be seen at Almack's, dancing it with Princess Lieven. This elegant society did not wash much. Creevey tells us that the heat and stench at one of the Regent's routs at Brighton Pavilion were so great that he left early.

The eighteenth-century passion for executions was not dead; they continued to be public spectacles, and Newgate was now as popular as was Tyburn during most of the eighteenth century. It had been the custom to hang criminals near the scene of their crimes; as late as 1807 a sailor, named Coleman, was hanged in Skinner Street, opposite the shop he had broken into and burgled. The Pillory, too, was still going strong.

Pillories stood at the Royal Exchange, Temple Bar, Lincoln's Inn Fields and Charing Cross, and were in active use until 1830.

Such was the London of 1804—aristocratic, virile, dissolute and picturesque, contemptuous alike of Jews, Turks, and Infidels—what place was there for Benjamin among its ruling class?

II

THE records of Benjamin's early childhood are few, but it is evident that even at four years old his memory and alertness were remarkable. His father, in a letter from Brighton to the publisher, John Murray, says, "My Ben assures me that you are in Brighton. He saw you! Now he never lies." When he was six, Benjamin was sent to a school at Islington, kept by a Miss Roper, which was described as "a very high-class establishment." Curiously enough, a number of Miss Roper's boys came from Buckinghamshire, so when his father settled at Bradenham House in that county, he was among some of his old schoolfellows. From this Dame's school, he went to one of greater pretensions, kept by an independent minister, the Rev. John Potticany. It was in Elliott Place, Blackheath.

Was he happy there? One imagines not, for in after years he never alluded to it. Potticany seems to have held liberal views in religious matters, as in those days few schools could be found for a professing Jew. Benjamin, we are told, was not only allowed to stand aside during morning prayers, but a Rabbi visited the school every Saturday to instruct him and another little Jew in Hebrew, that "tiresome, incomprehensible language, with its strange letters and archaic literature." It was the first time he realized that he was not as other boys were. Why, thought Benjamin, was he a Jew? He had not chosen to be one. Who would, unless an unbalanced eccentric like Lord George Gordon? And yet, in a way, he was proud of the ancient history of his race. His father was neither proud, nor ashamed of it: he simply did not care. A born agnostic, he believed in no dogma, practised no rites, and, happy among his books, smiled indulgently at the odd passions and beliefs of humanity. Among the boy's contemporaries at Blackheath was Milner Gibson, a radical politician, who, in after years, sat opposite him in the House of Commons. Benjamin must have been a kind-hearted little boy, for another of his contemporaries gives us this pleasant picture of him. He writes: "When my father took me to school he handed me over to Ben, as he always called him. I looked up to him as a big boy, and very kind he was to me, making me sit next to him in play hours, and amusing me with stories of robbers and caves, illustrating them with rough pencil sketches which he continually rubbed out to make way for fresh ones. He was a very rapid reader, was fond of romances, and would often let me sit by him, good-naturedly waiting before turning

171

a leaf till he knew I had reached the bottom of the page. He was very fond of playing at horses, and would often drive me and another boy as a pair with strong reins. He was always full of fun, and at midsummer, when he went home for the holidays in the basket of the Blackheath coach, fired away at the passers-by with his pea-shooter." Another boy, who apparently did not like him, says he was lazy and shone in none of the school work. He says, too, that he was fond of bargaining and also of acting, but that in a school performance of the *Merchant of Venice*, in which he played Gratiano, he was unsuccessful. It is curious, seeing that he was at Blackheath for several years, how little we know about his childhood at school and at home. But from that little it appears that he was kind and affectionate, sensitive and rather lonely. Even at that early age his favourite game during his holidays was "playing at Parliament," always, said his brother Ralph, "insisting on being himself the spokesman and leader of the House, keeping the others on the opposition benches!" Of his studies at Blackheath we know nothing. The only letter of his early years which has come down to us is laconic enough—it runs: "Dear mama—I have arrived safe. B. D'Israeli." There is a letter from his grandfather, who was very fond of him, and wrote, when Benjamin was very ill during one of his summer holidays: "We are now in great anxiety for poor little Ben . . . I am very much alarmed by the account I have from Isaac and very much afeard. God preserve him and grant that he may get the better and recover!" Little Ben recovered, but shortly afterwards his grandfather died.

Indirectly Benjamin gained by his death. His father, having inherited the old man's fortune (about £35,000) moved in the following year to 6 Bloomsbury Square, a better house with—for him—the immense advantage of being close to the British Museum. Then, too, the translation of grandfather to another sphere enabled Isaac to put into operation a scheme he had long had in mind. Both he and some of his wife's family disliked the narrow orthodoxy which was still practised in the synagogue. But until his father's death his (Isaac's) children had been brought up as orthodox Jews. Benjamin, as we have seen, was instructed in the faith, even at his school.

Now, though Isaac neither attended the synagogue, nor interested himself in its affairs, he continued to pay his dues until, for some reason or other—probably to push him into a stricter observance of his *soi-disant* religion—the elders of the Bevis Marks Synagogue elected him as warden of the congregation. Isaac wrote to remonstrate with them, and refused to act, whereupon they fined him forty pounds and told him his election was in strict accordance with their laws. A long acrimonious correspondence followed, which three years later ended in his insisting that his name should be erased from the list of their members. But though Isaac ceased officially to be a Jew, he never became a Christian, and was apparently quite satisfied for his children to dwell in limbo. It was owing to the persuasions of his friend, Sharon Turner, then well known as an historian of Saxon England, that he finally consented, much against his will, to take out celestial fire insurance policies for them. Benjamin was baptized on 31st July, 1817, after his two brothers; and his sister underwent the same ordeal a little later on.

Had the Chamber of Elders at the Bevis Marks Synagogue shown a little less fanaticism and a little more tact, says Monypenny, that strange political career which was to fascinate a later generation might well have been impossible.

Did Mr. Potticany's school close, as there is reason to believe, or did Isaac think that Benjamin's regenerate state made a new school desirable? In any case, he was sent to a private school near Walthamstow, called Higham Hall. It was kept by a Mr. Cogin, whose acquaintance Isaac had made at a bookseller's shop. Cogin was a lover of fine first editions, a Greek scholar of the Porson school, and a first-rate teacher; nature had intended him for a college don. "There," says Benjamin, "I remained four years and was quite fit to have gone to a university when I left Cogin—I mean I did not require any preliminary cramming at a private tutor's. Not that I was more advanced than other boys of my age; not so advanced, and never could reach the first class, which consisted of only one boy, Stratton, afterwards at Trinity College, Cambridge, and who, it was supposed, was to have carried everything before him there and everywhere else, but I have never heard of him since." He goes on to speak of his classical studies and his favourite Greek and Latin authors. In later years his memories of Higham Hall seem to have become a little confused, and to have included much that happened before and after he went there. He himself does not seem to remember exactly how long was his stay. In one account of his schooldays he gives it as four years; in another he reduces it to two or three years. But in all probability he left when he was about sixteen, and continued to study at home for a year or so more, most likely with a private tutor. That he regretted all his life not having been to a public school, one senses when reading *Vivian Grey*, but at that time and, indeed, until 1869, no professing Jew would have been admitted to one. But it is difficult to understand why his father did not send him to Oxford or Cambridge, as, having been baptized, he could have passed the religion test, which was in force till 1870. His race, as such, did not debar him from entry. Perhaps Isaac wished to spare him the chagrin of the social inferiority which it entailed. After he became famous he was often accused of being superficial, slipshod, and artificial. Certainly—though, as Monypenny says, he was a fair Latin scholar—the mental training he would have gained from the study of the classics, as they were taught in those days in public schools and universities, would have been invaluable to him. One gathers from his diary how great was his natural aptitude and love for them.

From an early age he was full of *l'esprit moqueur*. A friend of his, annoyed by his irony, described him as a Voltairian. This, of course, he was not. Despite his change of faith, his was a thoroughly Semitic mind, and the Voltairean spirit of revolt was utterly alien to him, brought up as he was in the most authoritarian of all religions. There is in his diary a pencil note: "Resolution—To be always sincere and open with Mrs. E——. Never to say but what I mean—*point de moquerie*, in which she thinks I excel." That Mrs. E——whoever she was—had reckoned him up astutely, we see by an anecdote concerning his schooldays at Higham Hall. The boys, who were, of course, members of the Established Church, had to walk a long way to morning service on Sundays. This they resented intensely, as, when they got back from church, dinner was cold and half over. Benjamin was one of the malcontents, and being far from willing to undergo martyrdom for his new faith, he suggested to his fellow victims that it might be just as well if they were to turn Unitarians for the rest of their stay at Higham Hall!

When Benjamin was seventeen years old, his father decided that he should become a business man. He (Isaac) had a great friend, the head of a very eminent firm of solicitors in the city: a Mr. Maples. He was apparently rich, intellectual, and a connoisseur of art, and, to add to his good fortune, providence had endowed him with one fair daughter, a maiden of surpassing charms. Benjamin didn't want to be a lawyer: even then he was dreaming of Parliament; of swaying men and events by his golden oratory. But for once Isaac was firm, and insisted on having his way. Perhaps he, too, had his dreams; visions of his beloved Benjamin—like the industrious apprentice—marrying his master's lovely daughter and becoming head of the business. Maples certainly gave the boy every chance. He made him his private secretary, and when important clients—among whom, as Benjamin wrote, were "great city magnates, bankers, and East India Company big-wigs"—came to discuss their affairs with the lawyer, Benjamin remained in the office taking notes, thereby gaining a knowledge of business methods, finance, and human nature, which was to prove exceedingly useful to him.

Unfortunately he hated the city, and after three years of it he absolutely refused to make law his career. As a child he had told his sister that he wanted to be something "great and dazzling." There was nothing dazzling at the office! "You have too much genius for Frederick's Place," said a friend to him, "it will never do." But what *would* do? To begin with, he was dying to travel. Isaac feebly suggested Oxford, but he no longer wanted to go to a university. "I was unmanageable," he wrote. Mr. Maples—writing long after the event—said that he had been entirely satisfactory as a business man. Were his recollections, perhaps, illuminated by Benjamin's subsequent fame? There is evidence that other opinions were less flattering.

So far, the only society in which he had moved was in that of the people Monypenny calls "the middling classes." Isaac was a bookworm *and* a Jew, and in neither capacity could he have gained a footing in the fashionable society of which Benjamin dreamed. Some of his biographers have suggested that he was launched in the world of fashion by men he had met at his father's house. This is highly improbable. Isaac's friends were mostly either bookish people he had picked up at the British Museum, or authors with whom his literary activities had brought him in contact. One of his Museum acquaintances was the Francis Douce to whom Nollekens so unexpectedly left the bulk of his fortune, possibly because his upright, disinterested, and kindly character made him so striking a contrast to the harpies by whom he (Nollekens) was surrounded in his latter days.

But Isaac's best friend was his publisher, John Murray; they lived on terms of the closest intimacy. Murray had known Benjamin as a small boy, and had always been struck by his remarkable gifts, so much so, that, before he was eighteen, he valued his opinions on literary matters and talked to him as an intellectual equal. Benjamin was a welcome guest at Murray's famous literary dinners. There, indeed, he met many celebrities, but not of the social or political worlds. In his diary he records a conversation which took place at one of those dinners.

November 27th, 1822—Wednesday—Dined at Murray's. Present Tom Moore, Stuart Newton, John Murray, my father and self—Moore very entertaining.

Moore: This is excellent wine, Murray.

D'Israeli: You'll miss the French wines.[1]

Moore: Yes: the return to port is awful.

D'Israeli: I am not fond of port, but really there is a great deal of good port in England, and you'll soon get used to it.

Moore: Oh! I have no doubt of it. I used to be very fond of port—but French wines spoil one for a while. The transition is too sudden from the wines of France to the Port of Dover!

D'Israeli: Pray, is Lord Byron much altered?

Moore: Yes, his facing has swelled out and he is getting fat: his hair is grey and his countenance has lost that "spiritual expression," which he so eminently

---

[1] Moore had just returned from his long residence abroad.

had. His teeth are getting bad, and when I saw him he said that if ever he came to England it would be to consult Wayte about them.

D'Israeli: Who is since dead, and therefore he certainly won't come.

Moore: I was very much struck with an alteration for the worse. Besides, he dresses very extraordinarily.

D'Israeli: Slovenly?

Moore: Oh, no! no! He is very dandified, and yet not an English dandy. When I saw him he was dressed in a curious foreign cap, a frogged greatcoat and had a gold chain round his neck and pushed into his waistcoat pocket. I asked him if he wore a glass and he took it out, when I found fixed to it a set of trinkets. He had also another gold chain right round his neck, something like a collar. He had then a plan of buying a tract of land and living in South America. When I saw Scrope Davies and told him that Byron was growing fat, he instantly said, "Then he'll never come to England."

Moore: Rogers is the most wonderful man in conversation that I know. If he could write as well as he speaks he would be matchless, but his faculties desert him as soon as he touches a pen.

D'Israeli: It is wonderful how many men of talent have been so circumstanced.

Moore: Ha! Curran, I remember, began a letter to a friend thus: "It seems that directly I take pen into my hand, it remembers and acknowledges its allegiance to its mother goose!"

D'Israeli: Have you read the *Confessions of an Opium Eater*?

Moore: Yes.

D'Israeli: It is an extraordinary piece of writing.

Moore: I thought it an ambitious style and full of bad taste.

D'Israeli: You should allow for the opium—you know it is a genuine work.

Moore: Indeed!

D'Israeli: Certainly. The author's name is De Quincey. He lives at the Lakes. I know a gentleman who has seen him.

Murray: I have seen him myself. He came to me on business once. He was the man whom the Lowthers procured to edit a paper against Brougham's party. He read me the prospectus, and the first thing he said was to tell the reader the whole story of his being hired by Lord Lonsdale.

Moore: Ha! ha! ha!

Murray: From this you may judge what kind of man he is, and I need not tell you that there never was a being so ignorant of the world's ways.

Moore: I read the *Confessions* in the *London Magazine*, and I had no idea that it was a genuine production.

These dinners must have been eagerly looked forward to by Benjamin, when working in the law office he so detested. As his diary shows, he remembered the table-talk he heard, and he used it when he began to write novels. He himself was the "elegant, lively lad" with a touch of dandyism and a sharp tongue, who became *Vivian Grey*. Even in those

A monument by Nollekens in Westminster Abbey

Disraeli speaking at the High Wycombe election

days his passion for fine feathers had already manifested itself. The wife of one of the partners of the law firm said that he used to visit her house, dressed very differently from the other clerks. He would wear "a black velvet suit with ruffles and black stockings with red clocks." These, plus his carefully oiled black ringlets and Jewish cast of countenance, must have rather startled the respectable city magnates and their wives, who dined with the good lady. No doubt the "devil of a tongue" helped the success which throughout his life he had with elderly ladies. He discovered that "there is no fascination so irresistible to a boy as the smile of a married woman." No doubt, too, he flattered the city ladies to the top of their bent. The knowledge of men and women—especially women—thus gained in early youth, served him well in dealing with Queen Victoria.

Having repudiated the law, he decided to take up literature. Murray encouraged him, and he wrote a tale which he intended to be a satire on "the present state of society", and sent it to Murray. It was a crude effort. What, indeed, did Benjamin know of any society beyond the small literary coterie he had met? The kindly publisher kept it so long that Benjamin, realizing that it could not be very valuable, asked him to burn it.

In 1824 Isaac yielded to Benjamin's incessant entreaties, and the two of them, accompanied by a young friend, named Meredith, set out for a six-weeks' tour on the Continent. They went by steamboat to Ostend, then by post-chaise through Belgium to Cologne, and then up the valley of the Rhine to Heidelberg. Benjamin enjoyed every moment. He has left his impressions of it all, both in his diary and in letters to Sarah. In these letters he already displays considerable powers of description, a keen sense of the ridiculous, and a feeling for beauty. There is also a Jewish *flair* for art, and, for so young a man, a surprising love of good food. He writes from Bruges: "The Governor was most frisky on his landing and on the strength of mulled claret, etc., was quite the lion of Ostend." He found Ostend detestable, but Bruges enchanted him; the "city of cities" he called it. He writes: "I never knew the Governor in such fine racy spirits . . . Sir John is certainly rather a bore but

"upon my life
    he has two daughters and a ladye wife."

The first are regular prime girls, both fine women, the younger devilish handsome. He has introduced us with the greatest *sang-froid*, and Meredith and myself intend to run away with them!" At Ghent they found "each thing more wonderful than another, but the work of art Benjamin most

M

appreciated was a *fricandeau*", the finest I ever tasted, perfectly admirable, a small and very delicate roast joint, veal chops dressed with a rich sauce piquant, capital roast pigeons, a large dish of peas most wonderfully fine, cheese, dessert, a salad, pre-eminently fine, even among the salads of Flanders, which are unique for their delicate crispness and silvery whiteness, bread and beer, served up *ad lib* in the neatest and purest way imaginable." This frugal meal cost them only six francs. After eating it, Benjamin was resigned to the "bad paper, infamous ink and 'wusser' pens of Belgium."

At Brussels they had a "debauch of Rubens." No *table d'hôte*, but capital private feeds. "Our living for the last week has been the most luxurious possible and my mother must really reform our table before our return. I have kept a journal of dinners for myself and of doings in general for my father. Mechlin, too, was kind to him. Oysters as small as shrimps but delicately sweet, dinner good and cathedral magnificent! Wine does not seem to have had so much interest for him as food. From Mainz he writes to Sarah: "We travel, as I wrote to you, in a most elegant equipage and live perfectly *en prince*. The Governor allows us to debauch to the utmost and Hochheimer, Johanisberg, Rudesheimer, Assmannshauser, and a thousand other varieties are unsealed and floored with equal rapidity." Ems, delightfully pictured, Frankfurt, where his father—lucky man—bought some Rembrandt prints, "magnificent impressions and very reasonable," and Darmstadt, all fascinated young Benjamin. At Coblenz, where his own record of the tour ends, "dinners, if possible, improve. Game is rushing in in all directions. Partridges abound. The roebuck is superb beyond imagination. At Mannheim we had *sour-craut*, but this is not the season for it."

At this time Benjamin had not finally left the law office, but when speaking of the Rhine he wrote: "I determined when descending these magical waters that I would not be a lawyer." Isaac, failing utterly to alter his decision, was reluctantly obliged to yield.

III

So, to the great regret of Isaac, Benjamin renounced the law—*and the profits*! What next? That the fates had cast him for a leading *rôle* in the *Comédie Humaine*, he did not doubt for a moment. He tells us all about it in *Vivian Grey*—"In the plenitude of his ambition he stopped one day to inquire in what manner he could obtain his magnificent ends: the Bar—pooh! law and bad jokes till we are forty; and then, with the most brilliant success, the prospect of gout and a coronet. Besides, to succeed as an advocate, I must be a great lawyer, and to be a great lawyer I must give up any chance of being a great man. The Services in wartime are fit only for desperadoes (and that truly am I); but, in peace, are only fit for fools. The Church is more rational. Let me see: I should certainly like to act Wolsey, but, the thousand and one chances against me! and truly, I feel *my* destiny should not be on a chance. Were I the son of a millionaire, or a noble, I might have *all*. Curse on my lot! that the want of a few rascal counters, and the possession of a little rascal blood should mar my fortunes!"

The "rascal blood" was more than a little, but the possession of an unlimited stock of "rascal counters," plus the fact that he had become a potential inheritor of the Kingdom of Heaven, might well atone for it—rascal, or *racial*! Benjamin turned his eager young eyes to finance. While in the city he, and a fellow clerk named Evans, had speculated very mildly on the Stock Exchange. Why not try his luck again? At that time there was a wave of the speculation fever to which English people are subject. Companies were being hastily promoted to exploit the mineral riches of the new world. He got into touch with his old friend, and with another youth, the son of a rich stockbroker, they started operations in November 1824. Luck was against them from the first. Before Christmas they had lost £400; by the end of January, 1825, their losses had increased to £1,000; by the end of June, to £7,000. So, at the age of twenty, Benjamin had incurred debts of several thousand pounds. It took him thirty years to pay them off: he had by that time led the House of Commons and been Chancellor of the Exchequer.

During these disastrous speculations, he had made the acquaintance of a clever financier, named Powles, who had profited largely by the boom. Even at twenty, Benjamin had an extraordinary power of influencing and charming others, and very soon the two became friends and confederates. Benjamin saw fortune ahead through the alliance, while

179

Powles, though not impressed by the youth's financial abilities, saw in his imagination, his facile pen, and his connections with Murray and the literary world, assets of considerable value. Speculation had become wild, the Government was seriously alarmed, and it was necessary to reassure the public. Powles enlisted Benjamin's services, and the result was a long pamphlet—published on commission by Murray—entitled "An Enquiry into the Plans, Progress and Policy of the American Mining Companies." It was a clever, though rather impudent, effort, and it pleased Benjamin's patrons. Another followed, with a flattering dedication to Canning, and yet a third displayed the young author as an authority on the conditions in Mexico ! But whether or not the pamphlets served the purpose for which they were intended, they did nothing to help Benjamin's financial affairs, and Murray was not paid for their publication.

But Murray believed in him, placing a high value on his literary *flair* and constantly consulting him. The great success of the *Quarterly Review* had fired him with the ambition of issuing another magazine which would appear more frequently and appeal to a wider public. He took Benjamin into his confidence, and Benjamin at once saw in the scheme a possibility far beyond anything dreamed of by the sober publisher—nothing less than a daily paper ! True, there was *The Times*, now in an impregnable position; true, also, that neither of them had any journalistic experience; but, as Benjamin said, "If a person has imagination, experience appears to me of little use." With Murray's capital and the support of his own city friends, how could they possibly fail? The more cautious publisher reasoned with him, pointing out how large a sum would be required to establish the paper and keep it going until it paid its way, but Benjamin always found reason unreasonable if it clashed with his ambitions. In the end, Murray yielded, and an agreement was entered into by which Murray, Powles, and Benjamin were each to contribute one third of the capital needed. Where Benjamin's share was to come from, neither of them knew—least of all, he himself.

The next thing was to find an editor. Murray was all for Lockhart, Sir Walter Scott's son-in-law. Sir Walter had been very useful to him when he founded the *Quarterly*; so it was decided to send Benjamin to Scotland to charm them into supporting the enterprise. Benjamin was described to Sir Walter as "my most particular and confidential young friend," and Lockhart was asked to consider his voice as the voice of Murray. Benjamin was enchanted with his mission. He spent a night at York and found it bustling and "delightfully gay." The Minster surpassed anything he had seen on the Continent; "the splendid rivalry in liveries and outriders and the immense quantity of gorgeous equipages—

many with four horses—of the Yorkshire squires" astonished him; the four horses of the Apocalypse would not have allured him more. It was a sight you could witness only in that "mighty and aristocratic county." Edinburgh, too, was a revelation—"the most beautiful city in the world." From Edinburgh he wrote that Lockhart had invited him to Chiefswood. He decided to break the journey at Melrose, where the Scottish breakfast—especially the cold grouse—pleased him as much as did the Scottish scenery.

Like all civilized men he was interested in food. In one of his books he describes a family dinner in the early nineteenth century—no doubt from experience. "The ample tureen of *potage royal* had a boned duck swimming in its centre. At the other end of the table scowled in death the grim countenance of a huge roast pike, flanked on one side by a leg of mutton *à la daube*, and on the other by the tempting delicacies of bombarded veal. To these succeeded that masterpiece of the culinary art, a grand battalia pie, in which the bodies of chickens, pigeons and rabbits were embalmed in spices, cockscombs and savoury balls, and well bedewed with one of those rich sauces of claret, anchovy and sweet herbs in which our grandfathers delighted and which was technically called a lear. A Florentine *tourte* or tansy, an old English custard, a more refined blancmange, and a riband jelly of many colours, offered a pleasant relief after these vaster inventions, and the repast ended with a dish of oyster loaves and a pomepetone of larks."

Lockhart, who had expected to see the author of the *Curiosities of Literature*—not his son—was at first cold and reserved, but in a few hours the charm had worked—"*nothing could be more magnificent and excellent.*" The next day, Sir Walter came to breakfast, and they talked over the scheme. They agreed that Lockhart must not be *officially* connected with it. At the end of the talk, Benjamin had already all America and the commercial interest at his back; the West India interest pledged, half the political parties in his power, and Lockhart not merely the editor of a paltry newspaper, but "the director-general of an immense organ, and at the head of a band of high-bred gentlemen and important interests !" And to serve these interests worthily he must of course be in Parliament. The paper was to be called *The Representative.*

The next day, he dined at Abbotsford. The two families, he wrote to Murray, "have placed me on such a friendly and familiar footing that it is utterly impossible for me to leave them while there is any chance of Lockhart's going to England."

Murray was as pleased with Benjamin as Benjamin was with himself. "I may frankly say that I never met with a young man of greater promise. . . He is a good scholar, hard student, a deep thinker, of great energy, equal perseverance, indefatigable application, and a complete man of business," he wrote to Lockhart. Sir Walter, too, added his note of appreciation. "Here," he wrote "has been a visitor of Lockhart's, a sprig of the root of Aaron, young D'Israeli. In point of talents he reminded me of his father, for what sayeth Mungr's Garland?

> Crapaud pickanini
> Crapaud himself.

Which means a young coxcomb is like the old one who got him."

The question of Lockhart's participation in the scheme was not easy to settle. In those days, to be the editor of a newspaper—or even the "director-general of an immense organ"—was not considered a position fit for a gentleman. But it was quite respectable to edit a magazine. Now it happened that the editorship of the *Quarterly Review* was about to become vacant. Who could better fill the position than Lockhart? An agreement was made that he should be its editor at £1,000 a year, at the same time doing his utmost to assist Murray in producing *The Representative*. Benjamin returned to London in triumph, and with frenzied energy threw himself into the work of organization, engaging business premises, foreign correspondents, and enlisting the support of his city friends. Very soon difficulties began to arise; the Lockhart "secret" leaked out, and Murray, "the most timorous of all God's booksellers," as Byron called him, took fright. Benjamin was in disgrace, but a long conversation with Murray put things right.

Alas! Poor Benjamin, like the ancient Jewish law-maker, was fated to see the promised land from afar, but not to enter it. The wave of agitation which had swept over the city culminated in panic, and in December, 1826, the crash came, bringing ruin to thousands, including— one presumes—Benjamin's financial backer, for he disappears completely from the scene. Thus ended his second attempt to storm the business citadel. Murray went on with the enterprise, and *The Representative* duly appeared. Ill-managed, and badly edited, it led a precarious existence for about six months and then gave up the ghost. It had cost Murray some £26,000, as the crash had reduced Powles to bankruptcy. It appears, however, that to their credit he and Murray remained in friendly relations, and that eventually his creditors were paid in full. With the Disraelis, too, Murray maintained his old friendship.

In after years Disraeli—then Lord Beaconsfield—drew a pleasant picture of his visit to Abbotsford. "When I was a youth (1825) I was travelling in Scotland, and my father gave me a letter to Sir Walter Scott. I visited him at Abbotsford. I remember him quite well. A kind, but rather stately, person: with his pile of forehead, sagacious eye, white hair and green shooting-coat. He was extremely hospitable, and after dinner. with no lack of claret, the quaighs and whisky were brought in. I have seen him sitting in his armchair, in his beautiful library, which was the chief *rendez-vous* of the house, and in which we met in the evening, with half a dozen terriers about him: in his lap, on his shoulders, at his feet. 'These,' he said to me, 'are Dandy Dinmont's breed.' They were all called Mustard, and Pepper, according to their colour and their age. He would read aloud in the evening, or his daughter, an interesting girl, Anne Scott, would sing some ballad on the harp. He liked to tell a story of some Scottish chief; sometimes of some Scottish lawyer."

Bowed, but not broken, Benjamin went home, and returned to his first love, literature. He was only twenty-one; he had all the resilience of his race and unbounded confidence in his own genius. In less than six months he wrote *Vivian Grey*. It was published anonymously by Colborn, who was a master of the art of advertising. Hints began to appear in the newspapers and magazines that a novel in which—thinly disguised—all the social and literary celebrities figured, would shortly be published, and from the moment it was on sale, its success was assured. It soon became the talk of London, and various celebrated people—among them Theodore Hook and a well-known peer—were credited with the authorship. But it ended his friendship with Murray, who broke off all relations with the family. He considered the book "an outrageous breach of all confidence and of every tie which binds man to man in social life." Murray apparently fancied that he had been satirized in it— why, it is hard to say. Though in later years he renewed his friendship with Isaac, he remained to the end of his life Benjamin's implacable enemy.

Vivian Grey came out at a fortunate moment. The middle classes, to many of whom the industrial revolution had brought great wealth, were emerging from their social obscurity, buying country estates, and making their way into public life. There was a craze for books which professed to describe the life and manners of fashionable society, particularly if that society were satirized. Of course the name of the author soon leaked out, and Benjamin was mercilessly scarified by the more high-brow magazines and reviews, but, all the same, it survived and went into three editions, probably on account of its gaiety and vitality. In after years Benjamin was ashamed of it. In 1853 he refused to reprint it, but "as it had baffled even the efforts of its creator to suppress it," he allowed it to be published—much expurgated—in a collected edition of his books.

Very few modern readers, I imagine, would have the courage to wade through *Vivian Grey* or, indeed, any of Disraeli's works. But in all of them there are passages and epigrams worth remembering. And they have been a gold mine to many an author who, though having few ideas of his own, has the knack of presenting the ideas of others attractively. Even Oscar Wilde's wit occasionally suggests an acquaintance with them. "Men of genius are always indolent," said *Vivian*; "Happy people are always lazy," said Oscar.

"I am in a refining humour to-day. I could almost lecture at the Royal Institution" (the Marquess of Carabas), and "How those rooks bore me! I hate staying with ancient families: you are always cawed to death" (*Vivian*), are pure Wilde. But Wilde's wit is more subtle and more human than Disraeli's. There is, too, psychological truth in the saying, "Peace gets such a bore. Everybody you dine with has a good cook and gives you a dozen wines, all perfect. All the lights and shadows of life are lost. We really must have a war for variety's sake." *Vivian Grey* is full of clever epigrams. "Patience is a necessary ingredient of genius" is far better than the popular and foolish "genius is the art of taking infinite pains," which is precisely what genius is not. "Man is not the creature of circumstances. Circumstances are the creatures of man" is a *dictum* born of youthful enthusiasm, but even at twenty-one he could strike a graver note: "The disappointment of manhood succeeds to the delusion of youth. Let us hope that the heritage of old age is not despair." Many people to-day will echo his wish that "The world consisted of a charter of small states. There would be more genius, and, what is of more importance, more felicity."

In the triumphant success and happiness of Vivian as a boy at school, one senses—as I have said—Benjamin's deep chagrin at having missed that happiness. He writes: "At a public school, if a youth of high talents be blessed with an amiable and generous disposition, he ought not to envy the Minister of England.[1] If any captain of Eton, or prefect of Winchester be reading these pages, let him dispassionately consider in what situation of life he can rationally expect that it will be in his power to exercise such influence, to have such opportunities of obliging others, and be so confident of an affectionate and grateful return?" *Vivian* was "a leader of boys" and he belonged to the social world he so loved by right of birth. Did Benjamin ever curse the unhappy fate which had caused *him* to be born a Jew?

The great interest of *Vivian Grey*[2] lies, of course, in the very fact that Benjamin identifies himself so closely with his hero. No man writing

---

[1]Presumably, Prime Minister.

[2]The first volume of *Vivian Grey* is the only one worth reading. In the others he loses his grip.

of his own hopes and fears, joys and sorrows, can be *wholly* dull, however unattractive his style. And Benjamin's style, stilted and high-flown as it seems to-day—though hardly more so than that of George Meredith— rang true enough in 1825. Brilliant it was, and still is. There is a certain affinity between *Vivian Grey*, and *Dorian Gray*. Both are amoral, both amazingly good-looking and both unscrupulous to a degree. Even at twenty, young Benjamin had realized the value of flattery in dealing with the great. During one of the egoistic, but oddly sympathetic, Vivian's conversations with the Marquess of Carabas, he uses it shamelessly. In after life, as Lord Beaconsfield, Benjamin was to say to Matthew Arnold, "you have heard me called a flatterer. It is true. Everyone likes flattery, and when it comes to royalty you must lay it on with a trowel."[1] He had made the discovery that it was not truth which his biblical namesake found at the bottom of the well. It was something infinitely more valuable—tact!

Was the unscrupulous Vivian a confession of faith, or was Benjamin trying to convince his reader, and himself, that, as his delightful con- temporary, Jane Taylor, wrote in one of her poems for children,

> Wicked courses never can
> Bring good and happy days?

Who can say? The City of the Soul is forbidden territory. We do not really know those with whom we are in the closest relation: we do not know ourselves. A character so subtle, elusive and complex as that of Benjamin Disraeli leaves us hopelessly baffled.

Benjamin's first action on receiving a substantial cheque from his publisher was to pay Murray the £150 owing for the publication of the pamphlets. The money was acknowledged with cold, formal civility.

The strain of business worries, followed by the excitement of his sudden notoriety, caused Benjamin to have what we should now call a nervous breakdown. Just when he needed a complete change his, and Isaac's, friends, the Austens, invited him to accompany them on a tour to Switzerland and Northern Italy, each paying his own expenses. Mrs. Austen, by the way, had acted as a sort of Egeria to the young author. She had not only revised *Vivian Grey* for publication, but had herself negotiated with her friend, Colburn, to publish it.

Benjamin was delighted. In accepting the invitation he wrote to Mr. Austen, "I have perused your note with attention and considered your offer with care and, as the man says who is going to be hired, 'I think the situation will suit . . . I have a good character from my

[1] *Queen Victoria*. Lytton Strachey.

last place which I left on account of the disappearance of the silver spoons,' I defy anyone to declare that I am not sober and honest, except when I am entrusted with the key of the wine cellar, when I must confess I have an ugly habit of stealing the claret, getting drunk and kissing the maids. Nevertheless, I've no doubt we shall agree very well. You certainly could not find anyone better fitted for ordering a dinner!"

This second tour gave him as much pleasure as did the first, and he wrote long, enthusiastic letters to his father. "Paris is delightful. I never was so struck with anything in my life," he said. He was amazed to find Frenchmen—and women—so different from the English. It was the same in Switzerland; he saw Mont Blanc on a cloudless day, and rowed on the Lake of Geneva with Byron's celebrated boatman, Maurice —vain, handsome and spoilt. It was Maurice who was rowing on the night of the famous storm described in *Childe Harold*. One day, says Benjamin, "Byron sent for him (Maurice) and sitting down in the boat he put a pistol on each side (which was his invariable practice) and then gave him 300 napoleons, ordering him to row to *Chillon*. Ordering two torches to be lighted in the dungeon entered it, and wrote for two hours and a half." Byron, said Maurice, was most ludicrously ostentatious. He gave the *gendarme* at *Chillon* a napoleon. Maurice remonstrated, saying, "*de trop milor.*" "Do you know who I am?" was the proud reply. "Give it to him, and tell him that the donor is Lord Byron." One day he gave Maurice five napoleons for racing him across the lake. Byron won, for though he was a slow swimmer he never tired. Another morning when they went swimming, Byron brought his breakfast to the boat: a cold duck and three or four bottles of wine. He drank all the wine and threw the food into the lake, saying, "You see I eat no breakfast myself, so do *you also* refrain, for the sake of the fish."

They went to the Great St. Bernard. One of the monks—a young Englishman—expressed a wish to see them. They found that all he wanted to know about his native country was whether the Thames Tunnel had been a success! At Milan they saw the famous Leonardo, and also the cathedral, which, Benjamin was told, had no rival. "Was rivalry desirable?" he asked. Benjamin is not the only visitor to Milan who has felt the same about it. Verona, Vicenza, Venice, enchanted him, but his emotions did not differ greatly from those of other romantic youths of his period. His remarks on the art of Florence are interesting, as they illustrate the extraordinary change in *values* that has taken place. "The god of Bertolini's idolatry," and, indeed, of all Italians, "was Flaxman, whom he placed on a level with the great sculptors of antiquity and of the Renaissance. The picture he most admired in that city of art, was Vandyke's Charles I! But then, he neither understood nor cared for the great Christian art of the fifteenth and sixteenth centuries, and found Michelangelo "extremely disappointing." All the same, Florence delighted him—what a paradise it was before civilization died! Benjamin wrote to Isaac: "You may live in a palace built by Michelangelo, keep a villa two miles from the city in a most beautiful situation, with vineyards, fruit and pleasure gardens, keep *two* carriages, have your opera box, and live in every way as the first Florentine nobility, go to Court, entertain, etc., etc., for less than a thousand a year, and this with no miserable managing, but with the enjoyment of every comfort and luxury." Travelling, too, was cheap. The businesslike Austen kept careful accounts of their expenditure. They were away for about three months, during which they posted over 2,000 miles, stayed everywhere in the best hotels, and spared no expense. Benjamin's share, including about £20 spent in buying prints, was £150.

The tour, while temporarily improving Benjamin's health, did not cure it. Writing to Austen in June, 1827, he says, "I continue just as ill as ever . . . as I understand you are in want of a book, I send you the most amusing in any language—*The Memoirs of Benvenuto Cellini*. Jem is richer than ever, and struts about town in a kind of cloth shooting jacket made by the celebrated Hyde of Winchester—almost as celebrated as a tailor as Dr. Chard is as a musician. In this quaint costume, with the additional assistance of a sporting handkerchief, he looks very much like one of those elegant, half blackguard, half gentleman speculators in horseflesh, who crowd Winchester market and dine at the 'good ordinary at 2 o'clock,' for which grub, if you remember, the bell rang loud and long as we crossed the cathedral." Winchester seems to have been quite an interesting city in 1827!

Benjamin continued to be "just as ill as ever" for over two years. Chiefly on this account, Isaac left his beloved London and bought an old manor house in Buckinghamshire, Bradenham House, not far from High Wycombe. It was built, wrote "the venerable Camden," for Lord Windsor, in the reign of Henry VIII. Buckinghamshire had always attracted the Disraelis. In *Vivian Grey* one of the characters is called "Lord Beaconsfield." During these years Benjamin lived very quietly, seldom going to London. But he was not idle; he wrote another book on social life—*The Young Duke*. "What does Ben know of dukes?" exclaimed Isaac, but, after all, his dukes were probably more amusing than the real article; indeed, he was accused of crediting them with intellectual interests to which no self-respecting duke would have owned! He never liked the book; not so his sister. "As for *The Young Duke*, it is excellent—most excellent. There is not a dull half page—not a dull half line," she wrote. Sarah, by the way, had become engaged to his friend, Meredith, his companion on the journey to the Rhine. On Benjamin's visit to London to deliver *The Young Duke* to Colburn, they met, and Meredith writes: "B.D. to dine with me. He came up Regent Street, when it was crowded, in his blue surtout, a pair of military light blue trousers, black stockings with red stripes, and shoes !" "The people," he said, "quite made way for me as I passed. It was like the opening of the Red Sea, which I now perfectly believe from experience. Even well-dressed people stopped to look at me." "I should think so ! He was in excellent spirits, full of schemes for the projected journey to Stamboul and Jerusalem: full, as usual also, of capital stories, but he could make a story out of nothing."

Benjamin must certainly have presented a remarkable appearance, but the sensation he created was probably caused just as much by his pale Jewish countenance, his long, black, well-oiled ringlets, and dandified manner. Fine masculine feathers were common in those days. London was full of colour; on all sides you would meet men wearing blue coats, red waistcoats, and fur-trimmed overcoats of a cheerful yellow. Soldiers in their brilliant uniforms brushed shoulders with wonderfully attired young dandies, and gaily-dressed women with their amazing headdresses alighted from highly-varnished and painted coaches, driven by powdered coachmen wearing three-cornered hats, and with footmen hanging on behind. Perhaps Lord Erskine, dressed in a green coat, scarlet waistcoat, and silk breeches, would pass with his friend Dibdin, or the Prince of Wales, wearing striped green velvet embroidered with silver flowers, his powdered wig adorned with curls and finished off with a long pig-tail, would be seen strolling down St. James's Street, leaning on the arm of Beau Brummell, exquisitely, but more quietly, dressed. The famous Beau was then living at 18 Bruton Street, a house in which the present writer lived for several years.

Brummell could make a man's social reputation by a word. Many young sprigs of nobility owed their position in the Court to his patronage; many were ruined by aping his extravagance. To one angry father who accused him of leading his son astray, he said: "Why, sir, I did all I could for him. I once gave him my arm all the way from White's to Brooks's !" Did Benjamin meet him? Probably not. Brummell would barely have condescended to patronize a Jew !

On the same visit to London to which Meredith refers, Benjamin met Lytton Bulwer.

"Just at the commencement of the spring of 1830, if spring it could be called, I made the acquaintance of Lytton Bulwer, and dined with him at his house in Hertford Street. He was just married, or about just married: a year or two. We were both of us then quite youths: about four and twenty. I met three men at dinner of much the same standing, all full of energy and ambition, and all unknown to fame. Bulwer and I had, at least, written something. I, *Vivian Grey*, and he two or three years afterwards, *Pelham*. The other three were Henry Bulwer, Charles Villiers, and Alexander Cockburn. Writing this, nearly five and thirty years afterwards, it is curious to mark what has been the result of the careers of these five young men. I have been twice leader of the House of Commons, Edward Bulwer has been Secretary of State, Henry Bulwer is at this moment H.M. Ambassador at Constantinople, Charles Villiers is at this moment a Cabinet Minister, and Alexander Cockburn is Lord Chief Justice-of England."

Henry Bulwer, in writing of this dinner party, tells us that Disraeli "wore green velvet trousers, a canary coloured waistcoat, low shoes, silver buckles, lace at his wrists and his hair in ringlets. If, on leaving the table, we had been separately taken aside and asked which was the cleverest of the party, we should have been obliged to say, 'the man in the green trousers.' "

The eastern tour spoken of by Meredith in the letter describing his meeting with Benjamin in London, had long been discussed by them. It was made possible by Colburn, who gave him £500 for the manuscript of *The Young Duke*.

IV

BENJAMIN and Meredith set out for their tour in the Near East in May, 1830. It was to be one of the chief formative influences in his career. The results of it were seen later in his bold Egyptian policy; in the conception of the Indian Empire; at the Berlin Congress. The Jew is essentially an Oriental, and he sympathized with and understood the tortuous Oriental mind to a degree possible to no pure westerner. To find himself in the ancient lands trodden by the Twelve Tribes, was to Benjamin like going home.

In those days travelling opened up new worlds to the receptive and intelligent tourist. Every country had its own costumes, customs, and food, and when you crossed a frontier, the curtain rose on a new scene. And as in travelling by land you were entirely dependent on the horse, you had time to assimilate the beauties of the country through which you were passing, and the idiosyncrasies of its people. The tourist of to-day, rushing from one city to another in express or plane; finding everywhere the same *Hôtel de Luxe*, the same *soi-disant* French *menu*, and, speaking his own language, sees nothing, learns nothing. Thus, instead of leading to mutual comprehension and sympathy, travelling is more apt to make for narrow insularity. The internal combustion engine has had a large share in the world-wide relapse into barbarism. Well, as we were taught when young, "rapid communications corrupt good manners!"

They sailed by steamer to Gibraltar, and Benjamin was at once fascinated by its colour: the Moors with costumes "radiant as a rainbow;" the Jews with gaberdines and skull caps; the picturesque Spaniards. They travelled in the mountain district of *Sierra da Ronda*, infested by bandits, "who commit no personal *violence* on travellers, merely laying them on the ground, cleaning out their pockets and shooting them if they possessed less than sixteen dollars!" From Gibraltar they went to Spain—Cadiz, Seville, Cordova. Benjamin lived—or says he lived—for a week with brigands. Spain, he wrote, "is a country where adventure is the common course of existence." Cadiz made Florence seem "a dingy affair. Figaro is in every street: Rosina in every balcony." Murillo enchanted him.—"For the first time in your life you know what a great artist is—Murillo, Murillo, Murillo! He never fails." Then came Granada and the Alhambra, which he placed with the Parthenon and York Minster. At Granada he was taken for a Moor; back to Gibraltar, and then Malta, *en route* for the Mediterranean and Turkey. At Malta they found an old friend, James Clay, and Benjamin tells his father how he and Clay delighted everyone, Clay by his skill as a sportsman, and he himself by his accomplishments and his disdain of *hoi-polloi*. Long afterwards, when Benjamin had become famous, Clay gave a less flattering account of the effect he made on his *soi-disant* admirers. When they were alone together, Benjamin was unaffected and charming, wrote Clay, but in society his coxcombry was intolerable. He made himself so hateful to the Officers' Mess that while they welcomed Clay, they ceased to invite "that damned bumptious Jewboy." "There seems," says Monypenny, to have been no limit to the "buffooneries of Benjamin, as he himself had the grace to call them. He dined at a regimental mess in Andalusian dress." "He paid a round of visits," writes Meredith, "in his majo jacket, white trousers, and a sash of all the colours in the rainbow; in this wonderful costume he paraded all round Valetta, followed by one half the population of the place, and, as he said, putting a stop to all business." He, of course, included the Governor and Lady Emily in his round, to their no small astonishment. The Governor, a brother of Lady Caroline Lamb, was very exclusive and dignified, and by no means cordial. But Benjamin did not mind.

From Malta they set sail for Turkey, and Benjamin, after a look at Corfu, at last found himself in the land of his dreams. He writes extraordinary accounts of his adventures to Isaac, and to Austen. So highly coloured are they that we are left wondering how many of them are true, and how many are the offspring of his vivid imagination. In all of them he plays the *beau rôle*. He had always loved romantic tales about brigands and caves, and in some of those letters he pictured himself as the hero of adventures very like those which he invented long ago for his little friend at the Blackheath school. He liked to pose as the complete Turk. "*Mashallah!*" he writes to his brother, Ralph. "Here I am, sitting in an easy chair, with a Turkish pipe six feet long, with an amber mouthpiece and a porcelain bowl. What a revolution!" In another letter he says, "I can give you in a letter, no idea of all the Pashas, and all the Silictars, and all the Agas that I have visited and who have visited me; of all the pipes I smoked, all the coffee I sipped, and the sweetmeats I devoured . . . In a week I was in a scene equal to anything in the *Arabian Nights*—such processions, such dresses, such *cortéges* of horsemen, such caravans of camels. Then the delight of being made much of by a man who was daily decapitating half the province! I am quite a Turk, wear a turban, smoke a pipe six feet long, and sit on a divan. You have no idea of the rich and varied costumes of the Levant. When I was presented to the Grand Vizier I made up such a costume from my heterogeneous wardrobe that the Turks, who are mad on the subject of chess, were utterly astounded."

Meredith describes this remarkable costume. "Figure to yourself a shirt entirely red, with silver studs as large as sixpences, green pantaloons with a velvet stripe down the sides, and a silk Albanian shawl with a long fringe of divers colours round his waist, red Turkish slippers, and to complete all, his Spanish majo jacket covered with embroidery and ribbons."

"*Questo vestito Inglese, o di fantasia?*" asked a Greek doctor, who had lived at Pisa in his youth. "*Inglese e fantastico*" was the answer.[1] But Benjamin was utterly impervious to criticism and ridicule: there was, indeed, something rather superb in his supreme egoism.

Did he, when in after-life as Prime Minister he visited Queen Victoria, sometimes cease for a moment to act the *rôle* of the grave statesman (he was always acting) and assume that of *Scheherazade*? Did he charm his "Faery" Queen[2] into forgetfulness of Balmoral, Landseer, John Brown—even of Albert! by singing her—in costume—"Songs of Araby and tales of fair Kashmir?" And was there, deep in the subconscious mind of the tired, august old lady, a touch of the exotic: a *nostalgie de la boue*? That Disraeli could awaken it may well have been the secret of his strange fascination for her. He was so unlike Mr. Gladstone!

He can hardly have related to her the story of a night he spent at a military outpost in the Albanian mountains with a young Turkish Bey to whom he had a letter of introduction. He and Clay arrived late in the evening, tired and hungry. But unfortunately they had no interpreter, so for two hours they sat on the same divan with their host, exchanging eastern courtesies in dumb show. "We smoked. It is a great resource, but it wore out, and it was so ludicrous smoking, and looking at each other and dying to talk; then exchanging pipes by way of compliment, and pressing our hands to our hearts by way of thanks."

Suddenly Clay had a brilliant idea; he remembered that they had some brandy. They offered it to the Bey, who smacked his lips and asked for more—they were drinking it in coffee cups. By this time Meredith, who had left them on some excuse—returned and joined them. The bottle was soon empty. Soon, to their great delight, an excellent supper, accompanied by wine, was brought in. They drank rivers of it, and the Bey finished another bottle of their brandy. They were now reeling, shaking hands, and slapping one another on the back. Finally, in a drunken stupor,

[1]"Is this an ordinary English costume, or fancy dress?" "English and fantastic."
[2]"Perhaps it was a Faery gift and came from another monarch, Queen Titania, gathering flowers with her Court in a soft and sea-girt isle . . ." Lytton Strachey (*Queen Victoria*).

Benjamin Disraeli when he became a Member of Parliament

Isaac Disraeli—father of Benjamin

they subsided on the rugs by the great wood fire. Benjamin, the first to wake, says he found "Abraham's bosom in a flagon of water!"

He was steeped in the romanticism of his period, like Flaubert, who wrote, "I was born to be Emperor of Cochin-China, to smoke pipes six feet long, to have six thousand wives, scimitars to sweep off the heads of people whose looks I didn't like, Numidian mares, marble basins," and all the rest of it.

Certainly these eastern scenes called to every Oriental instinct in Benjamin's nature, yet, shortly afterwards, when looking at a Grecian sunset, he "recalled with disgust the barbaric life in which he had been taking part. Five years of my life have been already wasted, and sometimes I think my pilgrimage may be as long as that of Ulysses," he said sadly.

They sailed through the Ionian Islands on a summer sea, visited Navarino, Corinth, Mycenæ, and on 24th November landed in the Piræus. Athens was reached just before the Turks handed it back to Greece. It appealed to the poet in this young man of many facets, just as the "barbaric splendour" of his Turkish hosts had appealed to the Oriental Jew. He lamented the fact that civilization had deserted the regions most favoured by the gods: Persia, Arabia, Greece.

From Athens they went to Constantinople: it did not disappoint him. Here again he revelled in the picturesque: the gay costumes, the brilliancy of the Turkish dyes, the veiled women. He stayed there for over a month, loving it all. To Bulwer he wrote: "I confess to you that my Turkish prejudices are very much confirmed by my residence in Turkey. The life of this people accords greatly with my taste, which is naturally somewhat indolent and melancholy." It was pleasanter, he thought, "to repose on luxurious ottomans, smoke superb pipes, take baths which needed half a dozen attendants, and take the air by shores that are a perpetual scene, than to lounge in London drawing-rooms." Pleasanter, too, than musing on the troubled home lives of Agamemnon, Clytemnestra, and Hecuba; what, indeed, was Hecuba to him?

Jerusalem—spelt in large capitals—pleased him immensely. He tried to visit the Mosque of Omar, and escaped with difficulty from a crowd of turbulent fanatics. From Jaffa they set sail for Egypt, Alexandria, Cairo—"very dilapidated." A voyage up the Nile to Thebes, and then to the borders of Nubia, Cairo again, and then came a tragedy which was a terrible shock to Benjamin, and which clouded the rest of his sister's life: Meredith contracted smallpox and died. Benjamin returned at once to England, arriving in October, 1831.

Benjamin had his full share of that admirable Jewish quality, family affection, and he mourned sincerely the loss of his friend and prospective

N

brother-in-law. But his transitions from one emotion to another were extremely rapid, and he was too much in love with life to mourn long.

> Remembrance and the faithful thought
> That sits the grave beside,[1]

were not in his resilient nature. He had not been idle during his travels, especially on the voyage home, and he brought back the nearly finished manuscripts of *Conterini Fleming* and *Alroy*. Both books reflect the more thoughtful and poetic side of his character, especially *Conterini*. It is a revelation of his ideal ambition, just as *Vivian Grey* revealed his active and *real* ambition. Of *Conterini* he wrote: "I am desirous of writing a book which shall be all truth; a work of which the passion, the thought, the action, and even the style, should spring from my own experience of feeling, from the meditations of my own intellect, from my own observation of incident, from my own study of the genius of expression."

Perhaps, if we could wade through it, we should discover all that, but truth to tell, it, like all his works, is too stilted and high-flown for the modern reader. He could not, like his great (near) contemporary, Jane Austen, write for all time. But there is in *Conterini* a passage which is curiously in sympathy with the philosophy of to-day.

> I believe in the destiny before which the ancients bowed . . . I think that ere long, science will again become imaginative and that as we become more profound we may also become more credulous.

The other book he brought home, *Alroy*, was not a success. Its poetic-prose style was amusingly parodied by a wit of the day.

> O reader dear! do pray look here, and you will spy the curly hair and forehead fair, and nose so high and gleaming eye of Benjamin Dis-ra-e-li, the wondrous boy who wrote *Alroy*, in rhyme and prose, only to show, how long ago victorious Judah's lion-banner rose.

Benjamin's tour had completely restored his health. He had made a considerable literary reputation and could now count on his pen as a regular source of income. He had returned to London and was settled in very comfortable rooms in Duke Street. "Mr. Disraeli, sir, is come to town—young Mr. Disraeli—won't he give us a nice light article about his travels?" said Colburn to Bulwer, then at the height of his popularity. He and Benjamin had become bosom friends, and through him Benjamin had at last gained a footing in fashionable society and found himself in a position to discover how nearly his *Young Duke* resembled the dukes of Mayfair. To his sister he wrote in 1832:

"We had a very brilliant *réunion* at Bulwer's last night. Among

[1]A. E. Housman.

the notables were Lords Strangford and Mulgrave, Count D'Orsay, the famous Parisian dandy; there was a large sprinkling of blues—Lady Morgan, Mrs. Norton, etc., etc. Bulwer came up to me and said, 'There is one blue who insists upon an introduction.' 'Oh, my dear fellow, I cannot really; the power of repartee has deserted me.' 'I have pledged myself, you must come,' said Bulwer, so he led me up to a very sumptuous personage, looking like a full-blown rose, Mrs. Gore." Again he writes: "The *soirée* at Bulwer's last night was really brilliant, much more so than the first . . . I was introduced, 'by particular desire,' to Mrs. Wyndham Lewis, a pretty little woman, a flirt and a rattle . . . a man talked to me very much who turned out to be Lord William Lennox. In the course of the evening I stumbled over Tom Moore, to whom I introduced myself. It is evident that he has read, or heard of, *The Young Duke*, as his courtesy was most marked, 'I have heard of you as everybody has,' he said."

Benjamin's introduction to Lady Blessington in 1834 resulted in his invitation to Seamore Place. Lady Blessington—ostracized by the great ladies of society on account of her dubious love affairs—was as brilliant a woman as he was a man. Although such women as Lady Jersey, Lady Holland and Princess Lieven, gave her the cold shoulder, their menfolk crowded her beautiful rooms; indeed, her house was the nearest approach to a *salon* London has ever seen, with the exception, perhaps, of Holland House. It was there that Benjamin met many of the famous men he afterwards used so adroitly; among whom was Byron. The society in which he moved was, though not the inner circle of the great world, an extremely interesting mixture of literature, art, fashion, politics, and what the French call *la haute Bohème*. It suited him exactly, and in it he soon became *persona grata*. "Yesterday I dined with the Nortons," he wrote to his sister. "It was her eldest brother's birthday, who, she says, 'is the only respectable member of the family, and that is because he has a liver complaint.' There were there her brother Charles and old Charles Sheridan the uncle, and others. The only lady besides Mrs. Norton, her sister, Mrs. Blackwood[1], also very handsome and very Sheridanic. She told me she was nothing, 'You see, Georgy's the beauty and Carry's the wit, and I ought to be the good one, but then I am not.' I must say I liked her exceedingly: besides, she knows all my works by heart, and spouts whole pages of 'V.G.' and 'C.F.,' and the 'Y.D.' In the evening came the beauty, Lady St. Maur, and anything so splendid I never gazed upon. Even the handsomest family in the world, which I think the Sheridans are, looked dull. In the evening Mrs. Norton sang and acted, and did everything that was delightful. Ossulton came in—

[1] Afterwards Lady Dufferin.

a very fine singer—unaffected and good-looking. Old Mrs. Sheridan—who, by the way, is young and pretty, and the authoress of *Carwell*—is my greatest admirer: in fact, the whole family have a very proper idea of my merit! I like them all."

Lady Dufferin gives a description of Benjamin's fantastic get-up at her sister's party. "He wore a black velvet coat lined with satin, purple trousers with a gold band running down the outside seam, a scarlet waistcoat, long lace ruffles, falling to the tips of his fingers, white gloves with several brilliant rings outside them, and long black ringlets, rippling down upon his shoulders." One wonders what his friend, D'Orsay, whose taste in dress was perfect, thought of him!

To the end of his life his personal vanity was amazing. Sir Harry Austen Lee, Chancellor of the Embassy in Paris, and afterwards Disraeli's private secretary, went to see him when he was old and very ill. He found him sitting up in bed, his dyed locks in curl papers!

Was Benjamin aware during the years he was talking his way into society, that his personality did not conquer everyone? That there were many who spoke of him contemptuously as "that pushing young Jew"? Probably not: he possessed the thick skin which is impervious to slights and which is the armour of the complete egoist and climber. His conversation, too, though brilliant and sparkling with epigrams, offended some people. "He talks like a racehorse approaching the winning post," said one of his contemporaries.

He never seems to have formed a *liaison* with any of the ladies whom his gaiety and talent so captivated—indeed, he preferred the society of clever middle-aged women. Perhaps he shocked them agreeably by his views on marriage. "All my friends who married for love and beauty, either beat their wives, or live apart from them," he said. "I never intend to marry for love, which, I am sure, is a guarantee of infidelity."

V

BENJAMIN was now twenty-eight, and had every reason to be pleased with his progress in life. He was a successful novelist and he had gained an entrance into society by sheer intellectual brilliance and personality. But he was not satisfied that *Vivian*, the man of action, had conquered the dreamer. Even as a boy, politics had attracted him. Before he left England he had begun to consider the possibility of a parliamentary career, and while abroad he studied *Galigani* assiduously. No Jew had ever sat in Parliament—members not being paid, the profession did not attract them. What a triumph to be the first Jewish M.P.! But he was not yet sure of his own political convictions. In *The Young Duke* he had written —and one must remember that he always wrote himself into his books— "Am I a Whig or a Tory? I forget. As for the Tories, I admire antiquity, particularly a ruin; even the relics of the Temple of Intolerance have a charm. I think I am a Tory. But then the Whigs give such good dinners and are the most amusing. I think I am a Whig; but then the Tories are so moral, and morality is my *forte*; I must be a Tory. But the Whigs dress so much better, and an ill-dressed party, like an ill-dressed man, must be wrong. Yes! I am a decided Whig. And yet, I feel like Garrick, between tragedy and comedy. I think I will be a Whig and Tory alternate nights, and then both will be pleased; or I have no objection, according to the fashion of the day, to take a place under a Tory ministry, provided I may vote against them."

In spite of his waverings, however, his real sympathies were Tory. His social and literary popularity had not gained him entry into the great Whig Houses; indeed, to the Whigs he was a purely comic figure, incalculable and—a Jew! Even when he had become famous they ridiculed his partisanship of the landed interests, and as a champion of the Church of England, they found him still more amusing.

But Whig or Tory, he was highly patriotic.

"Oh, England! Oh, my country—although full many an eastern clime and southern race have given me something of their burning blood, it flows for thee! I rejoice that my flying fathers threw their ancient seed on the stern shores which they have not dishonoured," he wrote to his father. Rather melodramatic, but there is no doubt that his patriotic pretensions were sincere enough. To every passing interest he devoted the whole-hearted enthusiasm of his exuberant nature and, like most ego-centrics, he managed to identify his convictions with his interests.

Benjamin had arrived home on the day that Parliament was prorogued, after the House of Lords had rejected the second Reform Bill. During the rioting and political strife which ensued, he wrote to his friend Austen (*en vrai* Tory!) "The times are damnable. I take the gloomiest view of affairs, but we must not lose our property without a struggle. In the event of a new election I offer myself for Wycombe."

In a letter to his sister a little while after, he said, "I am writing a very John Bull book, which will delight you and my mother. I am still a Reformer, but I shall destroy the foreign policy of the Grey faction. They seem firmly fixed at home, although a storm is without doubt brewing abroad. I think peers will be created and Charley Gore has promised to let me have timely notice if Baring[1] be one. He called upon me and said that Lord John often asked how I was getting on at Wycombe. He fished as to whether I should support them. I answered, 'They had one claim on my support: they needed it, and no more.' "

At the outset of his political career Benjamin was all for Reform, but he distrusted the Whigs profoundly, and by the time the third Reform Bill was launched on its stormy voyage through Parliament he had become decidedly lukewarm. "I am still a Reformer," he wrote, but hinted that if the Bill were not passed he would not regret its failure unduly. "I am neither Whig nor Tory. My politics are described by one word, *England*," he wrote.

High Wycombe—a few miles from Bradenham, Benjamin's home—returned two members to Parliament, and they were then the Hon. Robert Smith, son of Lord Carrington, a local big-wig, and Sir Thomas Baring, both supporters of Grey's Ministry. At this time there was every likelihood of an election under the old system if the struggle over the Reform Bill brought about a dissolution, and the certainty of an election under the new system if the Bill passed both Houses. It passed, and received the royal assent on 7th June, 1832, and Benjamin, foreseeing the event, had already posted down to High Wycombe. "I start on high Radical interest, and take down strong recommendatory epistles from O'Connell, Hume Burdett, and *hoc genus*. Toryism is worn out, and I cannot condescend to be a Whig." It appeared afterwards that Hume, whose knowledge of Buckinghamshire was very slight, had confused Wycombe with Wendover, and had imagined that Benjamin was opposing two anti-Reformers! A letter he wrote to his friends, Smith and Baring, explaining the mistake, was published by their agents and did not help Benjamin. But he, quite undismayed, plunged into the

---

[1] Sir Thomas Baring, father of the first Lord Northbrook and the sitting member for Wycombe.

fray with his usual enthusiasm and self-confidence. Politics were for him a game; a battle of wits.

From the "Red Lion," Wycombe, he wrote to Austen, "I write you a hurried note after a hard day's canvass. Whigs, Tories and Radicals, Quakers, Evangelicals, Abolition of Slavery, Reform, Conservatism and Corn Laws—here is hard work for me who is to please all parties. I make an excellent canvasser, and am told I shall carry it through if the borough be opened." A few days after Benjamin began to canvass, the situation changed. A vacancy occurred for a seat in Hampshire, and Sir Thomas Baring resigned his seat in order to contest it, thus bringing about a by-election at High Wycombe under the old system. Bulwer did his best to get his friend returned unopposed, but, as Benjamin was hated at the Whig headquarters, he was unsuccessful. To Mrs. Austen, Benjamin wrote: "We are hard at it. Sir Thomas, you know, has resigned. His son is talked of; I have frightened him off, and old Pascoe Grenfell and Buxton. Yesterday the Treasury sent down Colonel Grey with a hired mob and a band. Never was such a failure. After parading the town with his paid voices, he made a stammering speech of ten minutes from his phaeton. All Wycombe was assembled. Feeling it was the crisis, I jumped up on the portico of the "Red Lion" and gave it to them for an hour and a quarter. I can give you no idea of the effect. A great many absolutely *cried*. I never made so many friends in my life, or converted so many enemies. All the women are on my side and wear my colours, pink and white. Do the same. The colonel returned to London the same evening, absolutely astounded out of his presence of mind, *on dit* never to appear again. If he come, I am prepared for him." He could certainly hold his own at all hustings. During his speech someone shouted, "We know all about Colonel Grey, but pray, what do you stand for?"

"I stand on my head," answered Benjamin promptly!

Isaac wrote to his self-confident son, sounding a warning note. "You are acquiring an European name," he said, "but invention and imagination are not the qualities for a representative of our modern patriots." Perhaps the terror he inspired in "Old Pascoe Grenfell" and the rest was less than he imagined. At any rate Colonel Grey—who was a son of the Prime Minister—was not frightened off permanently.

That Benjamin had a success with the crowd, is understandable; they had never seen anything like him, and must have felt much as they would have felt had Mephistopheles bobbed up from the underworld to address them. He was then at his most eccentric phase so far as dressing was concerned, and his pale face, Jewish features, black ringlets, lace ruffles and red waistcoat fascinated these simple country folk. Then, too, he had to the full that sense of the dramatic which was always to be so great a feature of his oratory. In concluding his speech he pointed to the Red Lion's head, saying, "When the polling is declared I shall be there and" —pointing to the lion's tail, "my opponent will be there." Alas for Benjamin! When polling was declared the results were:

Grey 20,
Disraeli 12.

He was furious, and attacked his foes right and left. Lord Nugent had called him "a Tory in disguise," the nearest thing to which, he said, "was a Whig in office." But still there was hope. The general election was bound to take place soon, and he continued his campaign at Wycombe. Parliament was dissolved on 3rd December, and Benjamin stood again, with a programme eminently calculated to appeal to the people. The purity of the ballot, reduction of taxes, education, the Corn Laws, the improvement of conditions for the working man, all figured in it. And he came "wearing the badge of no party and the livery of no faction." But he was again defeated. This time the polling was:

Smith 179
Grey 140
Disraeli 110

When the results were announced he said angrily that the secret of the Whigs' enmity to him was that he was not nobly born. "The election, or contest, did not cost *me* £80, the expense of hustings, etc., and Grey, not short of £800."

So far, Benjamin's political experiences had not been encouraging. He had been twice defeated and had gained the reputation of being a political adventurer, belonging to no party and having no fixed opinions. This was far from being true. He was, as a matter of fact, bursting with opinions, but he had not yet reduced them to order. Then, too, had he thrown in his lot decidedly with either party, a seat would easily have been found for him. Such gifts of energy and oratory would have been invaluable to Whigs or Tories.

His social popularity had become greater than ever. To his sister he wrote in 1833:

"My table is literally covered with invitations, and some from people I do not know. I dined yesterday with the St. Maurs, to meet Mrs. Sheridan. An agreeable party. The other guests, Lady Westmorland, very clever; Mrs. Blackwood, Lord Clements, and Brinsley. Lord St. Maur, great talent, which develops itself in a domestic circle, though otherwise shy-mannered. In the evening a good *soirée* at Lady Charleville's. I met Lady Aldbro' but the lion of the party was Lucien Bonaparte, the Prince of Canino. I went to the Caledonian Ball after all, in a dress

The Young Disraeli. Facsimile of the sketch by David
Maclise, R.A.

Disraeli making his maiden speech in the House of Commons

from my Oriental collection. Particulars when we meet. Yesterday at Mrs. Wyndham's, I met Joseph Bonaparte and his beautiful daughter. I am putting my house in order and preparing for a six months' sojourn and solitude amid the groves of Bradenham. London is emptying fast, but gay. Lady Cork had two routs. 'All my best people, no blues.' At a concert at Mrs. Mitford's I was introduced to Malibran, who is to be the heroine of my opera. She is a very interesting person." Notwithstanding Benjamin's many social engagements, he did not neglect taking physical exercise. Earlier in the year he had given his sister an account of a remarkable run with Sir Henry Smythe's hounds at Southend. "Although not in pink I was the best mounted man in the field, riding an Arabian mare, which I nearly killed; a run of thirty miles and I stopped at nothing!"

Lady Cork, who made much of Benjamin, went back far into the eighteenth century; she was born in 1746, and had been an intimate friend of Dr. Johnson. We meet her in Boswell, as Miss Monckton. Among her hosts of friends were Canning, Byron, Scott and, indeed, all the celebrities of her period. One day at her house Lord Carrington— who had no use for Benjamin—was damning him with faint praise. "He is a great agitator," said his lordship. "Not that he troubles us much now. He is never amongst us now. I believe he has gone abroad." "You old fool!" Lady Cork replied politely, "Why, he sent me this book this morning. You need not look at it: you can't understand it. It is the finest book ever written. Gone abroad indeed! Why, he is the best ton in London. There is not a party that goes down without him. The Duchess of Hamilton says there is nothing like him, Lady Lonsdale would give her head and shoulders for him. He would not dine at your house if you were to ask him. He does not care for people because they are lords: he must have fashion, or beauty, or wit, or something: and you are a very good sort of person, but you are nothing more."

That same year (1834), he met Lord Melbourne, who, he said, "asked how he could advance me in life, and half proposed that I should be his private secretary, inquiring what my object in life might be. 'To be Prime Minister.' Lord Melbourne, with a gravity not common with him, set to work to prove to me how vain and impossible to realize was this ambition."

But Parliament was still his goal. We read in Greville's Diary, December, 1834: "The Chancellor called on me yesterday about getting young Disraeli into Parliament (through the means of George Bentinck) for Lynn. I told him George wanted a good man to assist in turning out William Lennox, and he suggested the above-named gentleman, whom he called a friend of Charles. His political principle must, however, be in abeyance, for he said that Durham was doing all he could to get him, by the offer of a seat, and so forth: if, therefore, he is undecided and wavering between Chandos and Durham, he must be a mighty impartial personage. I don't think such a man will do, though just such as Lyndhurst would be connected with."

7th December. "Disraeli. He (George Bentinck) won't hear of him."

In the following year there was again an election at Wycombe, and again he contested the seat. But though, as one of his political enemies admitted, "he managed with extraordinary skill to steer between the shoals of toryism on one hand, and the quicksands of radicalism on the other," he was for the third time defeated. The figures were:

Smith 280

Grey 147

Disraeli 128

But this last failure convinced him that he could not hope for political success unless he identified himself with one or other of the two great parties. After long consideration, and an interview with the Lord Chancellor, he decided definitely for the Tory Party. He had one more failure—this time at Taunton, where in spite of the fact that his eloquence, courtesy and wit gained him golden opinions from both sides, the aristocratic Mr. Labouchere won by a majority of a hundred and seventy.

During the next two years Benjamin worked hard, making valuable political friends, speaking constantly, and going everywhere. His reward came in 1837. His party nominated him to contest the Borough of Maidstone in conjunction with Mr. Wyndham Lewis, and they were both returned. The election took place on 27th July, soon after Queen Victoria, whom he was to serve so long and faithfully, began her reign.

From that time on, his career belongs to the political history of Europe.

BOOKS CONSULTED

Life of Benjamin D'Israeli	Monypenny and Buckle, London.
	John Murray, London, 1910.
Disraeli	André Maurois.
Curiosities of Literature	Isaac Disraeli.
Life in the Regency and Early Victorian Times	Beresford Chancellor. Batsford, 1926.
Lady Blessington—Masquerade	Michael Sadleir.
Vivian Grey—Disraeli	
The Greville Memoirs	
Collections and Recollections	G. E. W. Russell.
My Recollections	Lord William Lennox.

INDEX

BARON STOCKMAR

GENERAL

Butt, Clara, viii
Caruso, Enrico, viii
Fouché, Joseph, Duke of Oranto, vii
I Hope They Won't Mind, viii, ix
Kreisler, Fritz, viii
Laver, James, vii–ix

Melba, Dame Nellie, viii
Napoleon, vii
Parr, Dr. Samuel, vii, viii.
Tallyrand, Charles Maurice de, vii
Ysaye, Eugene, viii